RECREATING JANE AU

Recreating Jane Austen is a book for readers who know and love Austen's work. Stimulated by the recent crop of film and television versions of Austen's novels, John Wiltshire examines how they have been transposed and 'recreated' in another age and medium. Wiltshire illuminates the process of 'recreation' through the work of the psychoanalyst Donald Winnicott, and offers Jane Austen's own relation to Shakespeare as a suggestive parallel. Exploring the romantic impulse in Austenian biography, 'Jane Austen' as a commodity, and offering a re-interpretation of *Pride and Prejudice*, this book approaches the central question of the role Jane Austen plays in the contemporary cultural imagination.

JOHN WILTSHIRE is a Reader in English at La Trobe University in Melbourne, Australia. His previous books include *Samuel Johnson in the Medical World: the Doctor and the patient* (Cambridge, 1991) and *Jane Austen and the Body: 'The Picture of Health'* (Cambridge, 1992). He is also a contributor to the *Cambridge Companion to Samuel Johnson* and *The Cambridge Companion to Jane Austen*.

RECREATING
JANE AUSTEN

JOHN WILTSHIRE

CAMBRIDGE
UNIVERSITY PRESS

PUBLISHED BY THE PRESS SYNDICATE OF THE UNIVERSITY OF CAMBRIDGE
The Pitt Building, Trumpington Street, Cambridge, United Kingdom

CAMBRIDGE UNIVERSITY PRESS
The Edinburgh Building, Cambridge CB2 2RU, UK
40 West 20th Street, New York NY 10011-4211, USA
477 Williamstown Road, Port Melbourne, VIC 3207, Australia
Ruiz de Alarcón 13, 28014 Madrid, Spain
Dock House, The Waterfront, Cape Town 8001, South Africa

http://www.cambridge.org

First published 2001
Reprinted 2002

Printed in the United Kingdom at the University Press, Cambridge

Typeface Baskerville 11/12.5pt   *System* Poltype® [VN]

A catalogue record for this book is available from the British Library

ISBN 0 521 80246 6 hardback
ISBN 0 521 00282 6 paperback

For Miki, with love

Contents

Preface and acknowledgments

This book derives its inspiration, in part, from the recent crop of films based on Jane Austen's novels. But it does not offer a systematic study of any one of these films: instead it makes use of them, or parts of some of them, in order to throw renewed light upon the classic texts from which they derive and depart, and to propose a general theory of adaptation. Films directly based on the novels are not the only ones discussed, for perhaps even more interesting are others which, besides imitating her work, raise in the course of their action and dialogue the nature and status of 'Jane Austen' within our culture. I am interested in the general topic of artistic recreation and remaking, and the role Jane Austen plays in the contemporary cultural imagination. I have wagered that 'object-relations' psychoanalysis, which has studied the various phenomena of human love, might throw some light on our love of aesthetic objects as well, but this theory is drawn upon selectively. As a consequence, this book's handling of psychoanalytic theory may strike professionals in the field as decidedly sketchy. My excuse is it has been rarely applied to the discussion not of the internal life of 'characters' but to the understanding of the artistic processes of recreation itself.

I should like to thank the friends and colleagues who have helped me with this book. Chris Palmer, Max Richards and Iain Topliss have encouraged me in dozens of ways for many years: it is something to be able to thank them now for their support. Dick Freadman and Kay Torney Souter read parts of the book in early drafts and they too gave me helpful feedback and support. Among others, Jo Barnes, Terry Collits, Gilliana Del Alectos, Susannah Fullerton, Paul Komesaroff, Karen Lynch, Alison Ravenscroft, Carl Stanyon, Bruce Williams and Ruth Wiltshire have made (possibly unwitting) contributions. I am especially indebted to Laura Carroll for my understanding of film criticism. Thanks, too, to James Healey for the cover photo.

I hope Lorna Clark and my other friends in the Burney Society will forgive my treatment of Fanny (oops! Frances) in this book. Marcia McClintock Folsom in Boston exchanged ideas with me and has been extraordinarily generous and supportive of my work on Austen over the past four years. With characteristic grace, she has allowed me to borrow the title of one of her papers for Chapter 3. Justin Kelly SJ helped clarify my thinking about *Pride and Prejudice* at an important moment. I especially thank Ann Blake for her conversation as we thought together about Jane Austen and Shakespeare. She has been generous in allowing me to make use of our work, in Chapters 3 and 4. My editor, Linda Bree, has taken an interest in this book which has been a constant encouragement. To my wife, Zaiga, I owe much more than I can say.

An early version of Chapter 1, 'Imagining Jane Austen's Life: Biography and Transitional Space' was published as a review in the *Cambridge Quarterly* 27: 4, 1998, pp. 372–84; a condensed version of Chapter 3 was given as a paper at the JASNA conference in Colorado Springs in October 1999 and published in *Persuasions* 21, 1999, pp. 212–23. Parts of Chapters 3 and 4 are based on papers which I gave with Ann Blake at conferences in Brisbane, July 1998 and Auckland, July 2000. I am grateful to Ann for allowing me to make use of this material. A much condensed version of Chapter 5 was given at the JASNA conference in Boston, October 2000. I thank Judy Simons for the invitation to contribute to a volume on Jane Austen and the cinema that resulted in Chapter 2, and Marcia McClintock Folsom for the invitation to contribute to one on *Emma* that led to Chapter 6.

A note on texts

Citations of Jane Austen's novels are made in the text by following quotations with the title and page numbers. The page numbers refer to the text which has been used throughout, the *Oxford Illustrated Jane Austen*, edited by R. W. Chapman, 6 volumes, 1923–54. Where a number of references to the same novel is made, the title is omitted after the first. Citations of Shakespeare are from *William Shakespeare, The Complete Works*, edited by Stanley Wells and Gary Taylor, Oxford: Clarendon Press, 1988.

Introduction: 'Jane Austen' and Jane Austen

TOM: . . . nearly everything Jane Austen wrote seems ridiculous from today's perspective.
AUDREY: Has it ever occurred to you that today, looked at from Jane Austen's perspective, would look even worse?

Whit Stillman, *Metropolitan*, 1990[1]

Lots of fun with Jane Austen's novels is had in Helen Fielding's two volumes of Bridget Jones's *Diary*. The man of Bridget's dreams, as is now well known, is called Mark Darcy.[2] She and Mark are introduced at a New Year's Day Turkey Curry Buffet, arranged by friends of Bridget's parents. When she first meets him, Mark (a 'top human rights lawyer') is standing aloof, scrutinising the contents of their bookshelves. Bridget, prejudiced against Darcy from the first, thinks him a snob, and her new boyfriend, the rake, Daniel, confirms this opinion when he tells her that he's known Mark since Cambridge and he's a nerdish old maid. Bridget and Mark continue to bump into each other at parties and cross swords, in a series of conversations, though Bridget gradually comes to see that Mark might really care for her. When Darcy goes to great lengths to rescue the family from the financial disaster that Bridget's insufferable mother's romantic escapade has plunged them into, she is ready to fall into his arms – or rather to climb the stairs to his bedroom.

Bridget – daffy, honest, good-natured Bridget, daughter of *Cosmopolitan* culture, traumatised by supermodels – resembles *Northanger Abbey*'s Catherine Morland more than she does Lizzy Bennet, but it's not hard to read the novel as a reworking of *Pride and Prejudice*. What is more interesting is that the book calls the reader's attention to the issues this involves, as in what one might call a meta-novelistic conversation where Bridget and her friends discuss television adaptations of classics. Bridget works for a publisher, and at a book launch Mark's stuck-up fiancée (as inclined to sneer at Bridget's enthusiasm for the TV show *Blind Date* as Miss Bingley was at Elizabeth's traipsing across the fields) weighs in against what she calls 'the ultimate *vandalisation* of the cultural framework' involved in using opera arias as themes for the World Cup, and the conversion of great novels into television serials. ' "I must say", said Natasha with a knowing smile, "I always feel with the Classics people should be made to prove they've read the book before they're allowed to watch the television version." '³ But this ploy seems to cut no ice with Mark.

Bridget Jones's Diary raises a question that is central to this book. In *Classics and Trash*, Harriet Hawkins described the 'cross-fertilisation' that so often takes place between classics and more popular films and novels with a broad appeal.⁴ But what is happening in the *Diary* is more like – to adopt a term from film criticism – a 'transcoding'.⁵ It is a kind of borrowing that plays fast and loose with the original but is, it might be argued, redeemed by its lightness of touch. Aware of the difference between our times and Austen's, it switches and changes and finds different ways to meet similar ends – which might be defined, roughly speaking, as exploring the pressures on young women to conform to the expectations of their culture. One could argue, as Natasha might do, that the novel simply makes off with the plot outline and a few references to *Pride and Prejudice*, and that *Bridget Jones's Diary* is more indebted to the 1995 BBC serialisation of the novel (of which Bridget, of course, is an avid fan) than Jane Austen's original fusion of social criticism and romance. There would be some truth in this, though at least Helen Fielding's novels would remind us that Jane Austen began and ended her writing life a satirist and that if Bridget, like her younger contemporary Cher Horowitz of *Clueless* (Paramount, 1995) finds *Men are from Mars, Women are from Venus* an absorbing read, that is more or less the contemporary equivalent of the Gothic bestseller of Austen's youth, *The Romance of the Forest*.

I suggest though that this novel is emblematic of a phenomenon that is typical of cultural production in this era of greatly diversified means of mechanical reproduction. Remaking, rewriting, 'adaptation', reworking, 'appropriation', conversion, mimicking (the proliferation of terms suggests how nebulous and ill-defined is the arena) of earlier works into other media is an important feature of the current landscape. If *Bridget Jones's Diary* is a different kind of product, and emerges from a different reading of Jane Austen than prequels and sequels like *Pemberley* or *Darcy's Story*⁶ – which are also interesting manifestations of contemporary culture – then it is important to consider why. Every age of course adapts, modifies and remakes, as the history of Shakespeare's reception indicates obviously enough. Every cultural creation, even a cathedral, has an afterlife, unpredictable, uncontrolled by its original architect, when another era, another cultural configuration, turns it, adapts it, to its own uses.[7] Texts (however we interpret that word) only partially belong to the original author: they are constantly being reworked, rearranged, recycled. Redesigning and plundering the creations of the past, indeed, rather than their preservation, is a process so continuous and so endemic, that it is arguable that it is the central motor of artistic development.

It is only recently, however, that the emphasis in representing Jane Austen has shifted away from notions of preservation and 'faithfulness', that Jane Austen has been so widely recreated, or, to use the deceptively simple word which will play an important role in the argument of this book, 'used'. How are we to understand this use, and how can it be distinguished from the more inert, more slavish 'usage'? The verb itself oscillates between exploitation and honourable deployment. But, as Meagan Morris puts it, '[w]hen any and every text can be read indifferently as another instance of "strategic rewriting" . . . something more (and something more specific) is needed to argue how and why a particular event of rewriting might matter.'[8] So that the conversation in *Bridget Jones's Diary* opens an important question: how do we sort out the various strands and styles of rewriting, remaking? What makes some more significant than others?

These recent adaptations, transcodings and appropriations of Jane Austen's original novels form one subject of this book, for they are instances of a more general phenomenon, the fantasies which surround the name 'Jane Austen'. The transformation of Jane Austen's novels into several television productions and films which by general consent are more substantial and interesting than previous versions has already led to at least two critical collections and a great number of papers and commentaries.[9] In her chapter, 'Piracy is Our Only Option', Kristin Fleiger Samuelian takes a remark of Edward Ferrars in Emma Thompson's script for *Sense and Sensibility* and reads it against its author. Samuelian, like several contributors to the same volume, *Jane Austen in Hollywood*, regards Thompson's screenplay as a virtual betrayal of the novel, a reversal of its system of values, and a capitulation to notions – simultaneously romantic and conservative – that the novel pits itself against. 'Piracy' she writes, is the appropriate term for Thompson's postfeminist usurpation of Austen's original text. 'Piracy – the appropriation and adaptation for profit of Austen's courtship novel – is for Thompson a way of deflecting what is unanswerable in the

eighteenth-century ideology the novel depicts.'[10] Such serious charges
are made repeatedly in different forms by other writers – that in
adapting Jane Austen to the needs of a modern audience, in seeking to
please that audience, not only has the difficult balance of Austen's irony
been lost, but history has been traduced, and the ethical emphases of her
work have been reversed. Some writers even go so far as to intimate that
the film versions may, for a modern audience, liquidate or 'erase' the
novels.[11]

   No one is likely at this point of critical time, to wish to underestimate
the material conditions of a text's production. That decisions about
products costing millions of dollars are influenced by what are perceived
as the desires and demands of their audiences is not in doubt, nor that
writers and producers dwell within the same cultural climate, broadly
speaking, as their audiences. But that these govern choices, are exclusively determinative, or even dominant may well be a more disputable
matter. Even in Hollywood films are still made because a writer or
producer wants to make them, believes in them, and pushes them
through.[12] It is just as evident that Jane Austen, who hoped to make
money by her books, was influenced to some degree by what she
thought her readers would enjoy and accept.[13] Material conditions
influence the ideological messages of films also, needless to say, in a less
crude and more radical sense. The technical conditions of their production mean that books and moving pictures occupy or employ quite
different signifying systems.[14] The very obvious points that films and
television serials are predominantly visual media, that they must largely
therefore signify emotion by symbol, by expression and action, that the
interiority of their characters is represented through such signs rather
than through language, that they encourage the gaze rather than the
immersed reader's imagination, are all factors that have cultural and
ideological implications. What can be represented in the visual media
emerges from these conditions and presents itself to the audience, or the
viewer, as the natural and inevitable. Furthermore, it can be argued, the
audience is formed in the image of that at which it gazes. Thus transcoding from one to the other system of signs may involve effects that, in
some instances, are incommensurate.

   'In the appreciation of a work of art or an art form, consideration of
the receiver never proves fruitful.'[15] Whatever one may think of Walter
Benjamin's sweeping aphorism, it can be suggested that this focus on the
films as commercial commodities largely governed by the consciousness
and expectations of their intended audiences tends to remove the

scriptwriter or filmmaker as a designing subject from view. So does the Bourdieuian notion of 'cultural capital', the question his work leaves aside being precisely what internal possession of such capital means for the individual.[16] The notion of piracy at least restores the notion of the author of the filmic text; brings him, her or them back as an agent. In this book I approach the question of influence and adaptation from this perspective – the supply side. I imagine that scriptwriters and film-makers are agents and creative consciousneses, and that film and television versions do emerge – all things considered – from intelligent and coherent encounters with the original works. I do not disregard the differing cultural conditions in which Austen wrote and in which, two hundred years later, readers receive her novels. As W. J. T. Mitchell has remarked, in the current stage of capitalism, 'the common thread of both the marketable and the unmarketable artwork is the more or less explicit awareness of "marketability" and publicity as unavoidable dimensions of any public sphere that art might address'.[17]

But if one is to focus on remaking or adaptation, and put the adaptation or remade product into some kind of relation with the 'original' (however different this original is) it is impossible not to impute or imply an intelligence or imagination which has made choices, either to preserve, rework, or refuse the predecessor text. A criticism that focuses on the cultural context of texts, though often making a grudging acknowledgment, à la Barthes, that a certain 'mixing' of the given signs takes place,[18] – that the activity of deployment or shift makes the object under consideration a novel and distinct thing – finds it difficult to theorise the author, or 'auteur'. I propose then that scriptwriter and filmmakers be understood as readers, and that one advantage of all such revisions is that they make public and manifest what their reading of the precursor text is, that they bring out into the discussably open the choices, acceptances, assumptions and distortions that are commonly undisclosed within the private reader's own imaginative reading process.

In the conversation I have quoted from Helen Fielding's novel, Natasha goes on to complain of the arrogance with which a new generation imagines that it can somehow create the world afresh. Mark Darcy replies 'gently', 'But that's exactly what they *do*, do.'[19] One might add that indeed each generation produces its own works of art, but not entirely out of their own materials. Rewritings of Austen are primary examples of this process. This book builds therefore on the perception of the psychoanalyst Donald Winnicott that works of art are not entirely made, but neither are they exactly found either.[20] Rather than thinking of these works as piracies or abductions of the original text, I argue that they are best read as recreations, and therefore need to reintroduce the concept of creativity – redolent of the sixties though it be – into critical discourse. Winnicott is one of the few writers to offer sustained attention to the origins of creativity. Never a systematic thinker (as his French commentators routinely point out)[21] and rather suspicious of systematising modes of thought, Winnicott nevertheless offers a series of ideas and concepts with which to approach a notion that was no doubt discarded because, together with a clutch of similarly dynamic notions, it was used 'to designate a locus of opacity'.[22] Winnicott, a paediatrician as well as psychoanalyst, introduces an understanding of the notion of creativity at its earliest moments, in the infant's originary gestures towards the world. In his thinking, creativity, which is understood as a quotidian quality as well as an extraordinary one, is often shadowed by its alternative, compliance. Moreover, since the notion of creativity is central to his thought, he relates it to questions of art and literary production.

Winnicott's theory differs strikingly from Freud's attempt to make sense of the aesthetic. 'Sublimation' offers to instantiate a realm outside the domain of sexuality and yet always seemingly leads back into sexual determinants.[23] Winnicott's theory of creativity, on the other hand, expands into the social and interpersonal rather than the erotic. In papers which I shall draw on later in the argument of this book, Winnicott shows that everyday creativity makes use of the other person, that progress in psychological life is a form of consumption of the other which simultaneously respects the other's independence. Sometimes, through a series of intuitions or jumps Winnicott extends his thoughts about the infant's creativity into the realms of art and culture.[24] But following work by the psychoanalytic social theorist Jessica Benjamin I argue that in a variety of ways, and in different contexts, Winnicott's thoughts can be helpful in formulating a theory of artistic creation, influence and recreation, which has (though neither Winnicott nor Benjamin explicitly makes this point) an ethical aspect. What Winnicott shows about the infant and about the psychoanalytic patient, throws, I suggest, some light into the hidden and problematic processes in which a text that is public property becomes taken up and effectively remade. If the mind is, as contemporary psychoanalytic theory proposes, actually built out of 'configurations of self in relation to others',[25] then it is possible that the relations between texts may be illuminated by this parallel.

This book does not, however, offer a full account of the film and television adaptations of Jane Austen's novels. In fact, aspects of the films are only drawn upon when they contribute to a larger project, which is to understand the internal logics of the process which I am calling 'recreation'. The topic of the book then, is not so much the imitations or recreations of Jane Austen, as the process of imitation or recreation itself, and its central task is to transfer concepts formulated in the psychoanalytic encounter into literary or cultural criticism, to transform descriptions of human psyches in their interaction into useful ways of thinking about the relationships between texts, even when these texts belong to different genres or media. I consider the various versions of the novels not as piracies, but – all thing considered – as coherent readings of the original books, which by their public, objective existence, can throw unique light on the nature of reading. An analogy to the contemporary remaking of Jane Austen, I suggest, is to be found in her own hardly reverent relation to Shakespeare and in the first of two chapters bearing on this I contrast the theory of creativity with the more commonly accepted notions of influence.

I had thought of calling this book 'Jane Austen, Our Contemporary', to signal that Shakespeare is its secondary plot, its shadow subject. This would itself be a pinch from the title of Jan Kott's influential 1966 book, *Shakespeare, Our Contemporary*.[26] But it would be stealing with a difference: Kott's book insisted on the contemporary 'relevance' of Shakespeare's plays, reading the Henriad, for example, in the light of the brutal politics of Eastern Europe. My intention is otherwise. In developing a theory of adaptation through discussion of the recent remakings of Jane Austen's novels I seek to confront those readers in the academy and elsewhere who still consider Jane Austen as a novelist who belongs to or creates a 'world' that is far-off, impeccably gracious and morally superannuated, who panders (in the author's own unfortunate phrase) to a taste like Susan Price's for 'the genteel and well-appointed'.[27]

Yet 'Jane Austen' is obviously not everyone's contemporary. The distributors of the 1998 Touchstone Pictures comedy, *Jane Austen's Mafia!*, decided to change the title in pre-screening publicity when surveys revealed that only ten per cent of their teenage target audience knew who Jane Austen was (perhaps the same audience that is reported to have queued for *Sense and Sensibility* thinking it was a sequel to *Dumb and Dumber*). But the producers clearly knew what 'Jane Austen' signified, and counted on a certain response to their title. They were playing on 'Jane Austen' as a cultural commodity, bound to produce an expectation even in those who have never read the novels. For what does 'Jane Austen' mean? Propriety, decorum, romance, English ladies – just the opposite of what 'Mafia' suggests – brutality, violence, crime, machismo. The oxymoronic trick had been played before when James Ivory and Ismail Merchant released a film I shall discuss later in this book, *Jane Austen in Manhattan*, in 1980. Racy, smart, modern Manhattan; staid, genteel, old-fashioned Jane. The mere title 'Jane Austen and the Masturbating Girl', Eve Kosofsky Sedgwick's 1989 MLA presentation and 1991 essay, flaunting the same incongruity, was attacked by conservative commentators, disturbed at the linkage of the familiar cipher for placid elegance and furtive, unsanctioned sexuality.[28]

This 'Jane Austen' is almost a brand name. You come upon 'Jane Austen' nightdresses in the same section of the heritage shop 'Past Times' as her *Letters to Cassandra*. The name signals a variety of cosiness, seductively close to that notion of domestic 'comfort' which, as an architectural commentator has noted, Jane Austen's novels play their role in naturalising.[29] 'Jane Austen' stands equally for a certain priggish concern with manners, a prudish unadventurousness, an anachronistic fascination with the ways of ladies and gentlemen. This 'Jane Austen' is irredeemably conservative and middle-class. In another recent British novel, for instance, a young teacher parries a girl's invitation to have sex with her on their first date. Fed up with him, she lets fly: 'I think he could see what I was feeling because he said he was sorry . . . and we should say goodnight – I ask you what a load of Jane Austen bollocks, that was nearly it, there and then, I was that close, it was on the tip of my tongue to say all right then fuck off for ever darling I cannot be doing with one second more of this Jane Austen bollocks . . .'[30] This angry reaction is B's in *B. Monkey* published in 1992 by Andrew Davies, frustratedly working at that time, one must presume, on the script for the famously successful BBC *Pride and Prejudice*, which went to air in 1995. 'Jane Austen' means then, no sex and antiquated manners.

For others, 'Jane Austen' signifies English imperialism, the dissemination of her work via the BBC and Miramax films, colonisation in a new form. This Jane Austen is perceived as an enemy of the indigenous, the literary queen (as Shakespeare is the king) of a dominant culture, her texts one arm of an oppressive educative project that inculcates the values of the 'mother country', her careful investigation of behavioural constraints and the inner life, confined to a small section of nineteenth-century society, absurdly anachronistic, inappropriate and fundamentally detrimental to nations, peoples and classes seeking their own identities. The films, with their seductive depictions of English land-scape and gorgeous interiors, their focus on exquisite manners and exclusively heterosexual romance, only reinforce the image such readers carry of a Jane Austen stultifyingly genteel, complicit with patriarchy, a velvet enforcer of convention and conformity. Within Jane Austen criticism the operation of this image is seen in the reaction it provokes – the eagerness to show that Austen is sassy, spunky, postcolonial, radical, transgressive, sexually complex and ambiguous.[31]

For the taint of the staid, the oppressively genteel can be used also to rule out any consideration of Jane Austen's critics and commentators from serious engagement in the current critical agora. Jane 'Austen criticism is notable mostly, not just for its timidity and banality', Sedgwick declares, 'but for its unresting exaction of the spectacle of a Girl Being Taught a Lesson.'[32] Criticism has made Austen's work into 'a dryly static tableau of discrete moralized portraits, poised antitheses, and exemplary, deplorable, or regrettably necessary punishments' (pp. 127–28). 'This tableau is what we now know as "Jane Austen", fossilized residue of the now subtracted autoerotic spectacle' (p. 128). Such a 'spectacle' is what Sedgwick discerns in *Sense and Sensibility*, reading a scene in which Marianne weeps in her bedroom as her 'unstanchable emission, convulsive and intransitive', the signal of 'an excess of sexuality altogether, an excess dangerous to others but chiefly to herself' (p. 114, p. 120). Elinor's supposedly envious censorship is presented in the light of later medical tracts against 'self-abuse' and Austen's critics as scurrying, all too readily, to follow her, to underscore the coercive or prescriptive elements in the novels' plots.

Part of Sedgwick's argument makes Morris Zapp of David Lodge's 1975 novel *Changing Places* uncannily proleptic. Zapp, the American exchange Professor who is an Austen specialist (he has left behind nine-year-old twins called Darcy and Elizabeth) lectures his reluctant English class on the topic of 'Eros and Agape in the later novels'. Getting up steam, he snatches up the text of *Persuasion* and reads from the scene where Wentworth lifts the child from Anne's shoulders. ' "*Her sensations on the discovery made her perfectly speechless. She could not even thank him. She could only hang over little Charles with the most disordered feelings.*" "How about that?" He concluded reverently. "If that isn't an *orgasm*, what is it?" He looked up into three flabbergasted faces.'[33] Perhaps this can stand as a moral lesson in its turn on those dangers of ahistorical reading that hedge about such an enterprise as this one. Nevertheless, it is true, as Sedgwick suggests, that a previous generation of critics scarcely read the novels except in the transferential light of their own pedagogic practices. As Howard Mills remarks, few teachers will escape cringing when one of Zapp's students describes his essay on Austen: 'I've done it on her moral awareness.'[34] But I don't know how to address Sedgwick's depiction of Marianne and Elinor except to say that I think it shows a lack of moral awareness. Marianne's condition is not pathological: it is so distressing and such a challenge to her sister precisely because it is not aberrant or perverse.

'Jane Austen' then, the cultural image, can be distinguished from Jane Austen, the texts. So can the more kindly inflection of this tendency, 'Jane Austen' as the object of idealising and romantic fantasy. Whatever the associations of 'Jane Austen' the term always, I think, signals distance from the contemporary. Both those who say they love Jane Austen and those who dislike 'her' intensely often predicate their assessments on this supposed remoteness from the harassments and incitements of modern urban life. The cognate term or phrase 'Jane Austen's world' suggests this even more strongly.[35] 'The private life in the foreground, history a distant rumble of gunfire, somewhere offstage', as Zapp's English equivalent declares, 'In Jane Austen not even a rumble.'[36] Like 'hermetically sealed from the vast anguish of her time',[37] Reginald Farrer's description in 1917 of the milieu of the novels, these accounts no longer command any form of assent from Jane Austen's critics, but the notion that 'Jane Austen's world' is both synonymous with an actual historical period and also blissfully, or blindly, outside of history still persists,[38] kept overdeterminedly alive perhaps by the novels' own internal coherence, as well as the positiveness of the author's organising 'voice'.

What then makes it possible to claim with some plausibility – some chance of being heard – that despite the popular myth, the critical fossil, there is another Jane Austen who is our contemporary? In one sense this question is answered by the proliferating transformations that are the stuff this book works in. As I hope to show, sometimes the films do genuinely achieve, within different terms, an equivalence to Jane Austen. Its task would not, however, be complete without an account of at least one Austen novel that attempted to substantiate through its own critical reading the implicit claim I have been making here, to speak of Jane Austen rather than 'Jane Austen'. The chapter on *Pride and Prejudice* also allows me to make explicit a theme which is present in a variety of forms throughout the book. It is a version (so I fondly imagine) of Jane Austen's own dislike of sensibility, of the late eighteenth-century cult of feeling that was premised on 'natural affection' and the assumption that in feeling for another one was in touch with their inner reality. In my reworking, it shows itself as suspicion of critical romanticism – that tendency to write as if the critic could inhabit the mind of the author – which manifests itself in some studies of influence and in the methods of literary biographers. This book is concerned at its heart with what love of Jane Austen's work means, and how we distinguish between varieties and forms of this love. I argue that recreating her work is only possible when the reader has moved away from, overcome an early form of love which is characterised by identification. For this to happen, identificatory love must be replaced by recognition that the other, exactly, is other. *Pride and Prejudice*, I contend, offers an exemplary instance of how this occurs.

This book begins with a discussion of some recent biographies of Jane Austen. It does not add to these treatments, but instead examines aspects of the biographical impulse itself, that desire for intimacy which, I suggest, is a particular side-effect of Austen's art, and introduces the notion of 'transitional space'. In biography the fantasy of knowing and possessing the subject has always to accommodate itself to the recalcitrant facticity of that subject's absence and resistance to being known. This is emblematic of the multiple relations between self and other, between one artistic text and another, that are the subject of this book. In the next chapter three late-twentieth-century filmic interpretations of Jane Austen are considered; not films which seek to offer literal transcodings of the novels, but films which both explicitly and implicitly raise questions about what 'Jane Austen', and Jane Austen's texts, signify in the contemporary world. I draw here on a later paper of Winnicott's in which he develops his notion of recreation as a destructive as well as relating phenomenon.

The next chapter discusses Austen's own association with Shakespeare and offers a theory of the later writer's relation to her predecessor that replaces the notion of influence by the more dynamic and fruitful notion of incorporation. Chapter 4 suggests that Austen's adaptation of the Shakespearean soliloquy to her own ends, crossing genre, gender and media lines, offers a parallel to the retranslation of her texts into the newly dramatic signifying system of the film. This chapter concentrates on aspects of *Persuasion* and *Mansfield Park*. Chapter 5, on *Pride and Prejudice*, which follows, offers a more complete 'reading' of the novel, stimulated in part by the television film, but which also allows the further development of an idea which is central to the book – how identificatory love becomes transformed into adult love. The final chapter 'The genius and the facilitating environment' which looks briefly at *Emma*, returns to the biographical motif of the opening discussion and more explicitly addresses the controversies of Austen criticism, and of 'Jane Austen' as a commodity, which the book's focus on aesthetic and psychological matters might otherwise seem to bypass.

Jane Austen then is a signifier with multiple meanings. The films, for their own ends, artistic or commercial, rewrite the texts on which they are based, and, because of the power of the medium, because of their dependency upon and swift uptake into, the criticism of this writer, form part of the meaning that 'Jane Austen' now has. Much critical activity is devoted to recuperating Jane Austen from these films, but this is not my intention. Instead I wish to use the films to understand what our relation to Jane Austen, that rich and complex writer, now is. I do not wish to proclaim, over the heads of new historicist critics, an ability to speak with the dead.[39] It is rather that I wish to underscore the belief that to possess the past it is necessary to remake it. Because the novels speak to us, we – as scriptwriters, as filmmakers and novelists, and as critics – can speak back to them.

CHAPTER I

Imagining Jane Austen's life

> We are divided of course between liking to feel the past strange and
> liking to feel it familiar; the difficulty is, for intensity, to catch it at
> the moment when the scales of the balance hang with the right
> evenness.
>
> Henry James, Preface to *The Aspern Papers*[1]

Constance Pilgrim's wonderful, ridiculous book *Dear Jane: a Biographical
Study* was first published in 1971, and reissued twenty years later.[2] It tells
a story that is mentioned in all lives of the novelist. When she was very
old Cassandra Austen recalled that she and her sister had met a
personable young man on holiday in Devonshire sometime in the first
years of the century. He was attracted to Jane, and the feeling was
apparently reciprocated. The Austens expected to hear from him again,
arranged even to meet him the next year, but instead the news came of
his sudden death. Pilgrim's book concerns this 'mysterious romance'
and its disappointing denouement. She set herself to uncover the identity of Jane Austen's admirer, with remarkable results.

Like many biographers, Constance Pilgrim's main source for information about the novelist's emotional life is the novels themselves.
Assuming that the air of reality which so many passages convey indicates their origin in autobiographical experience, and especially, as an
acquaintance of Jane Austen claimed, that 'Anne Elliot *was*' the novelist
herself, and moreover (as a scrap of reminiscence suggests) the young
man was a naval officer, one obvious candidate presents himself irresistibly to the biographer's mind.[3] The romance – a word I shall use with
all the latitude of reference it permits – resembles Anne's in leading to
painful memories, and *Persuasion*, written in 1816, is an imaginative
rewriting and resolution of the loss endured in the past. The name of
Anne Elliot's lover, Wentworth, is the most important clue to this lost
sailor's identity. For someone was holidaying in that part of England in
just the months that Jane Austen and her sister may have been there –

and readers may have nearly as intimate a contact with this person as they have with Anne Elliot. Who else can this mysterious stranger be but John *Words*worth, William Wordsworth's brother, captain in the merchant navy, who died when his ship, the *Earl of Abergavenny*, sank in a terrible storm off Weymouth Sands in February 1805, and whose character is touchingly remembered in the poet's own elegiac lines?

Jane and John meet first in Bath, perhaps, or at Lyme in 1797. They become secretly engaged, but Jane is persuaded to break off the engagement by her cautious and worldly wise friend Mrs Lefroy, and John spends the first nine months of 1800 with his brother and sister in the Lake District, probably nursing his wounds. Nevertheless, he sends Jane a copy of Wordsworth's *Poems in Two Volumes*, published that year, since it is known from a letter that he gave them 'to a lady, a friend of mine'.[4] Two years later, when John is in London, waiting for his ship, he sees Jane Austen in London at a performance of a play he certainly attended called (significantly for readers of *Emma*) *Delays and Blunders*. She, however, has read a notice in the *York Herald* of 9 October 1802, announcing the marriage of 'Mr Wordsworth of Grasmere' (actually William's marriage to Mary) and misapprehensions, very like those in *Persuasion*, ensue. Shortly afterwards, nevertheless, they come to a renewed understanding. Now it is the story of Jane Fairfax, the secret engagement entered upon at a resort, that reproduces theirs. In the spring of 1803, then, amid the 'romantic beauty' of the Isle of Wight, they secretly renew their engagement, only for it to be cut off for ever by John's tragic death.

It is easy to fault the logic of this account but not to convey the air of conviction, the sense of personal involvement, the warmth and ingenuity with which the passionate Pilgrim interweaves her historical research into her portrayal of the two figures. There is a genuine romance in this book, even if it is the involvement of the author with the idealised figures of the past. Pilgrim's study in fact brings home how much overlap there is, or might be, between biography, criticism and romance. One can imagine one knows this handsome, sympathetic sailor, encouraged by his brother's mourning poetry, just as one can imagine oneself the intimate of Jane Austen as one reads the works of her pen. This phantasmal marriage of two minds is not unique to Constance Pilgrim, or to the biographer, however: we shall meet it again in another form when we consider literary critics' dealings with Jane Austen's relation to Shakespeare himself.

Jane Austen lived two hundred years ago, and (if one thinks about it dispassionately) there can be very little new to be known about her own inner or personal life. Victims to the fire, and to her sister's scissors, her remaining letters are a small proportion of those she wrote, and Deirdre Le Faye's admirable 1995 re-editing contained no new discoveries.[5] Apart from her brother Henry's brief biographical notice prefacing *Northanger Abbey and Persuasion* in 1818, other accounts of her date from the mid-Victorian years, a period of growing fame and fading memories. They are the reports of now elderly brothers or of their children, who had only known the novelist as a jolly maiden aunt. Fay Weldon remarks in her introduction to the Folio Society reprint of James Austen-Leigh's 1870 *Memoir*, that this, along with 'one rather bad portrait of her by her sister Cassandra, and a quilt stitched (badly) by the novelist when young is just about all we have'.[6] Though this is an exaggeration, the archive, collected in Le Faye's *Jane Austen: a Family Record*, an enlargement of the volume originally published in 1913 by William and Richard Austen-Leigh,[7] is substantially made up of reminiscences coloured by sentiment and guarded by propriety and family pride. In one of the two remaining sketches of her, Jane Austen, perched outdoors, is half turned away and her face is hidden by her bonnet. Constance Pilgrim thinks that she is gazing out to sea, watching the China Fleet, with John Wordsworth's ship among them, sail away out of sight.[8] Anything is possible. Perhaps what the picture signifies most plainly is its subject's inaccessibility.

Reading Pilgrim's romance I feel what Samuel Johnson, in the second of his *Rambler* essays, said of Cervantes's Don Quixote, that 'very few readers, amidst their mirth or pity, can deny that they have admitted visions of the same kind'. 'Our hearts inform us', Johnson declared, that the book's hero 'is not more ridiculous than ourselves, except that he tells what we have only thought'.[9] Pilgrim's is not the eccentric product of 'Janeism', an amateur biographer's stitching together of an improbable narrative: instead it responds to that impulse to know the author's innermost secrets, which, in one form or another, is the keynote of all lives of Jane Austen. Moreover, her ingenious little book epitomises something that seems to be characteristic of work on Jane Austen – the construction of a composite 'Jane', compounded of biographical information, interpretation of the letters, readings of the novels, the whole enhanced – and apparently validated – by the still surviving geographical lineaments of the world she inhabited. This composite Jane (or 'Jane Austen's world') crosses generic and textual borders, so that Jane Austen's biography seeps into the most formal criticism, enters into a film based on a novel, and sequels are written in which the Reverend Edmund and Mrs Price bump into the Reverend and Mrs Elton at a ball.[10]

There may be special reasons why Jane Austen's novels engage their readers with particular seductiveness. These will have something to do with their narrative confidence, and this in turn with the novels' origins in family entertainment, and the ready expectation of a responsive audience. (One remembers Marianne Knight's account of hearing 'peals of laughter' through the bedroom door, her aunt and her elder sister Fanny shut up together reading aloud.[11]) For whatever reasons, it is a well-established social fact that Jane Austen fosters in her readers a peculiarly intense and personal devotedness. 'Jane Austen' is for many of them a human instance with whom they feel unusually intimate, with whom they have shared 'that optimism of the imagination', which, as David Nokes puts it, lies 'at the heart of romance'.[12] 'Every true admirer of the novels', as Katherine Mansfield perceived, 'cherishes the happy thought that he alone – reading between the lines – has become the secret friend of their author'.[13] One might do well to take such readers at their own word, and think of this as a kind of love, notoriously weird as most manifestations of love often do appear to outsiders. Hence, it might be claimed, the readers' desire to know more, to ferret out the smallest details of the loved one's life, to share the secrets of her heart, to participate in, or merge her world with their own.

The result is that, despite the dearth of important new material, substantial attempts to rewrite the life of Jane Austen appear every few years,[14] as well as studies with a broader focus, which, setting her life in historical context, seek to illuminate the cultural world through which she passed and in which she wrote – a world which her novels may, or may not, reflect.[15] The notion of 'Jane Austen's world', here as elsewhere, expands infinitely outwards from the novels themselves. This intense biographical interest in 'Jane', an artist of a particularly retiring kind, though symptomatic of the public's appetite for biographies of artists of all types, is a psychological phenomenon in its own right, and therefore suggests an appropriate starting point for this book.

We are accustomed to thinking of the biographer's task as the recovery of facts about a life, as the compilation of a 'record'. But it might be argued that biography – the biography of an artist – has other sources and motivations than that. Biography is not best understood as a branch of historical inquiry, making what philosophers call the 'truth claim' that it represents what actually occurred in the past: the biography of an artist would perhaps be better understood as a form of imaginative identification. Biography's appeal to readers is inseparable from the dream of possession of, and union with, the subject (a dream which the successful author of a biography must in part share). As Terry Castle put it in a review of Le Faye's edition of the *Letters*, the reader of Jane Austen's fiction is 'hungry for a sense of the author's inner life'.[16] Writers and artists give so much – how understandable, then, that we should want even more! And of all writers in the canon, Jane Austen is the one around whom this fantasy of access, this dream of possession, weaves its most powerful spell. It is a branch of that 'collective exercise in romantic imagination'[17] that is a plausible account of the total phenomena named 'Jane Austen' within our culture.

That biography, and Austenian biography in particular, has elements of fantasy in it is not the argument of this chapter, however, nor that biography is a branch of fiction. The case is more interesting: biography is a hybrid form, a compromise formation between fact and make-believe, in which imaginative possession continually comes up against, and engages with, stubborn resistance. We might call this resistance by a variety of names – 'fact', 'reality', the limitations of knowledge, the paucity of the records, the recognition that the historical past is (much like the interior life of another person or subject) alien and inaccessible. The biographer's task is somehow to manage both the urgencies of fantasy identification and the recalcitrance of facts – their absence as well as their presence. If we accept that biography appeals to a longing for further intimacy with an artist who has seemed to partially, and therefore tantalisingly, disclose themself in their work, we can perhaps accept also that biography replicates the painful lesson we all learn at our mother's breast, that identification cannot be continuous or complete, that the fulfilment of our hunger must be interrupted and disappointed. Biography then in this account may certainly feed the reader's interest in and intimacy with the subject: but it must also deny the reader, and create in him or her a mature recognition of this subject's existence as an independent being, apart.

Perhaps this is the true significance of a celebrated moment that is often cited in Austen biographies, since it was first described in the *Memoir* of 1870. Commenting on his aunt's fertility of composition in the last years of her life, her nephew described her working 'in the general sitting-room, subject to all kinds of casual interruptions'. But, he declared,

She was careful that her occupation should not be suspected by servants, or visitors, or any persons beyond her own family party. She wrote upon small sheets of paper which could easily be put away, or covered with a piece of blotting paper. There was, between the front door and the offices, a swing door which creaked when it was opened; but she objected to having this little inconvenience remedied, because it gave her notice when anyone was coming.[18]

Unremedied still, this door offers visitors to Chawton cottage a physical sign of the past's continuity into the present. But its figurative or symbolic value is more complex than this.[19] The creaking of this door promises a moment of identification: for a second, the reader (or visitor) may imagine that they are close to the author – see her, in the mind's eye, listening for the door, putting her papers away; feel an intimacy, just for a fleeting second, with the activity of the creative writer. Austen-Leigh gives us a glimpse of something that was defined in the title of Jane Aiken Hodge's *The Double Life of Jane Austen* (1972). The hiding places of her power seem open, but Jane Austen, at the very moment before the visitor enters the room, conceals the evidence of her creative process. One is greeted by the polite, conventional lady, that is all: to enter is to be denied, and the surviving biographical material presents little more than this tantalising social self.

Many of the most interesting moments of biographical writing, indeed, occur at the points where the dream of possession and recognition of resistance converge: the moment when the biographer pulls back, when the unreachable nature of the past becomes as apparent as its call to the imagination. The child at the breast must learn that its mother is not always at its service, is not part of itself, is a being, distinct from itself;[20] the reader of the biography in a parallel or analogous way learns that that which he or she identifies with, imagines the possession of, is other, a distinct and separate entity, unreachable, so that, as Park Honan puts it, 'most assuredly, biography is in one sense a poor and failing enterprise'.[21] The self-confessed 'romantic biographer', Richard Holmes, declares that a form of love of his or her subject is necessary for the enterprise to succeed. 'If you are not in love with them you will not follow them – not very far, anyway.' In Holmes's version, the biographer makes a pilgrimage, following in his subject's footsteps, seeking to recapture him or her through an affective affinity encouraged by experiencing the surroundings in which that experience took form. 'But the true biographical process', Holmes suggests, 'begins precisely at the moment, at the places, where this naive form of love and identification breaks down'. 'Impersonal objective re-creation' (as Holmes puts it) requires the admission that the subject is inaccessible, that he or she inhabits the other side of a divide. The moment at which this perception forces itself upon Holmes is telling. 'For me, almost the earliest occasion was that bridge at Langogne, the old broken bridge that I could not cross, and the sudden physical sense that the past was indeed "another country".'[22] And this autobiographical confession is at the same time a contribution to biography, literally a bridge between the two.

It is not surprising that this tension between identification and resistance becomes most apparent when the material of Austenian biography concerns her 'romantic' attachments. Such is the moment in Elizabeth Jenkins's admirable 1938 life when Jane Austen's youthful flirtation with Tom Lefroy is recorded. In 1796, when the author was nineteen, Lefroy was staying with his aunt, Mrs Lefroy, Jane's friend at nearby Ashe, and a ball was held:

In the Rectory at Ashe they made room for dancing by opening the folding doors between the drawing-room and the morning-room; the windows of the latter looked out on to the lawn, on one side of which was a great yew hedge. The yews, black under the brilliant moon of winter, and the gravel that crackled and glistened under carriage wheels, were exchanged as the guests jumped out of their carriages and ran into the house, for the warmth of high-piled fires, the magic radiance of candlelight, the tuning up of violins and the welcoming, gracious gaiety of Mrs Lefroy. Jane in her rose-coloured silk dress had a reason besides her love of dancing for being excited; whether Tom Lefroy saw her first on the stairs or in the hall or in one of the halves of the ballroom; how soon they danced together, how much Mrs Lefroy, in the midst of her cares as hostess, had leisure to keep an eye on them, can never now be known. Tom Lefroy lived to be Lord Chief Justice of Ireland, and as an exceedingly old man he said that he had once been in love with the great Jane Austen; 'but it was a boy's love', he added.[23]

The detail about the rose-coloured silk dress is based on a mention in the first surviving letter of 9 January 1796 that 'all my money is spent in buying white gloves and pink persian',[24] the rest presumably on Ashe Rectory as it survives today. (It seems unlikely though that the light thin silk, commonly used for lining or underwear, would be made into a dress, or that the dress would have been ready in time for the dance a week later.) 'At length the day is come when I am to flirt my last with Tom Lefroy,' Austen writes to Cassandra in her next, on the 15th, 'and when you receive this it will be over. My tears flow as I write at the melancholy idea.' Austen typically forestalls a sentimental response, yet despite this, her other biographers have found the incident with Tom

Lefroy difficult not to embroider with the flowers of romance, as we shall see. But here it is interesting that the flush of authorly participation and readerly seduction is swiftly countermanded by the biographer's conscientious return to the mundane ground of recorded fact.

Such excursions into imaginative reconstruction are rare in Jenkins's biography, but more common in the recent lives. During the past decades, indeed, British biography has evolved into a genre with much closer affinities to fiction, or rather one in which the boundaries between history and fictionality have become indistinct. Though a great deal of history might well have always been, as Catherine Morland complained, 'invention' (*Northanger Abbey*, p. 109), most contemporary biographers of Austen unashamedly borrow techniques from the novel, and attempt in a variety of novelistic ways to eke out the bare provisions of the historical record. The desire to delve into the recesses of the author, to know the secret origins of creativity, is one which can only be satisfied by appropriation of techniques for the simulation of consciousness developed by the nineteenth-century novelists, and all of Austen's most recent biographers include passages in which the author's thoughts, plans and desires are rendered in a form adapted from that mode of her own that is inelegantly termed 'free indirect speech'. This enables the biographer simultaneously to mimic the figure's inner thoughts, and still to reserve to themselves the dignity belonging to an historian. But if biography now almost self-consciously admits its affinity to fiction, this is a tense rather than a gracious relationship. Fiction – by which in this context one means realist fiction – attempts to persuade its reader of the 'truth' of what it represents, but this is a different order of 'truth', obviously, as Aristotle taught, from that which the historian might claim for his or her material. There remains an uneasy instability within the biography between these two claims for truth.

If the notion that biography appeals to dream and fantasy is a tenable one, and if the analogy with the infant learning that its hungers must occasionally be disappointed seems plausible, one might take the comparison a stage further. Freud's argument in his well-known 1907 lecture 'Creative Writers and Day-Dreaming', was that private fantasies of power, omnipotence and sexual gratification illuminate the appeal of successful authors. The identification of the reader with the hero or sometimes with the villain, harnessing egotistic daydreams of various kinds, he claims, is the mechanism that drives the imagination forward and the source of much of the pleasure of the novelistic text. But as Freud admitted, this account could say nothing about the public or shared nature of art, the factor that links it with play, and distinguishes it from daydreaming and fantasy; nor does it differentiate classics from best-sellers, Jane Austen from Barbara Taylor Bradford. Freud asserts that 'a piece of creative writing, like a day-dream, is a continuation of, and a substitute for, what was once the play of childhood',[25] but in effect it is substitution rather than evolution that he stresses. D. W. Winnicott, too, linked creative experience with a child's play, but unlike Freud he sought to emphasise its essential continuity with the earlier experience of the child, which, he emphasised, is not like daydreaming at all.

The appeal of biography is obviously distinct from the appeal of the novels, for it straddles the space between the inner life of the subject and the objective world of 'real' historical fact. As Holmes's moment of revelation implies, it is a bridge between the two. I suggest that biography in effect occupies what Winnicott in one of his key papers described as 'transitional space'. As a paediatrician, he saw dozens of children, healthy as well as sick, in his clinic each day, and observed closely how they developed in relation to their mothers. It was he who formulated the notion that the ordinary – the 'good enough' – mother helps her child progress normally by occasionally disappointing and failing the infant. In this way, her existence as a distinct being, other to itself, is gradually made manifest to the child. Winnicott also observed that small children commonly carry about with them, and often cannot go to sleep without, a piece of soft cloth or rag, which he named a 'transitional object'. The term is a kind of pun, playing with the jargon of psychoanalysis in which the 'object' or 'internal object' refers to the presence in a person's psyche of precipitates of encounters with people who have been important to them. At the same time it acknowledges that these comforters of the child really are 'objects', in the sense that they exist in the actual world, can be thrown in the washing machine, and have a pet name recognised by the family. The soft rag or cloth represents the mother and is infused with the child's inner reverie of the mother's softness, comfort and closeness. It is 'transitional' because it enables the child to move towards the relinquishment of the fantasy of identity with the mother and towards the acceptance of that real world of which it simultaneously forms a part. Winnicott's thinking thus accommodated both the 'intrapsychic' life of the child and the 'real' realm of social interaction. Sooner or later, when the child can do without the soothing presence of this piece of cloth, he or she has internalised a care-giving mother, and is ready to enter the world of reality.

From the 'transitional object' (an observed phenomenon) Winnicott elaborated the theoretical concept of 'transitional space'. Transitional space is that area of simultaneously psychological and social life occupied by all activities in which illusion and reality coexist, such as the arts. 'Transitional space' offers us what, in an enigmatic formulation, he called a 'resting place for illusion'. Explaining the phrase to his French translator, he wrote, 'I mean that there is a constant struggle in the individual throughout life, distinguishing fact from fantasy, external from psychic reality, the world from the dream. The Transitional Phenomena belong to an intermediate area which I am calling a resting place because living in this area the individual is at rest from the task of distinguishing fact from fantasy.'[26] In transitional space, shared experiences coexist alongside private fantasy and dreaming, and the paradox is tolerated. Broadly speaking, the concept resembles others that have at times been elaborated by literary critics or anthropologists to define the distinctive nature of the objects they address – the 'third realm' of the poem or the 'liminal space' of ritual[27] – but it is distinguished by its emphasis on the satisfactions of fantasy, on the continuity between later experiences and the infant's earliest psychological life, and therefore by the hints it offers for understanding the satisfactions and power of art. Yet Winnicott's emphasis here on a 'resting place' seems less than exact where biography is concerned. For while transitional space names that arena or genre in which fantasy and reality coexist, it does not pinpoint anything of the tug-of-war between dreaming and history that is characteristic of the biography.

The view of life-writing practice that I have been developing has some distinguished opponents. There is a school of biographical theory, most forcefully articulated in Bernard Crick's *George Orwell, a Life*, which argues that the job of the biographer is to avoid 'the empathetic fallacy', to decline all attempts to represent the subject's thoughts or inner life.[28] Crick writes that '[a]ll too often the literary virtues of the English biographical tradition give rise to characteristic vices: smoothing out or silently resolving contradictions in the evidence and bridging gaps by empathy and intuition . . . None of us can enter another person's mind; to believe so is fiction.'[29] Yet as David Ellis comments in his recent *Literary Lives*, '[a]ll biography is a way of thinking about other people and that is a process virtually impossible in our culture without the use of expressions which imply knowledge of their states of mind.' To reconstitute the subject's 'internal soliloquy' is a necessary part of the biographer's enterprise, he suggests: what matters, as Ellis demonstrates, is the degree of plausibility, and the code of explanation that the biographer draws upon. But even he seems reluctant to use a term like imagination, which might appear to collapse the genre into a mode akin to fiction.[30]

A biography that seems to stick to the facts is Deirdre Le Faye's revision of *Life and Letters of Jane Austen* into *Jane Austen: a Family Record*. Scrupulously collecting, collating and presenting the reports of nieces and acquaintances, whilst acknowledging gaps and uncertainties, only the occasional 'no doubt' seems to signal the book's tentative extrapolation from the available information to hint at Jane Austen's state of mind. Whilst excerpts from the early reviews of the novels are presented (for these certainly belong to the historical record and may have had consequences for Jane Austen's sales) it is not assumed that the novels can be used as material to reveal the author's emotional life. The impression of bedrock historical reliability this abstention gives may explain why subsequent biographers have quoted from this 'record' virtually verbatim, without either recognising their borrowings, nor acknowledging that Le Faye, too, necessarily interprets the material she presents. 'On 5 December 1794', she reports, for example, 'Mr Austen purchased at Basingstoke, "a Small Mahogany Writing Desk with 1 Long Drawer and Glass Ink Stand Compleat" for 12/-': bald fact enough. Perhaps, she continues, this was given to his daughter on her nineteenth birthday; if so, 'it may have inspired her during 1794 to embark upon her first full-length project' – 'Elinor and Marianne.' 'Family tradition' suggests that this was written in letters. 'However, to convert *Elinor and Marianne* later on into the straightforward narrative of *Sense and Sensibility* must have involved Jane in considerable difficulty and labour, and so decided her against using the epistolary style for any further novels.'[31] Step by step, the reader is led across the stepping stones of 'seems', 'if so', 'perhaps', 'family tradition' and 'must have' into a region of pure speculation that nevertheless seems to be authenticated by the factual documentation out of which it apparently arose.[32]

Nor need biography be sympathetic nor its subject the receptacle of identification of an obvious kind to contain the work of wish-fulfilment. John Halperin's *The Life of Jane Austen* (1984) was self-consciously bent on disrupting the image of the author and her family given in the *Memoir* and repeated in previous books, like Elizabeth Jenkins's. His view is that Jane Austen's novels reveal their author to be very different from the modest and sympathetic figure of family tradition. Jenkins insisted that 'to try to deduce from her novels a personal history of Jane Austen, is completely to misunderstand the type of mind she represents', and argued that the writer was in this respect akin to Shakespeare.[33] Halperin asserts on the contrary that the critic can deduce the artist's temperament or mood from the works, and that figures in them are unmediated 'portraits' of acquaintances.[34] His 'academic' biography might appear to be at the opposite extreme to Pilgrim's, yet it too is seduced by the novels' promise of autobiographical disclosure, and attempts to generate a romantic or affective life for the novelist from their materials. Readings of the novels represent his main attempt to penetrate the inner sanctum of Austen's emotions and to reveal here not their benign, but their abrasive, reality. 'Irony, bitter irony, is the mode of *Northanger Abbey*', he writes, for instance (however improbably): it is 'the work of a caustic, disappointed woman':

In Catherine's early failures with men, we may perceive the novelist's. 'She had reached the age of seventeen, without having seen one amiable youth who could call forth her sensibility: without having inspired one real passion, and without having excited even any admiration but what was moderate and very transient.' What heartbreaking disappointment lies behind those words! Catherine aches to be popular. Instead, when she enters a public room in Bath no one notices her, no one asks who she is, no one sings her praises. Jane Austen's own despondency is clear in this . . . When Isabella says 'I have no notion of loving people by halves . . . My attachments are always excessively strong', we may catch the novelist's tone in her voice. 'I believe my feelings are stronger than any body's; I am sure they are too strong for my own peace', Isabella adds. That last phrase is a telling one. Jane Austen's 'peace' was surely on the brink of destruction, in her early twenties, as a result of loneliness, of sexual longing. *Northanger Abbey* shows her asking the old question: Where is the man for me?[35]

Though Professor Halperin is a literary critic, he knows the ways of the heart. To anchor one's presentation of the emotions of the author to analysis of a text, it seems, is no more a guarantee of impartiality than other methods. On the face of it, the approach is plausible, even necessary: only through her novels one might learn what were the deepest, most pressing preoccupations of Austen's life, since it would be the presence in them, however oblique, however disguised, of some such personal need that accounts for their hold upon readers. But Halperin's practice demonstrates again how reading the novels autobiographically cannot be separated from projection, the fantasy life or personal demand of the biographer, though it takes a quite different form from Pilgrim's romance. Here the biographer's desire – to establish his thesis, to see his inner representation of Austen vindicated in her 'objective' texts – compels him into otherwise inexplicable self-blinding. How else account for the complete disregard of elementary rules of critical analysis that allows him to take the slangy expressions of a caricature figure like Isabella as the author's own, or to regard the amused sanity of these narrational comments as evidence of heartbreak?

Three more recent biographies – those by Park Honan, David Nokes and Claire Tomalin – have faced with keener metabiographical alertness the challenges faced in recovering or narrating a life so reticently conducted and (comparatively) so parsimoniously preserved as Jane Austen's. All three are aware of the role that identification and imagination play in the biographer's task, and are conscious that in writing about Jane Austen they are trespassing, in some degree, into other readers' psychic space, involved as much with a figure of myth or collective fantasy as with a series of historical occurrences. 'Jane Austen', the denizen of the cultural imagination, stalks transparently through these texts. Of the three, David Nokes's *Jane Austen, a Life* (1997) is the most ambitiously provocative. Deliberately assuming a quasi-fictional format, beginning before Austen's birth and in a setting far removed from Hampshire, and representing serially the thoughts and motives of many other persons beside the novelist, Nokes's work marks a deliberate rupture with the previous styles of Austenian biographical narrative, just as it claims to break with earlier traditions of secrecy that have surrounded the author's family life. Explaining his intentions in his Introduction, he writes

This is a biography written *forwards*. In formal terms, it does not adopt the 'objective' view of a modern biographer but, like a novel, presents events through the perceptions of its principal characters (with only such occasional authorial interventions as might be permitted to the 'omniscient narrator' of a fictional work) . . . In this biography, the speeches put into people's mouths are *not* invention, and those who wish to verify their accuracy may find the sources in the footnotes. Nothing is spoken which cannot be authenticated, and no incident presented for which there is not documentary evidence. But in the disposition of a character's thoughts, as in the interpretation of his or her actions, there is some degree of invention.[36]

In effect, David Nokes adopts for his biographical narrative the convention of historical realism,[37] one in which events are perceived by a range of figures, including the novelist's father, her cousin Eliza de Feuillide, and Cassandra, as well as Jane Austen herself. With its wide sweep from the Sunderbunds of Calcutta to Revolutionary France,

Cadiz and the South Pacific, Nokes's epic narrative seems conceived in contradistinction to the narrower focus of his subject's art, an opening out of Austen's 'world' that replicates the recuperative strategies of recent filmmakers. One difficulty that the reader of the biography quickly comes upon is that since it is largely presented through different consciousnesses, a deal of what seems obvious 'invention' seems to occur.

Nokes is aware too, of the dangers of accepting familiar traditions as if they were self-evident truths. He rereads the available material in an infernal sense, to dispute interpretations that consensus has solidified into truths. He calls his readers' attention to the 'hearsay' nature of the information that the author 'fainted away' on being abruptly given the news in December 1800 that the family were to leave their country life in Steventon and remove to Bath, for example, and remarks on Austen's other biographers' keenness to 'repeat a story which accords so well with their own view of how she *ought* to have reacted' (*Jane Austen*, p. 221). Such scepticism is refreshing. In contrast to the tradition which makes her deeply unhappy at the removal from all that she cherished, and reads the absence of surviving letters from the ensuing years in Bath as evidence of unhappiness and frustration, Nokes suggests that Jane Austen might have been in fact delighted at the opportunities for social life the fashionable city offered. 'For years, Jane had dreamt of a larger world', he reveals: if Cassandra suppressed the letters in the weeks following the announcement, was this not because they were full of an 'unseemly excitement'? Maybe: but in one sentence in her letter of January 1801 – the first which survives after the news had broken – Jane Austen writes that 'I get more & more reconciled to the idea of our removal',[38] which Nokes omits.

Following his adversarial, revisionist scheme of disrupting the received image of the Austens' family life, Nokes is able to read into a letter of George Austen written when his wife is in London in 1770 evidence of 'disturbance' that she is enjoying the city's entertainments too much. So that when she in her turn writes to a correspondent that 'Town' is 'a sad place. I would not live in it on any account', he can construe this not as a candid statement of preference for the country (and even her husband's company), but as evidence that she is responding to his pressure (*Jane Austen*, p. 40). But why should dubious or mean motives be more plausible than generous and sympathetic ones? The adoption of Jane Austen's brother Edward by his rich relatives the Knights becomes a sinister 'dynastic transfer'. 'There is something so shocking in a child's being taken away from his parents and natural home!' Isabella Knightley declares in *Emma*. This is offered as evidence for Jane Austen's opinion of 'Frank Weston's similar adoption' (*Jane Austen*, p. 76) – though Edward was sixteen when the Knights formally took him as their heir, and Frank was removed to Yorkshire when he was about two. The fiction of a seamless continuity between the novels (distinct from each other as are their created worlds) and the biography is not the only troubling thing here: as with John Halperin's earlier book, statements of foolish characters are lifted out of context and distorted to serve the biographer's overriding destructive intent. There is no adequate reason to think that Henry Austen resented his brother's good fortune, though Nokes attempts to put such a construction on Henry's reminiscences (given to Anna Lefroy in 1858 when he was seventy-seven). Jane 'felt saddened and disturbed at his sudden disappearance from the Austen family home', Nokes relates. Edward's removal had been on the cards for four years, since he was twelve – and James had previously left home for Oxford at the age of fourteen.

The imagination, I have been arguing, must inevitably play a role in any biographical enterprise. Why, then, does this challenging attempt to reconfigure Jane Austen's life provoke the reader into such an attitude of surly scholarly virtue? Is the hostile reception of this biography merely resentment at having familiar illusions disturbed? One might have a good deal of sympathy with the belief, heralded most explicitly in Nokes's chapter headings – 'Noisy and Wild', 'Profligate and Shocking', 'Wild Beast' – that Austen cannot have been the anodyne figure of family tradition, the demurely Christian lady who never said an unkind thing nor thought a bad one. Austen was a genius, and her relations with her environment cannot have been all smooth sailing. How to read this into the surviving and censored record is the challenge.

'The history of a writer', George Eliot once declared in a letter, protesting against biography in general, 'is contained in his writings – these are his chief actions'.[39] If her novels are Jane Austen's chief actions (certainly a more plausible idea about her than about Burney or Stendhal or Scott) it is only through an account of them that her genius – which set her apart from her world – can be represented. It can only reside in the novels and can only be expressed or signalled through the novels themselves, or at least through their intellectual energy and style somehow lighting up the biographer's own narrative. (One might suggest that this is why the critical enterprise has a better chance of putting us in touch with the essential Jane Austen, whatever that is, than the biographical.) Perhaps to catch something of the essence of Austen is what Nokes is attempting in his simulations of free indirect speech. Yet his accounts of the novels themselves are brief and conventional.

Jane Austen, a Life is at the opposite end of the scale to Le Faye's. Its solution to the challenge of biography is to give fictional reconstruction pride of place. But this fresh interpretation of character and events occurs under the aegis of historical realism, and that is the core of the problem. One cannot, within this convention, and bound to realism's ends, simultaneously proclaim the speculativeness of one's representation. To do this is to subvert and disorganise the very premises on which the realist enterprise depends, so memorably expressed when Henry James greeted Trollope's authorial avowal that he might make his characters do what he wished with the comment '[S]uch a betrayal of a sacred office, seems to me, I confess, a terrible crime'.[40] A realist text only works if the reader's assent to its claim to represent the historical truth can be secured. The narrative's pursuit of immediacy – 'How well George remembered the day . . .' (*Jane Austen, a Life*, p. 19), 'Philadelphia took up the letter once more, which trembled in her hand as she read it' (p. 27) – can scarcely be read within this convention but as transcription of known historical fact. Was Jane Austen's cousin Eliza really the illegitimate daughter of Warren Hastings, whom her mother had known in India, and who bestowed munificent gifts on them both? It is a cornerstone of Nokes's account that she was. 'No proof at all has ever been found to substantiate this claim', wrote Deirdre Le Faye in a scathing review of his book.[41] The issue is not really though of 'interpretive imagination run riot', as she put it, it is that within the dictates of this convention, there is no leeway for supposition or hesitation or the latitude of speculation: she either is or she isn't. David Nokes may have enjoyed imagining how her sister might have looked to Cassandra, or writing an approximation of eighteenth-century prose to render George Austen's thoughts. But there is no sense of the fanciful or the provisional woven into his narrative. Nor is there space within his adopted model for the imagining self of the biographer. The reader becomes imprisoned within narrative conventions whose authority stifles collaboration. In other words, what is missing here is something that – using one of its many and varied meanings – one might designate as authorial 'play'.

Winnicott's transitional phenomena were the precursors of much more widely extended activities. 'There is a direct development from transitional phenomena to playing', he wrote, 'and from playing to shared playing and from this to cultural experiences'. The infant toys with its blanket or rag: the toddler plays. The child who is playing is preoccupied, nearly withdrawn into the world of fantasy and illusion, but not quite. Into this play area he or she, as he put it, 'gathers objects or phenomena from external reality and uses these in the service of some sample derived from inner or personal reality'. The psychic motor, so to speak, is the dreamlike activity, but the child takes account of material conditions and objects. 'Without hallucinating the child puts out a sample of dream potential and lives with this sample in a chosen setting of fragments from external reality.' [42]

Just as Winnicott's theory suggests, the term 'play' itself expands towards a whole universe of cultural activities, as if language itself were recognising the infinite extensibility of the phenomena it designates. One plays soccer or the violin or the stock market or observes the shifting play of light. 'Who can keep pace with the fluctuations of your Fancy, the Capprizios of your Taste, the Contradictions of your Feelings?', Jane Austen wrote with intense mimetic zest to her niece Fanny in 1817, 'I shall hate you when your delicious play of Mind is all settled down into conjugal & maternal affections.'[43] It is such qualities that Winnicott perceived as central to all the activities to which we apply the verb 'play' – latitude, variation, imaginative flexibility within specific constraints – and which brings to life cultural productions. If one accepts Winnicott's rather grand leap from child's play to 'cultural experiences', biography would be an example of the elaborated activities which derive their salient characteristics from the child's play. Similarly imaginative possession of the subject is the motor, and a similar cognisance of external reality ('the facts') and its constraints (including the absence of facts) must be negotiated whilst at the same time continuity or consistency of imaginative life is sustained.

Like David Nokes, though not in his biography itself, Park Honan offers a response to Crick and a defence of writers who attempt to enter their subject's minds, in his articles collected in *Author's Lives: on Literary Biography and the Arts of Language*, published in 1990, three years after his biography of Austen. In the introductory chapter, 'Beyond Sartre: theory and form in modern biographies', he comments that Sartre's biographies of Genet 'have an inward reflective comment that suits the quality of their subject's mind', and that he 'lends out his own mental vitality to animate a mind equal to his own – and lends out his attributes, of course, to that mind in both cases. He subverts truth in interpretation.'[44] This seems in part to describe Honan's own practice, in which the mind of Jane Austen and the narrator's own construction of it seem to merge. The effect, at its best, is of literary criticism fused with biographical interpretation. When he writes 'Richardson seemed to her not at all sentimental, but realistic in showing that what goes through the mind is chiefly emotive and not so cold, privileged and settled as retrospective narrative tended to suggest',[45] he is indeed 'lending' his own critical understanding to the elucidation of his subject. He does not mean that at a given historical moment Jane Austen thought these scholarly thoughts, but that these ideas offer a plausible reconstruction of the kinds of motives that might have been intuitively at the root of her artistic practice.

This is a dangerous tactic, though, for it is claiming historical truth whilst actually resting on imaginative truthfulness. When Honan, like other biographers, offers to enter Jane Austen's mind, the reader detects the sound of thin ice cracking. This is the case with the most momentous passage of Jane Austen's life of which we have record. He devotes several pages of *Jane Austen: her Life* to her meditations the night after her acceptance and before her subsequent rejection of Harris Wither's proposal in December 1802, deftly weaving commentary and quotations from the novels, comments on the period, fragments of evidence from witnesses (or at least from Fanny Lefroy who heard from Anna Lefroy who had heard from her mother) and invocatory gestures, into a tapestry that offers a plausible simulacrum of a person revolving difficult issues. This enables him – perhaps more importantly – to pace his narrative so as to accord this occasion its appropriate weight.[46] As with Austen's characteristic late deployment of free indirect speech, Honan's writing here, and elsewhere at key moments, tends to move from the narrator's position, in which the subject is 'she' or 'Jane' to a rhythmic propulsiveness which picks up and resonates with something of the emotion he is rendering ('She had made a major mistake. She was to blame, to blame'). This is an unabashed claim to enter the consciousness of the writer in 'a prose style attuned' to the subject's mind, which Honan also speaks of in suggesting what Austen might have found useful in *Camilla*.[47] But the effect is not altogether convincing. Nothing can disguise the fact that we simply do not know what Jane Austen thought or felt on this occasion, that to concoct it seems like an intrusion on her privacy; the very scrupulosity of the biographer's attempted reconstruction seems to read as a confession of this.

Occasionally in Honan's book a figure called 'one' appears. 'One' marks the incursion of the author, glimpsed whenever the past surroundings of Jane Austen's life still survive, or when 'one' is able to handle family documents.[48] One, for just a moment, is understood to live in the present and to imagine the past. Such a strategy becomes a key element in the third of the biographies published in 1997, Claire Tomalin's *Jane Austen: a Life*, which foregrounds the narrator as an imagining modern writer.[49] Without blending autobiography and biography, as Richard Holmes does in his reflections on the biographical enterprise, *Footsteps*, she manages to suggest her own presence, as an imagining, thoughtful, reconstructing being. This enables Tomalin to treat Austen as a writer too. When the novelist was staying with Henry in London in August 1814 'she describes herself walking in and out between house and garden', Tomalin writes, and adds 'it is very much what someone settling down to write does, getting up, pacing, thinking, returning to the page she is working on' (*Jane Austen, a Life*, p. 243). And, at an earlier period, 'Now that Jane had begun, she must often have walked alone along the lanes, made passable by the frost, her feet clinking in their pattens, her imagination working.' 'You can imagine her at work in the blue-papered dressing room upstairs before coming down for dinner at three-thirty, or after tea at six thirty, testing her dialogue first on her own ear, cutting and amending whatever embarrassed her or struck a false note in the dialogue, as you do if you are going to be reading aloud to others; and marking her text in the neat hand she had developed, paper always being expensive.'[50]

Tomalin's *Jane Austen: a Life*, then, is openly a work of the identificatory imagination (though it is also conscientiously researched). 'The family trees need to be sorted out', she remarks, 'by anyone who aims to inhabit the world in which [Jane Austen] was at home'. Such a comment defines both the need to 'inhabit' that world, and the sense of that project's difficulty, a distance that the imagination alone can bridge. Tomalin achieves this by actually bringing forward her fancy as a figure on the textual stage, and by underlining, rather than obliterating, the distinctions between past and present. 'Looking back from our easier century, you feel how wretched it must have been when a longed for marriage brought pregnancy and illness', she writes, adding, 'but this is a strictly anachronistic piece of sympathy' (p. 200). Writing of Jane Austen's interest, or lack of interest, in clothes she says '[t]he impression we get is that, had she lived 200 years later, she would have rejoiced in the freedom of a pair of old trousers'. Neither the term 'identification', nor the notion of biography as 'transference',[51] though, can capture why this technique works so persuasively.

'You' in Tomalin's biography is both the biographer and a space that the reader himself, or herself, is invited to fill. This 'you' simultaneously inhabits the past – 'you did not expect the luxury of piped water in a country cottage' – and harkens to the present. At moments present imaginings are reflected back onto the past: 'Cass's bereavement seemed to be pushing them both into – aunthood? spinsterhood? self-sufficiency? – it was hard to say' (p. 142). Perhaps this might have been more accurately written 'It is hard to say', but even here the questioning mode allows space for a provisionality that is not uncertainty but play. In Tomalin's narrative the presentation of 'you', temporarily both reader and biographer, enables the otherness of others, historically remote from ourselves, to become fleetingly apparent. By allowing her imagination to wonder (though not to wander) and by making plain that she is wondering, Tomalin begins to solve the epistemological problem that besets the biographical enterprise. Tomalin's book occupies a genuine transitional space then, engaging, if not satisfying, the desire for both the real, the historical, and the yearning to know, to possess, to enter the experience of the great writer.

Yet it remains the case that, as Henry James suggested, '[w]here [Jane Austen's] testimony complacently ends, the pressure of appetite within us presumes exactly to begin'.[52] The enigma of this writer – whose subject, above all, is love, love in all its varieties – is that so little sense of her own erotic or emotional attachments is available in the surviving documents. 'Is not my soul laid open in these veracious pages?',[53] Jane Austen's 'dear Dr Johnson' had written teasingly to Mrs Thrale, and followed it up with an elaborately artificial letter brimful of formal phrases which convey nothing at all – the sort of passing parody of literary stylistics in which Austen's own letters delighted. Everything we infer from her work about the novelist's attitude towards the literature of sensibility suggests how heartily she would agree about the untrustworthiness of directly avowed sentiment. Austen's letters do not lay her soul open: they are above all artefacts written to please (by their information and wit), certainly not to communicate the deepest emotions of the author. Yet the yearning, in the biographers of Austen, and her readers, to know about, to believe in, the inner life, yields to the foregrounding of sexual and emotional motifs she would herself have disdained. The young Jane Austen is imagined, anachronistically, on the model of a romantic heroine.

Which brings us back to Tom Lefroy. Nadia Radovici's *A Youthful*

Love?: Jane Austen and Tom Lefroy tells a story not unlike Constance Pilgrim's, but with a different hero, and with even more artless ingenuity.[54] In a letter from Bath in 1805 Jane Austen writes that 'this morning we have been to see Miss Chamberlayne look hot on horseback. – Seven years & four months ago we went to the same ridinghouse to see Miss Lefroy's performance! – What a different set we are now moving in!' For Radovici this is unquestionable grounds for believing that Jane Austen's relationship with Tom Lefroy did not end with their flirtation in 1796. Have we not the autobiographical evidence of *Northanger Abbey* and *Persuasion*, scenes of which are both set in Bath, for the continuance of their relationship? Tom is partially Henry Tilney (for he and Catherine talk about history, and Tom was an enthusiastic member of the Historical Society of Dublin): Mrs Lefroy's dispatching Tom from Ashe is the 'mirror image of what is told in the novel', General Tilney's 'hurrying away' Catherine from the Abbey. What these two young lovers saw in each other was 'true value, pure, unalloyed gold', and Jane Austen's love for Tom was to last her lifetime. Anne Elliot's early loss is her's, and Tom reappears in the figure of Captain Wentworth. Lady Dalrymple remarks that Wentworth is 'a very fine young man indeed. More air than one often sees in Bath – Irish, I dare say'. Doesn't Jane Austen refer to Tom Lefroy as 'my Irish friend'?[55]

Like Constance Pilgrim's, Radovici's book is suffused with an enthusiasm that has its own power to persuade. But all of Austen's recent biographers find the episode with Lefroy an irresistible invitation to their creative and sympathising imagination. 'For him, Jane's feelings were poised on the knife-edge between flattered amusement and the exciting apprehension of possible romantic commitment', Le Faye narrates, with apparent knowledge of the writer's intimate life. 'This ambivalence is reflected in the first two of her extant letters, those which she wrote to Cassandra during January 1796.'[56] Nokes makes explicit his enrolment of Austen in the ranks of romance. A dance where a greenhouse was 'illuminated in a very elegant manner', as Austen tells her sister, in the first of these letters, turns into 'a splendid ball . . . where the greenhouse was magically illuminated with several hundred candles'.[57] Jane becomes a Cinderella figure, her happiness at the ball tragically cut short. Tom is called off by his family and all her hopes turn 'to ashes': they dance together, 'savouring the sweet melancholy of a final embrace' – how can a reader of Jane Austen unblushingly write such a phrase? – and never meet again. Nevertheless, Jane's pain is mitigated 'by the status that this episode had conferred on her of being a woman who had loved and lost. It was no small consolation to her wounded pride to be able to view herself in the tradition of romantic heroines.'[58] Which is rather hard to swallow.

Taking his tip from a 'Lefroy descendent who states that "she did all the running" ', Park Honan's much more thorough and subtle interpretation of the same episode presents the young Jane Austen as a sexual adventuress. Though he too puts himself at times in Austen's shoes ('She knew more of flirting and finesse than the tired owner of three debating medals who stood before her . . . she had decided to fall in love'[59]), it is Tom's experience at the hands of a vivacious predator that arouses his interest, as when he lists the lavish provision of food and describes how 'red-faced hunters were present on these occasions . . . a flushed man swollen with drink might grab at a girl in the supper interlude and mutter "Let's to bed" . . . Who cared if people gossiped till they burst?' (Red, flushed, swollen, burst: and just whose unconscious is showing here, I wonder?) Austen's own reminiscence of such a raucous world was rather more dainty. 'He has but *one* fault', she wrote of Lefroy to Cassandra, 'which time will, I trust, entirely remove – it is that his morning coat is a great deal too light. He is a great admirer of Tom Jones, and therefore wears the same coloured clothes, I imagine, as he did when *he* was wounded.'[60] Despite this incursion into his sketch of a hunted rather than hunting Lefroy, Honan is sure that the tables were turned on Austen, and the flirtation is once again pumped up into serious romance. 'Jane . . . despite herself fell deeply in love; a positive fact reflected in her long obsession with Tom Lefroy.' This claim is backed up by the new evidence (exciting enough to be inserted into the 1997 edition of his book) that 'she was to copy out Irish love-songs for a considerable time.'[61]

Claire Tomalin does not eschew the romantic motif occasionally either: Tom Lefroy enters as 'this dazzling stranger' in her presentation of the episode. But her staging is of Austen writing the first letter, not of Austen at the balls, and her account is avowedly a kind of reading over the author's shoulder as she writes. Thus a certain light speculativeness is infused into the account, and the intimate touches that in David Nokes's narrative seem woodenly fictive become delightful: 'She can't keep him out, this "gentlemanlike, good-looking, pleasant young man", as she covers the sheet of paper so cheerfully, dipping her well-sharpened pen into the little ink bottle at her side.' (*Jane Austen, a Life*, p. 113). Phrases such as 'there must have been', 'no doubt', 'something of the kind' do not function in Tomalin's writing like the nervous reassurances of other biographers that what they are claiming has the status of historical truth, but the opposite way, as signals of alertness to the fact that much of this must in the end be conjecture.[62] The writer is constantly reminding the reader that the past can only be captured through a kind of make-believe, at the same time as she is engagingly willing to try her hand.

'We can't help knowing that her personal story will not go in the direction she is imagining in the letter' (*Jane Austen: a Life*, p. 117). Tomalin's book is as much about the reader, and about what the eager reader wants to think, and about her own imaginative sympathy, as it is about Austen. 'Then, if you turn back to the very beginning of the letter, you find its opening sentence suggests there was some thought of the future in her mind as she wrote.' Then, Tomalin offers a simulation of what Jane Austen might have dreamed of as she wished Cassandra on her twenty-third birthday, which is the occasion of the letter, 'twenty-three years longer'. She imagines Jane Austen dreaming of her own and Cassandra's future. The effect is uncanny. 'Eighteen-nineteen: the date in another century was almost unimaginable, conjured out of the air by Jane's pen.' Conjured out of the air by Clare Tomalin's wordprocessor, nearly two centuries later, one is brought close to the past, but also reminded in the same gesture, of how unimaginably remote, at two removes, it is: the past strange and the past familiar seem to hang together, tremulously in balance.

It has not been the purpose of this chapter to contribute to Austen biography, but rather to explore some of the epistemological and psychological aspects of the biographical impulse. As I have tried to indicate, we actually know much less about Jane Austen than her biographers would have us believe. The case is not hopeless: much genuine illumination of Austen's circumstances can be found in books, not committed to narrative, which blend historical research with attention to the outer circumstances of her life.[63] An entirely different twist to these readings of Austen's emotional life was given, however, when Terry Castle, reviewing Le Faye's edition of the *Letters* in August 1995, suggested that the true, the real, object of Austen's most passionate feelings was not male at all, but this sister to whom most of them are addressed. In this light, the facetious tone of her youthful treatment of heterosexual sentiment, her intense portrayal of sisterly relations in *Sense and Sensibility* and *Pride and Prejudice* (though not of course in *Mansfield Park* and *Persuasion*), her comments on physical appearance in the letters, even her interest in dress and dress-making, – and, one might add, her acceptance and then retraction of the proposal of Harris Wither – might be pressed into the service of quite another thesis about the inner life, the central mystery, of this writer.

Castle's general proposition, that Jane Austen's companionship with her sister was 'unquestionably the most important emotional relationship of her life' is really not at issue.[64] It is salutary to be reminded of this, when so much of the biographers' energy is devoted to amplifying hints of heterosexual romance, as if only this could authenticate or dignify the author's claims to speak, as she does so convincingly, about love. The strength and solidity of this relationship has crucial consequences for the novels' characteristic qualities, for, as Jocelyn Harris comments, 'since she could expect readers to have read the same texts as she, starting with her beloved sister Cassandra, reader response theory is everywhere an assumption in her work'.[65] Castle went further and, supported by Claudia Johnson in the ensuing correspondence, suggested that this key emotion was homosocial, if not homosexual. 'Was Jane Austen Gay?' roared the headline in the issue of the *London Review of Books* in which her article appeared. Many readers wrote in, some underlining the flimsiness of the evidence (the assumption that Austen and her sister shared a bed, made throughout Terry Castle's article and subsequent letter, was effectively refuted by Edward Copeland), but that is not the point I would make here, which is merely to note that, however controversial her suggestion, Castle is obeying the same impulse, responding to the same call, as other biographical speculators.

In the vein of Castle's transgressive suggestion, Johnson sketched the history of Austen's reception as a struggle between what she called 'the elegiac tradition' – 'pressing fantasies about the wholesome serenity of Regency England into the service of nostalgic yearnings after intelligibility' – and an 'anti-normative tradition' which has always suspected that if, in Charlotte Brontë's words, 'the passions were entirely unknown' to Jane Austen that was, as Johnson puts it, 'not because she was such a good girl but because in some secret, perhaps not fully definable way, she was so bad'.[66] Brontë's remark is one of the crassest ever passed about Austen, but this – and the fact that Jane Austen herself might have looked askance at any way 'perhaps not fully definable' – is no reason why this suggestion should not be taken seriously. In the final chapter of this book – not being exempt from biographical yearnings myself – I attempt to read the novels in a psychological light that produces a similar result.

'Nostalgic' or traditionalist attitudes towards 'Jane Austen' are certainly a feature of her cultural reception, and perhaps grow more tenacious as the 'world' she is supposed to inhabit recedes ever more rapidly away. As recent a book as Nigel Nicolson's *The World of Jane Austen* offers an example of the way acknowledgment of the awkward historical facts is swept instantly aside by the upsurge of romantic nostalgia:

She loved the luxury of Godmersham . . . Above all she loved its countryside which in Kent is nowhere more beautiful than where the Stour breaks through the North Downs towards Canterbury, with woods and pasture and tenderly sited farmhouses and mansions, where everyone seemed perennially at peace with each other and the external world, even when the poor were suffering cruelly and Buonaparte was gathering his armies at Boulogne. It gave Jane Austen an experience from which she selected only the most pleasing aspect, for that was how she chose to view the world.[67]

The tendency to rewrite Austen's life in the terms of romance that I have been identifying in this chapter is replicated in those versions of her novels that fall under the general rubric of the 'heritage' or 'nostalgia film', in which we 'are offered the pleasures of a spectacle of history immune from contemporary uncertainties around gender identity, personal and political struggles for economic independence, and personal autonomy'.[68] Many writers and readers, like Castle and Johnson, would insist that precisely those problems course through her texts (that's why we still read her).

In the Merchant Ivory film *Jane Austen in Manhattan*, which I discuss in the next chapter, the conflict between these two attitudes – the nostalgic and the progressive – is dramatised, as rival theatre companies tussle over the right to produce a play written by the author when young. One can read this battle as a commentary on what Winnicott, extrapolating from the notion of transitional space, described as 'the interplay between originality and the acceptance of tradition as the basis for inventiveness'.[69] 'It interests me', he wrote, 'that in any cultural field *it is not possible to be original except on a basis of tradition*' (Winnicott's italics). How is continuity maintained as difference is affirmed? Just how can the past author's work be simultaneously conserved and remade? *Metropolitan* and *Clueless* in their different ways address this question too.

CHAPTER 2

Recreating Jane Austen: Jane Austen in Manhattan, Metropolitan, Clueless

> To articulate the past historically does not mean to recognise it 'the way it really was'. It means to seize hold of a memory as it flashes up at a moment of danger . . . In every era the attempt must be made anew to wrest tradition away from a conformism that is about to overpower it.
>
> Walter Benjamin, 'Theses on the Philosophy of History'[1]

'Re-vision' – 'the act of looking back, of seeing with fresh eyes, of entering an old text from a new critical direction'[2] – has been the name of the game in literary and cultural criticism for the last three decades. Meanwhile 'revision', in the sense of borrowing from an original to further one's own artistic purposes, has been pursued even more vigorously within the novel, the theatre and film. Inevitably, perhaps, it has been Shakespeare who has served as the cultural hero against whom most artists have wanted to measure themselves, playfully or angrily rewriting the plays from radical, postcolonial, feminist, lesbian or gay points of view, or borrowing from his plots to give added resonance to their own enterprises. There is an immense range and variety of such 'appropriations'. From the disconcerting eruption into Gus Van Sant's tale of Seattle rentboys, *My Own Private Idaho* (1991) of lines and even whole scenes of *Henry IV*,[3] to the incestuous Lear of Jane Smiley's *A Thousand Acres* (1991)[4] Shakespeare has been 'plundered' to serve purposes as diverse as diligent modernisation and outright burlesque.[5]

Shakespeare is often conceptualised in the critical rhetoric that surrounds these versions as an oppressively patriarchal figure, the father who, blending with more recent fathers, must be torn away from and even repudiated.[6] But a different set of considerations comes inevitably into play when the 'canonical' author, the cultural icon whose work is being remastered is not a playwright but a novelist, and not a man of the theatre but a woman – and a woman writer who was, perhaps notoriously, 'a proper lady', too. But whilst responding to the mother text may well involve different challenges from reinventing the master text, there is no reason to think that Jane Austen has less power over her subsequent adaptors than Shakespeare over his. The very tightness of Austen's plotting, the very timbre of her confident prose – these themselves seemed until the late twentieth century to inhibit and constrain into genteel replication all endeavours to transpose the novels into another medium. The BBC *Northanger Abbey* (1986) was the first version which dared to reinvent the text, blend it with current cinematographic influences and produce what was in effect a re-Gothicisation of Austen's original anti-Gothic satire. Despite his 'bardolatry', David Garrick, the eighteenth-century actor–manager, had no qualms about making drastic cuts to his beloved Shakespeare, nor about adding to the plays when he felt like it.[7] Today Jane Austen's novels, transposed to the screen, are treated with a similar freedom.

What is the nature of the pleasure the reader of the novels might take in such a recreation? Does one judge filmic adaptations by 'fidelity' to the original – in which case the further question is 'whose original'? Or (as film buffs tend to insist) as a movie in its own right? (But it is impossible to forget what one knows.) The problematic – the puzzling area – can be defined in various ways. Critics who have discussed the relation between literature and film have mostly employed a structuralist, or quasi-structuralist method. They have set out typologies which order the field – categorising filmic remakes as transposition, commentary, analogy, or alternatively as borrowing, intersecting, and transforming, for example.[8] There are many problems with such procedures. This modernist critical enterprise of division and separation fails to take account of the many cross-species that the field contains, or of the divisions, involutions and transitions within specific films. Their usefulness is limited by the fact that, watching any one film, one is often aware of its blurring or overlapping the suggested categories.

I assume here that what we are dealing with is something to do with relationship, rather than to do with typology, and that theories of relationship developed to account for human interaction may be helpful in understanding the nature of the connection human beings make between artefacts. Perhaps thinking developed in the affective sphere will throw some light on the aesthetic, especially, as the films I shall discuss seem to suggest, the question whether one 'loves' or 'possesses' Jane Austen, and if so how one loves her, and what this means for the practice of transposition, come to the fore as soon as adaptation of the work is an issue. In this chapter, then, I offer a beginning to the creation of a theory of transposition of texts, not a comparison of filmic texts with

Austen's originals, but an account of the inner process of transformation into other media. I consider a group of films which, either within themselves, or through the nature of their enterprise, raise prior questions about Jane Austen's cultural image, and what reinventing or reconceiving her work might mean. In *Jane Austen in Manhattan* and *Metropolitan*, discussion about Jane Austen, about what ways her novels are alive today, is central to the films' own dramatic content. But in *Clueless* it is as if such issues have already been resolved, and the film thus can be used to substantiate some key features of the argument.

Jane Austen in Manhattan was produced by the team of James Ivory and Ismail Merchant in 1980; *Metropolitan*, written, directed and produced by Whit Stillman, on a comparatively shoestring budget, was released in 1990. These films address the question of Jane Austen's contemporaneity directly. They are about 'Jane Austen' as cultural icon just as much as they are about reading Austen's texts, and delighting in them, today. The oxymoronic *Jane Austen in Manhattan*, unlike Louis Malle's similarly titled *Vanya on 42nd Street*, points to a significant rupture that runs through the film. Whereas *Vanya* effects a seamless transition between the preliminary chatter of the players over polystyrene cups of coffee and their speaking the opening lines of *Uncle Vanya*, and implies a similar continuity between contemporary lives and Chekov's characters, *Jane Austen in Manhattan* is agitated by the problematic of cultural distance. 'Jane Austen' figures as something that has either to be drastically reinvented for today or presented, self-consciously, as a period piece.

Metropolitan presents Jane Austen in both modalities. A tribute to Austen's art is embedded in the social milieu, comedy and wit of the script, and at a more discursive level, her choice of heroines and their values are examined for their contemporary sustainability. Audrey Rouget, the film's 'proper' heroine, is aligned with Austen's protagonists; surprisingly, with Fanny Price, apparently the least sympathetic of them to modern audiences. Whereas the young men in the film suffer from absent and uncaring fathers, Audrey, a woman who identifies with a great woman writer, the film suggests, may turn out to be the true heir of the patrimony. Thus these two films are explicitly interested in the very questions of continuity, discontinuity and reinvention that are the topic here. How do we think about the relationship between a modern text and a Regency one? Does one need to abduct, remake, reinvent and transgress the original in order to make Austen's work heard by a contemporary audience? Can one work of art be true to its predecessor only through a kind of creative destruction?

Reaching back on my own account into the eighteenth century, I begin with the suggestion that the theory and practice of the 'Imitation' raises some important issues and answers, and then proceed to consider what guidance can be found in the most widely cited modern text about the relation of artists to their predecessors, Harold Bloom's *Anxiety of Influence* (1973). Limited as it is, as I suggest, Bloom's account, which emphasises the element of destruction in the later writer's relation to the earlier, does open the door to a psychoanalysis of influence and indebtedness. 'Jane Austen' is no longer a person, of course: but around that name have gathered such associations and affections that one might plausibly write of the love of the author's novels as if it were not too dissimilar to the love of a person. So I propose a psychological theory of adaptation. In the adaptor's response to the text two different modes of relation combine. In the first, the filmmaker seeks to 'translate' the original into another mode – to consign it, as a treasure might be consigned across a frontier, across a technical and cultural divide. This is adaptation conducted under the rubric of fidelity. In the second, the secondary text can be said to destroy and then to remake the original. This is a more complex and dangerous trajectory, and involves other motives than fidelity. So what I am suggesting is that the terms, 'reinvention', 'inter-textuality', 'rewriting' and 'appropriation' ('fine word, "appropriate"!'[9]) commonly used as if they refer to unproblematic, homogeneous pro-cesses – as if all 'rewriting' were the result of the same impulses and designs – need to be broken down or analysed. These two dispositions towards the original are like two modalities of love, and it is the second form, that which harnesses the impulse to destroy, that paradoxically is the more fruitful.

The script of *Jane Austen in Manhattan* is by Ruth Prawer Jhabvala. The film concerns two rival New York theatre directors, each of whom wants to put on *Sir Charles Grandison*, a play, or playlet, that Jane Austen adapted from the novel by Samuel Richardson. At the time the movie was made this little play, said to have been composed by the novelist for her niece Anna in the years before 1800, and thus well before her great period, was unpublished. The auction of the manuscript, which actually took place at Sotherby's in 1977, forms the film's opening sequence. When edited and published by Brian Southam in 1980, it consists of five short Acts in rather less than eighteen small pages.[10] *Sir Charles Grandison* was originally brought out in seven volumes in 1753 and 1754 and contains close to half a million words, so Jane Austen could be said to have anticipated the *Monty Python* 'summarise Proust in thirty seconds' competition by two hundred years. In effect the playlet dramatises only one occurrence of *Sir Charles Grandison*, the abduction by Sir Hargrave Pollexfen of Harriet Byron from the masquerade in Volume I, which is followed by his attempt to force her into marriage. Though the rival producers have very different approaches to this central event of the text, they both concentrate on Harriet's attempts to escape the machinations of the villain.

In a haunting naturalistic sequence of *Jane Austen in Manhattan* (a clip, as it were, from Richardson's novel) chairmen hurry across the screen, stealing Harriet away from the masquerade. Like the novel and the playlet, the film is concerned with abduction. Pierre, the young and supposedly charismatic director of one company – the Manhattan Experimental Theatre Workshop – steals the leading actress from the more conservative director, Liliana Zorska, who later entices her back. Pierre's abduction of the actress is used to suggest that a similar violence of appropriation is at work in his projected production of Austen's text. Pierre's approach to 'Jane Austen' is to make her speak to the late twentieth century, and this means giving the play a bizarrely experimental production in which the performers screech their lines dancing up and down on rubber mattresses. The attempted rape of Harriet is played as a farcical but erotic chase as the half-naked Pollexfen careers after the heroine in and out of the doll's house construction which is the set.

When the backers come to the preview, they are dismayed. Pierre, undaunted, lying on the studio floor, delivers a speech about the violence and chaos of the modern world, of which Jane Austen knew nothing. 'But Jane Austen was never aware – ' interrupts a backer. 'That's what we're here for, to make her aware, to bring her up to date. That's what we agreed when you gave me the manuscript, to bring her up to date?' 'This much up to date – ?' The backers withdraw their support. His rival, the traditional director, envisages the play as an eighteenth-century operetta, in period costumes. Extracts from her production are presented in counterpoint to Pierre's version. It is a campy, over-decorated, over-dressed staging which does not 'respect the manuscript' any more than his does, since bits of Richardson are spliced into Austen's text; but whether the movie's intention is to subvert both productions is unclear. Concluding with this performance, the film seems to hand it the palm.

One problem for the film is that, as Brian Southam puts it, *Sir Charles Grandison* 'is at a far remove from the great Jane Austen.'[11] This Merchant Ivory production is thus dealing not with Jane Austen's texts, but with a vague cultural notion of 'Jane Austen' – an Austen which might stand for any canonical work of the past. The film is an attempt on the part of the producing team to come to grips with some of the controversies surrounding the 'heritage' film. One intention is certainly a repudiation of attacks on 'costume drama', though its own experimental qualities – its juxtaposition of different modes – qualifies this. But the irony is that it was Jane Austen herself who performed the original abduction. It was she who took a solemn and authoritative patriarchal text and turned it into a comic skit for family entertainment. The play presages Austen's later authorial relation to Richardson, in which, as Jocelyn Harris says, she transposes 'events, characters and speeches from his context to her own, she misapplies his tones and registers, she inverts his priorities and she wildly exaggerates his scenes.'[12] Austen's burlesque of the original is in effect far closer in spirit to the adventurous and irresponsible Pierre than to the heritage theatre style that seems to be demanded by his backers.

Translating Jane Austen's novels to the screen involves at the very least a shift from one, a print, to another, a visual, culture, or as Brian McFarlane puts it, from a conceptual to a perceptual mode.[13] An analogous shift was performed in the eighteenth century when many writers published versions of texts belonging to classical Greek or Latin literature (and hence to pagan thought and culture) for English and Christian readers, who might also often be, unlike the original audience, female. Reusing, remaking, borrowing, is of course part of the stuff – the warp if not the weft – of literary history. But in the eighteenth century the genre of the 'Imitation' was particularly popular, its terms and conditions clearly understood. An Imitation was not, as its name might suggest, a copy but a version of a classical original into English which transposed events, characters and allusions into contemporary equivalents. All three of the films discussed here are American, and saturated, 'thick', with modern American culture. It is the very density of their immersion in the particular cultural milieus they depict, each quite distinct, and the abrasion or friction between these and the culture of Austen's novels, that generates their dramatic dynamic. Similarly, the gap between classical Rome and England of the eighteenth century was huge. It was their security within their own culture that enabled writers to embark successfully on the enterprise of remaking. The simultaneous presence of difference and affinity, of originality and recognition, is essential to the genre.

The Imitation was a kind of translation, but the theory distinguishes it firmly from translation proper. As Howard Weinbrot in his extended account of this practice comments 'In their imitations . . . Swift, Pope and Johnson demand that the reader both recognise the poem's model, and be aware of how it has been changed: this demand was generally absent in modernisation and pure translation.'[14] The consequent effect is summed up by James Beattie in an essay 'On Ludicrous Composition' in 1778, writing of Pope's 'The Rape of the Lock'. 'Clarissa's harangue in the fifth canto . . . gives pleasure to every reader', he declares, 'but to those who recollect that divine speech of Sarpendon [*Illiad* xii, 310–28], whereof this is an exact parody, it must be entertaining in the highest degree.'[15] This kind of pleasure is present then even when the Imitation varies in tone from the original: it is difference in mode, style and context, that makes for the delight.

To ensure that their readers were entertained in the highest degree, Rochester, Pope, Swift and others who practised this art often reprinted the original poems on the opposite page to their text or quoted parallel passages in their footnotes. Weinbrot argues this practice shows that the Imitation (however solemn, as in Johnson's *The Vanity of Human Wishes*, 'the tenth satire of Juvenal imitated'[16]) has its origins not in the earnest wish to translate, but in the comic parody, travesty, or burlesque. Unlike translation, the Imitation and the burlesque depend for their success on the reader's awareness of what Weinbrot calls 'the parent-poem', the original. The motive for translation on the other hand is to replace the original, to substitute a version in another language, so as to communicate something of the power of the original to a new public. Like parody or travesty, the Imitation invites the active to and fro comparison between the original and its updated version. Yet the new text will, if successful, have its own individuality and inner coherence. The Imitation extends 'from virtual translation to virtual rejection of the parent-poem', but it is, paradoxically, when the parent is most rejected that he (always 'he') looms most powerfully.

This takes one into the territory staked out by Harold Bloom in *The Anxiety of Influence*.[17] Bloom's was not a theory of translation, but an account of the relationship of later poets to their predecessors in the same language. The 'strong poet' is imagined to be locked in a wrestling match with his poetic parent, or rather – since Bloom's theory is wholly androcentric – his poetic father. 'Poetic Influence', he writes, ' – when it involves two strong, authentic poets, – always proceeds by a misreading of the prior poet, an act of creative correction that is actually and necessarily a misinterpretation.'[18] He reverses the common assumption that the later poet seeks to do homage to, or extend, or develop the earlier's achievement. The later poet is out to destroy the earlier, to replace his work with his own. And in a series of vivid tropes and metaphors, Bloom presents the poet as involved in a Nietzscheian struggle which defines one's originality against the otherwise consuming power of the father.[19]

The model, however, is unsound. This is certainly not an adequate characterisation of Jane Austen's relation to her predecessors, argues Harris, who draws on Nancy Chodorow's gendered conception of human development in order to suggest that 'while male writers may indeed inevitably play out their oedipal role of separation and murderous competition, Jane Austen's womanly bonds with her predecessors, male as well as female, provide rich and productive origins for her fictions'.[20] A theory of influence which omits bonding, the recognition of affinity, which omits in effect the love the later artist feels for the work of his or her predecessor is inadequate. Artistic fathers (and mothers) are not biological parents – they have to be discovered and felt *as* parents. Bloom's book says nothing about the admiration, the identification, the assimilation, which found the younger poet in thrall to the older, the prior process that led him to this ideal parent of his creative romance. On the other hand, an emphasis on female bonding and affinity seems to omit the element of mischief, of play, of wilful destruction or distortion of the older writer's achievement. Between ensorcellment by the great model, the desire to possess and imitate the original (to be at one with him or her) and the creation of the genuinely new work, some other psychological process must intervene.

Some contemporary psychoanalytic thinkers, focusing not on the father, but on the mother, and on the child's earliest development in relation to her, have given especial attention to the nature of imitative relationships. We could do worse, I suggest, than begin with such a passage as this from Jessica Benjamin's *The Bonds of Love* (1988). Drawing here on the work of Daniel Stern, Benjamin offers a little drama of her own, which describes how the infant and mother come together in play, a moment at which the infant recognises the mother as both like itself and different:

Now, when the infant reaches excitedly for a toy, he looks up to see if mother is sharing his excitement; he gets the meaning when she says 'Wow!' The mother shows that she is feeling the same, not by imitating the infant's gesture (he shakes the rattle) but by matching his level of intensity in a different mode (she whoops). This translation into a different form of expression more clearly demonstrates the congruence of *inner* experience than simple, behavioural imitation. Technically the mother is not feeling the same feeling as her child: she is not excited by the rattle itself; but she is excited by his excitement, and she wants to communicate that fact. When mother and child play 'peekaboo' (a game based on the tension between shared expectancy and surprise), the mother takes similar pleasure in contacting her child's mind.[21]

The child, in the words of Robert Frost's poem, receives 'not its own love back in copy speech / But counter-love, original response.'[22] For Benjamin, such exchange is a paradigm for later relations with beloved others. Such 'intersubjectivity' does not mean, as this vignette demonstrates, the passive obliteration of one self, putting itself at the service of another, nor merging, nor the careful translation of one achievement into analogous terms. It is the recreation of the original gesture in a different modality that gives the assurance of genuine recognition. The congruence of inner experience is manifested not by copying, but by response in this other mode.

Benjamin's thinking is influenced by a number of researchers into parent–child relations, but by none more so than Winnicott. A key text for her thought is his 1968 paper 'The Use of an Object and Relating through Identifications', and it is the argument that Winnicott makes there which throws most light on this issue.[23] Here Winnicott focuses on a formative moment in mother–child relations, seeking to understand what he calls at one moment 'the most difficult thing in human development' (p. 89), the transition whereby the infant places 'the object outside the area of the subject's omnipotent control', or in other words, the birth of the child's awareness that another person really does exist. In this paper Winnicott is describing and theorising a clinical phenomenon; here he makes no attempt to extrapolate his argument into the field of the arts and creativity. Yet it can be suggested that by focusing on the nature of relationship he puts his finger on a psychological distinction that is crucial to the understanding of recreation.

What Winnicott calls 'destruction' of the object plays a key role in his argument. Like 'use' in his title the word is given an unorthodox meaning. 'It is generally understood that the reality principle involves the individual in anger and reactive destruction', Winnicott writes (p. 91). (It is this, Freudian, account that is the basis of Bloom's theory. The strong poetic 'father' stands there, like Laius at the cross-roads, an incarnation of the reality principle, blocking the way to his Oedipal son's achievement, and must therefore be fought against.) Winnicott, who had observed many more children than either Freud or Klein, was for years unhappy with this notion that destructiveness is a reaction to the frustrations of externality, believing that it separates out the negative quality of destructiveness in the earliest infantile excitement too early. In this late contribution he comes up with the idea that reality does not impose itself on the infant from the outside – as the positivist Freudian view would suppose – but rather that the infant's rage is actually its breakthrough *into* externality.

It is a fundamental premise of psychoanalysis that the relationship between the patient and the analyst allows the reproduction of earlier dispositions of the patient's life. Transference (or 'transference love'[24]) means that the analyst features not as a personality but as the means by which earlier important figures can be revivified, and earlier relations replayed, interpreted and, perhaps, adjusted. By keeping his or her demeanour as low key as possible, the analyst facilitates this process. In this sense the consulting room becomes the analysand's psychic theatre, with the analyst's person a player within the patient's subjectivity. In Winnicott's terms, the analyst is usually related to as a 'subjective object': and this is, moreover, he implies, overwhelmingly the mode in which we relate to other human beings in the usual commerce of life – as revenants, carriers of our projections. We relate through identifications. But, as he argues, there are crucial moments when something else must happen.

Winnicott begins his exposition by contrasting two babies feeding at the breast. 'One is feeding on the self, since the breast and the baby have not yet become (for the baby) separate phenomena. The other is feeding from an other-than-me source, or an object that can be given cavalier treatment without effect on the baby unless it retaliates' (p. 89). One baby has, one has not, been carried over from relating to 'usage', which here means not exploitation but being able to benefit from the existence of another person. It is 'destruction' of the object which makes the object real. By this Winnicott does not mean one single act of destruction, but 'on-going destruction in unconscious fantasy' (p. 90). This initial destructive thought or impulse, Winnicott says, is the moment at which the other emerges. The infant moves from a realm in which itself and the other are a seamless fabric, in which the other is present merely as the realm of projections, fantasies and identifications, to a realm of being in which the foreignness (and therefore the resistance) of the other can be acknowledged.

At certain moments or phases of the treatment, the patient may live temporarily in a world in which the analyst as a person does not exist, or rather exists only as raw material for the analysand's purposes. He or she attacks the analyst in all sorts of ways, using the analyst as a target for the rage and destructiveness stored up from earlier relationships. If the analyst becomes discomposed by these attacks, if his or her analytic disinterestedness is undermined, then the analyst has become sucked into the patient's world, and the inner, fantasy world, to all intents and purposes, has spread itself into, has become, all there is. But if the analyst, like the mother-person, can stand these attacks calmly and not retaliate, then the child or the patient may begin to relate to the other as to a real subject. The object is placed outside the realm of omnipotent control: he or she starts to exist for the patient or the baby as something independent of their own needs and wishes – recognised, within the psyche, as a distinct being. Winnicott illustrates his point with what Adam Phillips[25] calls 'his own Punch and Judy dialogue':

The subject says to the object: 'I destroyed you', and the object is there to receive the communication. From now on the subject says: 'Hullo object!' 'I destroyed you.' 'I love you.' 'You have value for me because of your survival of my destruction of you . . .' (90)[26]

When Jessica Benjamin, twenty years later, takes up Winnicott's ideas, she places them within a philosophical tradition, and relates them to a broad and telling distinction between the 'intrapsychic' and the 'inter-subjective.'[27] Within these are modalities, Benjamin suggests, of love. The most common form of love can be defined in a quotation from Goethe that Harold Bloom cites. 'To be loved for what one is, is the greatest exception. The great majority love in another only what they lend him, their own selves, their version of him.'[28] In other words, what is loved is usually loved as part of the subject's internal world, as a subjectively perceived object. The other, a rarer form of love, results from successful destruction and survival, and it results in 'recognition' of the other's reality, their true and unco-optable separateness. This psychoanalytic theory of relationship between persons carries with it necessarily an ethical overlay. This is partly why it can clarify the nature of the judgements we instinctively make when we see a film based on a book with which we are familiar.

There are obvious impediments to applying ideas elaborated within the clinical setting, in which the parent or the analyst's interventions are a substantive part, to reading a text, which does not alter in response to the reader.[29] The text is not 'there to receive the communication' in any sense approximating to Winnicott's picture of the attentive and open analyst. Yet I propose that just as the infant shifts from one mode of relating to another, we can imagine that the reader oscillates between one mode of relating and another when they come to 'love' a text. The usefulness of Winnicott and Benjamin's theory in this context is that they provide a concept of 'strong' love which is free from any connotations of idealisation and reverence. Their theory enables one to incorporate the element of opposition or destruction into the notion of artistic development, whilst still retaining a sense of the later artist's tie to his or her predecessor. Love of an author at its strongest, the true 'contacting of another's mind', does not mean mimicry or painstaking attempts at authenticity. It does not involve the fantasy, present in so much writing about or 'continuations' of Austen, of union with the idealised original. Instead it defines a process out of which a new individual product can be made, a new thing that is in relationship to the predecessor, but which can treat it with insouciance, 'cavalierly'.

Southam remarks of the young Jane Austen's reading of *Sir Charles Grandison* that by 1790 (when she was fifteen) 'she was sufficiently in possession of the novel and sufficiently confident to be poking fun at it in the early satires'.[30] The very word 'possession' may suggest that similar phenomena are in play when we read and are engrossed by a text: and therefore that love, or infatuation, rather than Oedipal rivalry, might be the starting point of our understanding of what this process signifies. To possess a text, one might suggest, is to know that this object has a reality beyond one's own mental construction of it. That is why it can survive destruction, why 'poking fun at it' will not destroy one's serious esteem, why, like Punch's Judy, one can be confident that it will bounce back again. On the other hand, there is the discourse of 'fidelity'. One hears talk of adaptations of the novels as 'betraying', of being 'unfaithful' to, 'stripping Austen of her social awareness', even of 'violating' the original.[31] The question to ask here is faithful 'To what?'[32] This relational, affective, even erotic vocabulary is not incidental for it points, I suggest, to the inner psychic reality of such readers' relation to the texts they have enjoyed. 'Great liberties were taken with the text' one hears people say: the text unconsciously imagined as a virgin abducted by the rakish filmmaker, insisting that the finished product bear the mark of his own will. In such a response the text is, to use Winnicott's term, a subjectively perceived object. It has not undergone that process of psychic destruction which would enable it to survive. In this modality, the novel is not outside, but within the narcissistic enclosure of the self. If it is damaged, the self will be damaged, so the prevailing desire, the prevailing motivation, is transcription, preservation. 'Respecting the manuscript', as the traditionals in *Jane Austen in Manhattan* proclaim, is what counts, the index of success.

Metropolitan, on the other hand, is a text that tries to undo, and then recreate, Jane Austen. Stillman's witty film is in no sense a 'tribute' to the author, any more than it is a tribute to Scott Fitzgerald or Woody Allen – though both are obvious influences. But if 'Jane Austen' features in the film as a signifier for anachronistic morals and style, that reputation is also disputed and contested. Set in New York, 'Not So Long Ago', as a title card reminds us, the film follows a few days in the life of a group of rich young socialites, and threads its romantic narrative through a succession of pastimes – the parties, games, balls and conversation with which these naive, but self-confident 'preppies' fill the Christmas season. Tom Townsend, a bright boy from the West Side with socialist ideas, somehow finds himself taken up by this set of young people, who have all known each other from their schooldays. It is not long before Audrey, one of the women, becomes very fond of him, but Tom is still infatuated with the glamorous Serena.

The relation of *Metropolitan* to Jane Austen can be discerned in two modes, which I shall call the manifest and the latent. The manifest relation occurs in a string of explicit references to Jane Austen and her novels. The friendship of Tom and Audrey develops through a series of tête-à-tête conversations about Austen's books, filmed as intense moments of communication within settings crossed by the movements and talk of others. Tom is initially amazed that anyone could still enjoy Austen, especially *Mansfield Park*, because 'nearly everything Jane Austen wrote seems ridiculous from today's perspective'. This is evidently the 'Jane Austen' of the cultural image. It turns out he hasn't read any of the novels and when in their next conversation Audrey vigorously defends both it, and Fanny Price, its heroine, he thinks again, and in the course of the film comes round to admitting that once he reads *Persuasion*, he enjoys the book. In the film as produced, though not in the script, these allusions to Austen are intensified when Audrey, out sadly Christmas shopping, is drawn irresistibly towards a Fifth Avenue bookshop window, in which a set of Jane Austen's novels is displayed, alongside a toy signifying their suitability as a gift.

The suggestions here are uncertain. Perhaps Audrey's love of Jane Austen (or is it 'Jane Austen'?) is juvenile and nostalgic, a mark of the novels' incompatibility with the modern world; perhaps the novels are her life-line. At the climax of the film, Audrey disappears, and it seems possible that she has gone away with (if not been actually abducted by) Von Sloneker, the titled rake. Continuing this set of manifest allusions, Charlie, the amateur philosopher of the group, pronounces that Audrey would never have anything to do with the goings-on at Von Sloneker's pad because '[s]he has very clear views about these things – you know she's a big admirer of Jane Austen', a comment that leads quickly to his imagining that 'she's probably at home asleep right now, with the pink coverlet tucked in tight, and her stuffed animals looking over her'. Thus one might say that the film plays, at times uneasily, as much with 'Jane Austen' as a cultural signifier, 'Jane Austen' as code for gentility and 'old-fashioned' virtues, as much as it signals its consanguinity with Austen's comic texts.

This 'Janeite' motif, though, is set within a comedy whose enclosed milieu, whose small cast of upper-class characters (most of whom are none too bright) whose quick feeling for the selfish and absurd, re-sembles Austen's own art. This latent level of reference to, perhaps influence by, Austen passes also through the film's focus on Audrey. She is not merely presented, as Charlie defines it, as a person of 'principle', she is put into a relationship with Tom that resembles Fanny Price's with Edmund Bertram. It may be just coincidence that Tom and Audrey's first real contact in the film occurs on a stair with others casually passing, and so can allude to the first meeting of Fanny and Edmund, but like theirs, the relationship's emotional depths are always mediated or hidden by their ostensible conversational topics. What is clearly Austen-like (and offers the reader of Jane Austen that delightful sense of familiarity within difference that the Imitation brought) is that Tom is oblivious to Audrey's attraction to him, as Edmund is to Fanny's affection, and is drawn to her, not as a lover, but as a conversational partner and equal. Tom appeals to Audrey for understanding whilst they discuss Tom's feelings for Serena, just as Edmund used Fanny to air his misgivings about Mary Crawford.

Audrey then is put in the Austenian position. The identification with Fanny is even more apparent to the reader of *Mansfield Park* in the scene in which these idle and rich young people, taking over an apartment whilst the parents are away, play daring games. One of these is 'Truth', in which bad luck in the contest requires participants to answer a question honestly, however embarrassing it may be to them. Fanny/ Audrey refuses to play, and declares that such games are 'dangerous', that 'conventions' have come to exist because '[p]eople saw the harm that excessive candor can do'. The raised eyebrows and impatient gestures of the others suggest plainly that they think her stubborn, old-fashioned and priggish. Sitting on a sofa, squeezed between Tom and Charlie, the emotional cost of this resisting position is written all over her face. There is a long pause. Finally, accused of spoiling everyone's fun, like Fanny, she gives in.

It is as if Stillman offers a thematic string of allusions to Austen which can be read in several ways. The film is deeply preoccupied with the notion that its milieu, its people, the standards and values it espouses, are anachronistic, and one main purpose of the references is to focus this anxiety. At the conclusion of the movie, Tom and Charlie 'rescue' Audrey from Von Sloneker's country house, Tom using a toy gun that he had played with as a child, and that his father, much to his dismay, has recently thrown away. Audrey has not been abducted, nor seduced, but going to Von Sloneker's 'is not something Jane Austen would have done', they both agree. Much of the film is clearly troubled about the situation of its male characters, whose fatalism about their historical position is expounded by Charlie. These are young men whose fathers are absent, whose mothers (disturbingly) 'go out on dates', who have a ludicrous sense of themselves as the last of a declining race. Audrey, on the other hand, enjoys a supportive relationship with her mother, and seems to find in her identification with a literary mother a sustaining continuity and security. In Stillman's third film, *The Last Days of Disco* (1998) Audrey Rouget is glimpsed eight years on. She is, someone whispers, the youngest person ever to be made an editor at Farrar, Strauss. Isn't this the equivalent of being taken under the wing of Sir Thomas Bertram, the contemporary version of welcome into the patriarchy? *Metropolitan* is filled with a kind of comic anxiety, not knowing quite how to frame its loyalty to the past.

Like other film and video treatments of Austen's novels, *Metropolitan* demonstrates within the public arena some of the psychological dynamics of reading that usually remain undisclosed within the recesses of private consciousness. It displays simultaneous loyalty to, and uneasiness about, Jane Austen. But it does not imitate, in the usual sense, and certainly is not faithful to, *Mansfield Park*. Rather it takes elements from the novels, and breaks them down, redistributing them and reconstituting them into something recognisably contemporary. The film represents both 'relating through identifications' and at its best, 'the use of an object', recreating the texts it loves in another milieu and another mode. But *Clueless* (1995) as its reception already indicates, demonstrates an

internalisation of Austen that is much more complete, and more successful.

Clueless, written and directed by Amy Heckerling, is clearly analogous
to the Imitation. Like the eighteenth-century reader of 'The Rape of the
Lock', anyone familiar with *Emma* viewing the film enjoys the possession
of two orders of cultural capital and aesthetic pleasure at once – both
connection to the authorising past (the classic text read at college) and
participation in a youth culture apparently at the cutting edge of
(post)modernity. Maybe this is what is slyly signalled in the scene where
Christian makes Cher view *Spartacus* and the cinema screen fills with a
television showing Tony Curtis speaking about 'the children of my
master to whom I taught the classics' – though this is a clip with more
than one ironic reference. More directly, the motif of the 'makeover'
(both violence against and metamorphosis) which runs through the
script provides a metanarrative commentary on its own gestating impulse. The Imitation began in burlesque, but arrived at a quite different
kind of art. Critics and commentators have, of course, been delighted to
find resemblances between the film and *Emma*, but it is more pertinent
here initially to note *Clueless*'s unlikeness to its precursor. As Esther
Sonnet has suggested, 'the resolutely contemporary setting of *Clueless*
plays as much *against* its source as it does with it'.[33]

The notion that *Clueless* is a 'version' of the novel is, at one level,
simply a mistake. When Beverly Hills teenagers were asked what they
made of *Clueless* they not surprisingly responded that it was 'way exaggerated.'[34] Whoever thought otherwise? Though *Emma* begins with a
series of near-farcical cross-purposes, it is a novel deeply embedded in
realism: *Clueless* is a fantasy/burlesque, a mode signalled immediately in
Cher's opening voice-over commentary 'I have a way normal life for a
teenager', whilst viewing her wardrobe for the day on a computer
screen. True, this establishes Cher's innocent insouciance, and might
well resemble the combination of blithe assurance and complete insular-
ity signalled in *Emma*'s opening phrases about its heroine. The fantasy
elements in *Clueless* are evident enough, however, in Cher and Dionne's
exaggerated wardrobes (and Cher's sixty costume changes, according to
Vogue[35]) but more importantly in its utopian reinvention of social realities. Part of *Emma*'s realism is the exactness with which it depicts a
community in which some are rising into gentility and others are
slipping from it, a 'Highbury world' therefore in which the niceties of
social discrimination are everywhere woven into the action, but apart
from Cher's rebuke to Elton for being 'such a snob' class distinctions

appear to have little significance in *Clueless*, as Carol M. Dole points out.[36] After her makeover (carried out so swiftly and exuberantly as to resemble a magic transformation scene), the Bronx 'Loady' Tai suddenly acquires a new wardrobe almost as stylish as Cher's. Neither Dionne, Cher's black friend, nor her successful relationship with her boyfriend Murray have equivalents in *Emma*: that Cher and Dionne are buddies, social equals and co-conspirators is the film's imaginary reconciliation of real contemporary racial relations.

The film's engaging fantasy is most evident in the sequence that is completed before the overt correspondences with *Emma* are invoked, when Cher decides that she must bring her teachers, the dowdy Miss Geist and the miserable Mr Hall, together. *Clueless* allows Cher and Dionne an indulgence in match-making success that Emma Woodhouse could only dream of. There's a touching kindness as well as intimacy in the moment where Cher, from her school desk, tells Mr Hall softly that Miss Geist thinks him the most intelligent man in the school, and the camera, moving in on Mr Hall's face, finds him smiling to himself – a signal of Cher's power that completes the circuit of pure comic fantasy. Miss Bates, whose introduction after the first volume is essential to the novel's deepening of its interests in the community, has no equivalent in the film: her deletion, and the absence of Mrs Bates, and her niece, fringe-dwellers of gentility, disturbers in various ways of Emma's equanimity, is a necessary condition for *Clueless*'s fundamentally celebratory and utopian mode.[37] If Cher comes up against unyielding reality it is in 'the Messiah', as he calls himself, of the driving-test examiner, and her chagrin at his refusal of her licence has no element in it comparable to Emma's heartfelt distress after Mr Knightley takes her to task at Box Hill. (Though it might be argued that Mr Knightley is split between the two figures, Josh – a fellow-student, too young to possess the social weight of Mr Knightley – and this symbol of the Law.) All this is obvious enough. Yet the many readers who have felt that the film nevertheless has some real affinity with *Emma* are not necessarily mistaken.

Cher's voice-over narration is an important ingredient in the movie's success.[38] The contrast between her spoken appraisals and what the screen itself shows parallels Emma's equally mistaken assessments of the world delineated in the novel. Cher's commentary provides continuity for the action, but also supplies unspoken thoughts to supplement the visual images of her face. When Tai is regaling her classmates with the story of her 'near death' experience at the Mall, for example, Cher's dismay at being pushed from centre stage is written on her puckered brow and uneasy movements, and simultaneously expressed in the words of the voice-over, understood as her consciousness. This voice is sometimes immediate, dramatic, sometimes explanatory, retrospective; sometimes inside, and sometimes outside, Cher's head on the screen. Attending to Cher's unspoken thoughts, the viewer sometimes finds, to their surprise, that this virtual 'inner speech' has become real speech, as the train of thought emerges without a break into the action, or is broken into by someone else's words. The driving examiner's brusque 'Move into the right lane' intercepts Cher's preoccupied musings about Josh. Thus the use of the voice-over in *Clueless* avails itself of some of the effects of free indirect speech in the novel. Just as the shifts between narrator and character in the novel make for irony, so does the shifting match or mismatch between verbal and visual representations.

Sometimes the effect resembles Jane Austen's youthful parodies. 'I needed to find sanctuary in a place where I could gather my thoughts and regain my strength', Cher's voice declares – followed by a shot of the mall. This is the bathos of 'Love and Freindship', not *Emma*: 'The place was suited to meditation. A grove of full-grown Elms sheltered us from the East', followed by ' – a Bed of full-grown nettles from the West – Before us ran the murmuring brook and behind us ran the turn-pike road.'[39] At other times the technique is far more sophisticated. The voice-over's combination of commentary, with present tense and immediacy, is most intricate at the climactic moment of Cher's realisation. Attempting to recover from Tai's attack and to understand the mistakes she has made, she is walking home, swinging her designer label tote bag, the voice-over accompanying her: '. . .Josh needs someone to take care of him. Someone to laugh at his jokes – if he makes any. Then suddenly' ('then suddenly' being the equivalent of a narrator), Cher stops short before a fountain which (could it be with the speed of an arrow?) leaps into life and colour, and now the inner speech emerges into dramatic speech, as she exclaims, wonderingly, 'I love Josh.' All this is intercut with flashbacks which recover moments in their previous relation that Cher now understands: a constellation of different technical means for the representation of thought-processes that does not seem less complex than the novel's.

Lesley Stern makes a key observation when she notes that both scripts transform the quotidian by means of their own inventiveness, the worlds of both texts being parochial and mundane, the energy of both treatments being ingeniously transformative.[40] The delight in language and metaphor that is so unusual in the script of *Clueless* is part of this

regenerative response towards the silly and immature dramas that are
its substance (and in *Clueless*, as in all of Austen's novels, simultaneously
enjoyed and ridiculed.) Cher, like Emma, is beautiful and a natural
leader (but not vain), eager, bright, kindhearted, egotistic and intelligent. Both heroines, having known nothing but love, expect the world to
be kind to them. But it is the aesthetic treatment that both receive which
is of the essence, and if Emma, like Cher, is a radiant 'picture of health'
(*Emma*, p. 39) that is communicated in the novel, as in the film, by partly
sensuous means. For the buoyancy and vitality of the imagination that
conceives Emma is brought to the reader through the energy and brio,
not of metaphor, but of the rhythms of Austen's prose. By reenacting
this aspect of the original text so tellingly, the film rebukes that pedagogic criticism which reads Emma so earnestly as the disciplining of
Emma's errant imagination, more severely chastised by Eve Sedgwick.
It follows from the natural goodness of the heroines, though, that the
plot of *Clueless*, like *Emma*, delivers a moral outcome, even if in *Clueless*
this is presented as a 'makeover of the soul'. The film thus simultaneously parodies the tradition of the female *bildungsroman*, and inserts itself into
that tradition.

One particularly successful mimicry of the novel's treatment of
Emma's thoughts occurs towards the film's climax when Cher is seriously attempting to sort out her feelings. Emma's resolutions not to interfere
with Harriet's romances any more are crossed suddenly by the thought
of 'William Coxe' as a potential beau (*Emma*, p. 137). As she walks
through the city, anxiously pondering in voice-over what she has done
wrong, Cher's attention is caught by a dress in a shop window, and her
inner thoughts on the soundtrack become indistinguishable from
spoken excitement: 'I wonder if they have it in my size?' Defaulting to
bad habit is simultaneously the resurgence of 'youth and natural cheerfulness' (*Emma*, p. 137), a both ironic and celebratory moment. Only a
close and attentive reading of *Emma* could explain such corresp_onden-
ces, but no one would imagine that Amy Heckerling deliberately set out
to attain them. André Bazin once remarked of Jean Renoir's *Madame
Bovary* that its 'fidelity' was paradoxically compatible with 'complete
independence from the original'.[41] *Clueless* represents an imaginative
absorption of Austen that is perfectly reconcilable with taking liberties
and disregarding whole aspects of the original text, and, as I have
argued, transforming it into a different genre or order of art. *Clueless*
then plays with *Emma* and implicitly too with Jane Austen, the 'classic'.
Emma is not a mother text that is idealised or revered but an inner

presence that has been loved, destroyed in fantasy, survived and can now be treated 'cavalierly'.

Both *Metropolitan* and *Jane Austen in Manhattan*, have an undercurrent of anxiety: how do you reconcile loyalty to Jane Austen with contemporaneity, how do you manage the transition between a writer thought to be genteel and elitist with the modernity you seek necessarily to embrace? The apartment of the backer in *Jane Austen in Manhattan* is furnished in traditional style, filled with books and antiques, but its huge windows span an urban industrial landscape. When he is finally defeated, Pierre, the unscrupulous experimental director, makes off with a valuable vase from the collection. It seems there's an uneasy price to be paid for this victory of 'high' culture, this form of reverence for the past. Such an anxiety has been overcome in *Clueless*: it simply takes Austen for granted. But for this film the Austen taken for granted is not an image or model of high culture and gentility, but of creative zest and brilliance, not 'Jane Austen', the cultural image, but Jane Austen. The film is secure in its own sophisticated ironic presentation of brashness and innocence, its own brand of simultaneous mockery and imaginative complicity. *Clueless* may depict and enjoy a teenage world in which the 'cultural capital' that matters is consumerism and style,[42] but its own technical virtuosity, inventiveness and spirit seem to stand apart, secure and generous in its possession of some other cultural currency, which includes Jane Austen. But the form of possession is not adequately described by the metaphor of 'capital'; one might say it resides rather in the scriptwriter's psychological secretion of the essence of Austen's art – an analogy I shall develop in the next chapter.

All this, as my argument suggests, is perfectly compatible with the script's breezily deflating references to literary culture. 'It is a far, far better thing doing stuff for other people', Cher tells herself; 'Shall I compare thee to a summer's day?' becomes 'the way famous quote' from *Cliff's Notes*; *Hamlet* is remembered only because the film starred Mel Gibson. It is no coincidence that this treatment resembles that meted out to the collection of way famous quotes, mostly from Shakespeare, assembled in the opening chapter of *Northanger Abbey*. In the next chapters I suggest also how Austen's own relation to Shakespeare can be read as a parallel instance of recreation.

CHAPTER 3

An Englishwoman's constitution: Jane Austen and Shakespeare

His plays are out of joint; *O cursed sprite!*
That ever I was born to set them right!
Arthur Murphy, *Hamlet with Alterations: a Tragedy in Three Acts*[1]

Not long ago, the traveller in England was confronted everywhere – on railway stations, in bookshops, on hoardings and placards – with a message advertising Penguin Classics: 'Two Heads are Better than One'. The coarsely represented male face (high forehead, long hair, high collar) was juxtaposed with an equally blurred female one (lace collar, curls peeking out of cap).[2] With the crudity of images reproduced, and reproduced again, these faces seemed to have not the idiosyncrasy of individuals but the replicability of trademarks. It was not the merging together of these two icons that signalled their equivalence, so much as their familiarity, the expectation broadcast so clearly that if there were two writers whose images the British railway-travelling, and bookshop-frequenting, public would be sure to recognise, these were they – William Shakespeare and Jane Austen.

The association of Shakespeare's and Austen's images and names might well be said to belong to the history of promotion rather than of critical history. If you were concerned, as many of Austen's nineteenth-century critics may well have been, that the object of your enthusiasm – her world so circumscribed, her range so narrow – met none of the heroic criteria for great writing, what better defence than the use of Shakespeare's name? For there certainly has been a long tradition of associating such very different (as one might think) figures as the protean playwright and the author of six domestic novels. The name of Shakespeare was used not only to indicate the level of her achievement but to point specifically and repeatedly to Austen's 'dramatic' quality. One of her first enthusiasts, Richard Whately, writing in the *Quarterly Review* of 1821,[3] for instance, noted that Austen did not use the form of letters for her novels but followed the 'ordinary plan', directly describing scenes and conversations. Commenting on the 'dramatic air of the narrative', he then remarked that she conducts conversations with 'a regard to character hardly exceeded even by Shakspeare himself'.[4]

Lord Macaulay's claims were naturally more resounding and imperial: 'among the writers who have approached nearest to the manner of the great master', he wrote in 1843, 'we have no hesitation in placing Jane Austen, a woman of whom England is justly proud'.[5] (Another way of reading the poster is to see it as a Janus, or like two heads on a coin – the recto and verso, king and queen of the English literary empire.) George Lewes (1847), who declared that Macaulay had referred to Austen as a 'Prose Shakespeare' praised her as one who, in contrast to Scott, possessed 'Shakspearean' qualities of 'tenderness and passion', and 'marvellous dramatic power'.[6] Tennyson also spoke of Jane Austen as 'next to Shakespeare' in her 'realism and the life-likeness of her characters.'[7] This nineteenth-century tradition was consummated by A. C. Bradley in 1911. He wrote of Jane Austen's 'surpassing excellence within that comparatively narrow sphere whose limits she never tried to overpass . . . which . . . gives her in that sphere the position held by Shakespeare in his'[8] – an appraisal neatly replicated by the poster's positioning of the two writers side by side.

Austen's most important nineteenth-century critic, Richard Simpson, a Shakespearean scholar, writing in 1870, took up the by now orthodox emphasis on her dramatic quality. But Simpson also introduced the new idea that Jane Austen's relation to Shakespeare was one of indebtedness or influence. He implies this strongly when, giving a particular illustration of earlier critics' claims, he describes Miss Bates's talk in *Emma* as being made up of 'the same concourse of details' as that which makes up Mistress Quickly's.[9] 'Miss Austen', he then declares more explicitly, 'must surely have had Shakespeare's *Twelfth Night* in her mind while she was writing this novel [*Persuasion*].'[10] 'Anne Elliot is Shakespeare's Viola translated into an English girl of the nineteenth century.' He argued that the novelist will have remembered the dialogue between Orsino and the disguised Viola when she wrote the exchanges between Captain Harville and Anne Elliot in which Anne speaks of women's constancy, and indirectly of her own.

The comparison continued to be made throughout the last century. Reginald Farrer's great appreciation of 1917 begins by taking up Macaulay's claim that Austen is comparable only with Shakespeare: 'both attain their solitary and special supremacy', he wrote, 'by dint of a

common capacity for intense vitalisation'.[11] Caroline Spurgeon, the
Shakespearean scholar, read a 'fulsome eulogy' at the Royal Society of
Literature in 1927 'endorsing the association of Jane Austen's name with
that of Shakespeare and enlarging upon "why she is so characteristically
English"'.[12] In 1938, Elizabeth Jenkins, as we have seen, defined
Austen's type of genius by comparing her with Shakespeare. For later
critics, though, the critical proposition (Austen and Shakespeare share
something in common, the attempt to define which is tantamount to
describing literary greatness)[13] becomes or merges into the scholarly
one: Jane Austen read Shakespeare and the signs of his influence may be
detected in the novels. Contemporary critics have pursued this question
of Austen's possible indebtedness to Shakespeare with great assiduity.
When Fanny Price speaks to Edmund of 'looking out on such a night as
this', it has been suggested, for instance, that she is recalling the exchange between Jessica and Lorenzo at the opening of the fifth act of *The
Merchant of Venice* in which the phrase 'in such a night' is repeated.[14] In
the first act of *Romeo and Juliet*, Mercutio says 'Nay, gentle Romeo, we
must have you dance.' Park Honan suggests that these words are
'echoed' in Mr Bingley's first words, 'Come Darcy, I must have you
dance.'[15] One might remember Johnson's treatment of the suggested
evidence for the playwright's own classical learning in the *Preface to
Shakespeare*. 'I have found it remarked that in this important sentence
"Go before, I'll follow", we read a translation of *I prae, sequar*' (a line
from a play by Terence), he commented dryly. 'I have been told that
when Caliban, after a pleasing dream, says, "I cried to sleep again", the
author imitates Anacreon, who had, like every other man, the same wish
on the same occasion.'[16]

Association, affinity, influence – these are distinct phenomena. Yet
the mingled idea that Austen resembles, or was influenced by, or alludes
to, Shakespeare is still very current. Isobel Armstrong writes that when
nineteenth-century critics evoked Shakespeare's name 'they were thus
implying a range, depth and insight far beyond that of most poets as well
as that of most novelists'.[17] Much the same motive seems to apply to
their twentieth-century successors, the sub-text of their comparisons
being naturally that they are far from absurd. When Roger Gard for
example compares *Persuasion* with passages from *Pericles* he is underscor-
ing his general claim that Austen is an artist 'who is justly compared in
some of her powers with Shakespeare', rather than seeking to persuade
the reader of any specific indebtedness.[18] Yet Gard does compare the
'lethal rationality' of the conversation in Chapter 2 of *Sense and Sensibility*

between Fanny and John Dashwood with the dialogue in which Lear's daughters progressively strip their father of all his comforts.[19] More wholesale or consistent recapitulations of Shakespeare have been suggested. Armstrong has written of the many affinities between Shakespeare's *As You Like It* and *Henry VIII* and *Mansfield Park*.[20] In another book-length treatment, she has claimed that the absent father and the hysterical daughter are only two of the correspondences to be uncovered between *Sense and Sensibility* and *Hamlet*.[21] Jocelyn Harris has argued with flair that *Emma* is a rewriting or reimagining of *A Midsummer Night's Dream*.[22]

There would be little point in disputing any of these particular suggestions. Part of the pleasure their authors have in making them, and their readers in being intrigued by their accounts, is the sense they give of deep communion with two great minds at once. When one picks up an echo or a hidden quotation or allusion, and then detects – or feels one detects – more correspondences, starts to unravel the text, to conceive that the second writer is 'using' the first, that this allusion opens up a whole hidden creative design, one has a delicious sense of inhabiting the fertile mind of the successor author, a mind, one feels, not so different from one's own. But the truth claim here is probably more akin to the biographer's than to the historian's. The purpose of this chapter, then, is less to review and add to the bank of possible Shakespearean references and allusions in Austen than to raise some of the critical, epistemological and even psychological issues that surround the question of their relationship.

Many critics and scholars have of course placed Austen within a literary context whose achievements enabled her own. No one now would dispute how much she owed to Richardson and Burney, among others, in the forging of that impression of vivid life the novels give.[23] It is generally accepted also that the signs of Samuel Johnson's influence are manifest not only in the occasional citation or reference, but in passages where Austen's narrator makes explicit comments on the human mind and its workings.[24] These were prose writers of her own era whose effects she might naturally have assimilated. But the association with Shakespeare is worth probing further because of the bizarre disjunction between Shakespeare's and Austen's style, form and content. The poetry of Shakespeare's plays is intensely metaphoric, often convoluted and entangled, his range is immense, including, in many instances, the supernatural. Her style is correct, rarely ventures beyond the most commonplace metaphorical language, her form is the novel in prose,

her subject the lives and perceptions of young women within a confined
and, by and large, unvarying society. Moreover, a good many of
Austen's own references to Shakespeare are casual or ironic or disre-
spectful. Why then do readers link Jane Austen with Shakespeare? (In
Patricia Rozema's film of *Mansfield Park* (1999) Fanny Price's horse – her
escape from conformity – is even called Shakespeare.) One account
would argue that the association is indeed merely political, the two
figures thus brought together instituting or confirming a dominant
conservative view of English literary culture. In this chapter I shall
suggest that if Austen does indeed have some affinity with Shakespeare,
it is in vain to establish this through allusions and other signs of
conscious remembering. If Jane Austen was akin to Shakespeare, I
argue, the evidence is to be found not on the surface but within the
structure of her texts. Austen's relationship to Shakespeare's work may
thus throw light on the phenomenon of recreation itself.

Isobel Armstrong's reading of *Sense and Sensibility* as a version or rewriting of *Hamlet* is especially pertinent, though, because it entirely sidesteps
the question of influence, and puts the discussion on a different footing.
This is an account which is conducted without any reference to the
author as an agent. Instead, one text 'resonates' with another like two
musical intruments, played by ghostly, insubstantial hands, and the
question of who hears this resonance is not directly addressed. 'We have
never finished Hamlet, Marianne, our dear Willoughby went away
before we could get through it' (*Sense and Sensibility*, p. 75): Mrs Dashwood's remark is the only explicit reference to *Hamlet* in *Sense and
Sensibility*, but 'the play is everywhere in the novel', Armstrong suggests.
'It provides for that strange dreamwork structure – a kind of alternative
text – which always seems to be lurking in Jane Austen's beautifully
ordered writing, issuing in travesty, masquerade and dissidence.'[25] In
both narrative and tragedy, fathers are absent, there is 'the repressed
presence of war', brother is in conflict with brother. Above all,
Marianne's illness (akin to madness in the eighteenth century,
Armstrong suggests) resembles Ophelia's. Not only is Marianne's sickness brought on by being spurned by a lover, this lover returns contrite:
in *Sense and Sensibility* to what he imagines is his lover's death bed, in
Hamlet, literally to her grave. Many other 'concealed, cobweb connections and references' (p. 83) pervade the later text.

　　Armstrong does not suggest in Bloomian fashion that Austen's novel
has an 'Oedipal' relation to the play which she sees inhabiting it.

Rather, most interestingly, her discussion is conducted in quite other psychoanalytic terms, drawn from Freud's *The Interpretation of Dreams*.[26] The model Armstrong adopts for the relation between texts is the relation he posited between the dream thoughts – the latent memories and desires out of which, in his view, the dream is fashioned – and the manifest dream itself. Armstrong suggests that there is a 'fleeting and subtle network of *Hamlet* allusions, providing a latent dreamwork text which repeatedly intrudes into the manifest narrative' (p. 82) of the novel. In Freud, the 'dream-work' is the means by which inadmissible desires are reconfigured so as to emerge into consciousness and pass respectably in the remembered and manifest dream. It refers to such processes as displacement, condensation and representation by the opposite, and Armstrong finds such disguises present in the novel, suggesting, for example, that since 'it is the privilege of dreamwork to ordain changes of sex' (p. 18) the inquisitive, spying Mrs Jennings is a recasting of Polonius.

By situating the question of influence at an unconscious level, Armstrong is able to make a series of fascinating suggestions about the pulling power of the narrative – that for example, incestuous wishes are operative in the depiction of Mrs Dashwood's interest in Colonel Brandon, and that when Elinor listens to Brandon telling the story of his ward, she has 'the dreamwork satisfaction' of being her sister's lover's momentary object (p. 109). She provides one model for a relationship between two writers which moves it decisively away from conscious allusion. But the analogy itself seems shaky: *Hamlet*, the latent text, is itself a highly conscious artefact, and cannot plausibly be conflated with fantasy or desire. One can, of course, propose that Shakespeare's influence on Jane Austen penetrates so deeply, or is so pervasive that it can be thought of as belonging to the deep unconscious. In that case it will hardly retain the precise lineaments that enable exact comparisons or references. On the other hand Armstrong occasionally suggests that Austen's 'invocation' of the play is more or less purposeful: 'The brilliance of making *Hamlet* an undertext is that its dark, brooding complexities can be invoked and yet kept at bay by comedy: the tragic structures are transposed and re-inflected in the lucid sharpness of satire, irony and pun' (p. 108).[27]

If at such moments Armstrong implies a Jane Austen actively referring to the earlier text, her chosen vocabulary and metaphors actually open up another possibility. She has adopted as a theory of the relationship between texts an account that was framed as an avenue – in Freud's complacent phrase a 'royal road' – to the understanding of the individual unconscious, but her presentation usually avoids the suggestion of any individual psyche in which these connections are made. And because the place of the psyche, the agent, is left vacant, and yet is always presumed by the analogy, her mode of writing suggests ultimately that the site at which the interactions between these texts take place can be none other than where they meet, in her own imagination. In this sense her argument is a beautiful representation of reading, a phenomenological demonstration of what occurs within a well-informed, sensitive mind familiar with both authors' works. Its 'shadows', 'cobwebs' and 'resonances' catch not aspects of the texts, but are descriptions of the fleeting, nebulous associations and memories that occur in the hovering attention of such a reader's response. So the issue here – a general one for scholars investigating 'influence' – resembles that in biography: what kind of truth claim is being made? On the other hand, this quasi-psychological presentation paradoxically underlines a doubt I have already raised about the discourse which seeks to represent the relation between films and their originating novels in structuralist terms – that the evacuation of the psychology of the remaking agent leaves too many questions unanswered.

As Armstrong's project implies, however, if there is anything in the cultural association of Jane Austen and Shakespeare, what this is can scarcely be approached at the level of conscious allusion and reference. Yet there is a deliberate allusion to Shakespeare in *Sense and Sensibility* that, as Alice Chandler points out, clearly adds something to the text. 'When you leave Barton to form your own establishment, Queen Mab shall receive you,' says Willoughby offering his horse to Marianne (*Sense and Sensibility*, p. 59). Queen Mab 'is the hag, when maids lay on their backs, / That presses them' (*Romeo and Juliet* I, iv, 93–94): to readers who knew Shakespeare this would give a pretty strong hint as to what Willoughby is really proposing. Elinor, who 'instantly saw an intimacy so decided, a meaning so direct' (*Sense and Sensibility*, p. 60) may or may not be intended to gather this too.[28] There are several such purposeful allusions to Shakespeare in Austen's novels.[29] These do not, in themselves, provide much evidence for the pervasive and dominant presence or affinity that would justify the long tradition of associating the two writers. On the contrary, what they often seem to signal is irreverence. In *Emma* for instance, there is a discussion about the validity of a line in *A Midsummer Night's Dream* when applied to Harriet Smith's experience of love. Emma Woodhouse, with her scheme to marry Harriet off to Mr

Elton in full flight, excited at its success so far, declares that

'There does seem to be a something in the air of Hartfield which gives love exactly the right direction, and sends it into the very channel where it ought to flow.

The course of true love never did run smooth –

A Hartfield edition of Shakespeare would have a long note on that passage.' (*Emma*, p. 75)

'Hartfield' (an enterprise otherwise known as Miss Emma Woodhouse) apparently knows a thing or two that Lysander in *A Midsummer Night's Dream* did not. Emma in her 'enchanting hubris'[30] seems to be modelling herself momentarily on such a famous editor of Shakespeare as Johnson. She is gaily usurping the position of her male editorial forerunners, at the same time as she takes leave to differ from a famous line of Shakespeare himself. Later in the novel, a more chastened Emma is to make reparative use of both Johnson and Shakespeare when she cites 'the world is not their's, nor the world's law' to excuse Jane Fairfax.[31]

The youthful Jane Austen herself treats Shakespeare with similar irreverence in earlier instances, as at the opening of the 'History of England', by 'a partial, prejudiced and ignorant historian'.

Henry the 4th ascended the throne of England much to his own satisfaction in the year 1399, after having prevailed on his cousin and predecessor Richard the 2nd, to resign it to him and retire to Pomfret Castle, where he happened to be murdered. [Henry] . . . did not live for ever, but falling ill, his son the Prince of Wales came and took away the crown, whereupon the King made a long speech, for which I must refer the Reader to Shakespear's Plays, and the Prince made a still longer. Things being thus settled between them the King died . . . (*Minor Works*, p. 139)

Catherine Morland, 'in training for a heroine', acquires a store of 'those quotations which are so serviceable and so soothing in the vicissitudes of their eventful lives' (*Northanger Abbey*, p. 15). Among them are those lines from *Twelfth Night* that Simpson suggested were her source in *Persuasion*, which declare, as Austen disingenuously claims, 'that a young woman in love always looks' like Patience on a monument. Can such skittish or 'lightly ironic' treatments of Shakespeare be reconciled with any deep debt or affinity?[32]

One turns to the famous discussion of Shakespeare in *Mansfield Park*.[33] Responding to Edmund Bertram's congratulations on his reading of *Henry VIII*, Henry Crawford remarks: 'I once saw Henry the 8th acted. –

Or I have heard of it from somebody who did – I am not certain which. But Shakespeare one gets acquainted with without knowing how. It is part of an Englishman's constitution. His thoughts and beauties are so spread abroad that one touches them every where, one is intimate with him by instinct' (*Mansfield Park*, p. 338). Edmund Bertram's response is less indolent and more intelligent, his alteration of Henry's pronouns suggesting that he wishes to avoid the sexism of Henry's remarks and perhaps include Fanny (who has already been witnessed reading Shakespeare aloud to her snoozily uncomprehending aunt) in his commentary:[34] 'No doubt, one is familiar with Shakespeare in a degree', he says, 'his celebrated passages are quoted by every body; they are in half the books we open, and we all talk Shakespeare, use his similes and describe with his descriptions'. The *Recollections* of Mary Russell Mitford, among Jane Austen's contemporaries, confirm the accuracy of this picture of Shakespeare's currency among the genteel classes of the time. 'It may be reckoned amongst the best and dearest of our English privileges', she remarks, 'that we are all more or less educated in Shakespeare; that the words and thoughts of the greatest of poets are, as it were, engrafted into our minds.'[35] Frances Burney's late novel, *The Wanderer*, published in 1814, the same year as *Mansfield Park*, celebrates in similar terms 'the all-pervading Shakespeare'.[36]

Despite the references in *Emma* and *Sense and Sensibility*, it is odd then that Austen's own writing rarely slips in the Shakespearean phrases that her character declares are on everyone's lips and spill onto everyone's pages. This contrasts very strikingly with the habit of her contemporaries. Jonathan Bate has noted, for example, the 'allusive structure' apparent in Scott's references to the Henry plays throughout *Waverley*, also published in 1814.[37] In *The Wanderer*, the suicidal Elinor Joddrel, in love with a man who prefers the heroine, Juliet, expresses her weariness with life in phrases that plainly echo the soliloquies of Shakespeare. 'I am sick of the world yet still I crawl upon its surface', she laments (p. 189), mingling Claudio with Hamlet in the expression of her 'sickness of all mortal existence' and declaring 'call it what you will, sleep, rest or death – termination is all I seek'. Bidding her lover farewell, she borrows that 'very fine speech' of Cardinal Wolsey that Henry Crawford very likely hit upon,[38] so familiar was it to her contemporaries: 'Farewell! a long Farewell!' (p. 183), she exclaims. Perhaps the use of such phrases, as of many others – 'the finger of scorn', 'my almost blunted purpose' (p. 372) is purposive – a signalling to Burney's readers of the importance, or rather the dignity, of her feelings. But they are not confined to Elinor in *The*

Wanderer and their effect must be a muted or divided one: they tend to signal not so much authentic as stagy and therefore second-hand feeling.

Austen's characters do quote Shakespeare, but neither they nor the narrator pick up familiar Shakespeare expressions in the way that Burney, Scott and, to use a later example, Dickens, habitually did.[39] Jane Austen did not, like Dickens, see Shakespeare professionally acted at an early and impressionable age (though she may well have taken part in play-readings and she saw Edmund Kean in *The Merchant of Venice*[40]); did not spend three years in the library of the British Museum reading Shakespeare, did not carry Shakespeare's works with her when she travelled.[41] She certainly doesn't appear to share Dickens's hero-worshipping relation to Shakespeare. 'To know him in bits and scraps, is common enough', Edmund continues, 'to know him pretty thoroughly is perhaps not uncommon' (*Mansfield Park*, p. 338). But it is not difficult to show that Jane Austen in some sense 'knew' the works of Shakespeare. The difficulty is to give some precise and useable meaning to the verb to know.

Certainly, the casual references to *Henry VIII*, *Hamlet*, *The Merchant of Venice* and *Richard III* in *Mansfield Park* do suggest a certain familiarity. And perhaps Edmund's careful discrimination implies that the author took the knowledge of Shakepeare seriously. But one should not overestimate this – the passages Austen quotes, I think, never go beyond the common cultural lexicon of Shakespearen phrases, the sort of thing that might easily find its way into a keepsake book, to be found in Radcliffe or Richardson, perhaps, just as readily. If, as the conversation of Edmund and Henry might suggest, Austen knew some of Shakespeare's plays from early family reading, if she deeply admired him – both ifs – that did not mean that she sought to imitate or copy, or, as one says in an expressive phrase, to draw upon him. We might suppose, in contrast, that what occurs when a writer like Burney employs Shakespearean phrases or Dickens imitates a Shakespearean motif is psychologically speaking a form of merging, or a momentary obliteration of the distinction between self and other, what Freud called an anaclitic, or dependent relation. Temporarily the second writer allows the first to take over, to be a kind of surrogate or prosthetic expressive self. The momentary attempt is to blend with, incorporate, and become the other, as the metaphor hidden within the term 'influence' perhaps indicates.

Earlier in *Mansfield Park* Tom Bertram, furiously defending his enthusiasm for acting a play, recalls the boys performing in front of their father. 'How many a time have we mourned over the dead body of

Julius Caesar, and *to be'd* and *not to be'd*, in this very room, for his amusement!' (*Mansfield Park*, p. 126). Another indication of Austen's casual way with the plays, the phrasing of this quotation can also serve as a model for different kind of relation. A hint at what this might mean is given in K. C. Phillipps's study of Austen's language. Commenting that 'Jane Austen shows great freedom, and even daring, in her conversion and use of almost any part of speech as any other part of speech', he remarks that 'Shakespeare was the precursor to whom she might look in this . . . At least two of her conversions emanate from *Hamlet*.' He instances Mr Weston's '[e]ver since her being turned into a Churchill she has out-Churchill'd them all in high and mighty claims' (*Emma*, p. 310), which 'echoes' Hamlet's famous 'out-Herods Herod'.[42] His point is not that Austen imitates the semantic content but instead replicates the grammatical structure made possible by Shakespeare. This may suggest the level at which one might seek to grasp Jane Austen's relation to Shakespeare.

More importantly, one can question the very notion of influence itself. The word originally meant the action of the stars on human affairs, and as this suggests, it often implies some magical transmission, some unimpeded flowing, by which one sensibility imbibes the power or gift of another.[43] It is plausible to link this with the child's first experiences at the mother's breast, a link that is most strongly made in the writings of the Romantic poet, Wordsworth. There, conceptions of power flowing from the outside into the self, as with Nature, 'the nurse / The guide, the guardian of my heart' in 'Tintern Abbey' (lines 110–11), of hearts 'drinking in at every pore / The spirit of the season' ('Lines', ll.27–8), of the 'influx' of feeling (*The Prelude*, XII, 308) are explicitly modelled on, or have their archaic origin in, the experience of the child feeding on 'the innocent milk' (*Prelude*, V, 272), from the mother's breast, as the famous passage about the infant babe in *The Prelude* Book II makes clear (lines 237–80). Blest influences then, in Wordsworth, are received into the self in the similar unmediated way that milk is taken in, and similarly bring with them a sense of grounding in the world and community with other beings. The notion of literary influence similarly suggests a form of feeding, or nourishment, in which the pupil or secondary writer draws on the inspiring power of the first.

But the nourishing relation between two writers might equally be figured in other ways, as in the classical tradition. A comparison of the poet to a bee, gathering food from his predecessors and turning it to honey is made in Seneca's letters to Lucilius.[44] Ben Jonson reworks this idea, as well as a passage of Horace, in *Timber: or Discoveries* (1641). In a very different idiom from Wordsworth he writes

The third requisite in our poet or maker is imitation, *imitatio*, to be able to convert the substance or riches of another poet to his own use . . . Not as a creature that swallows what it takes in, crude, raw, or undigested; but that feeds with an appetite, and hath a stomach to concoct, divide, and turn all to nourishment. Not to imitate servilely, as Horace saith, and catch at vices for virtue, but to draw forth out of the best and choicest flowers, with the bee, and turn all into honey, work it into one relish and savour; make our imitation sweet.[45]

Perhaps the relation between two artists might be represented best then not as the direct, unmediated absorption of the drinking metaphor, but the complex, masticatory and digestory process of the feeding one. The first writer may certainly enliven and energise the successor, but the crucial emphasis here, as I understand it, is on the process of 'concoction' or digestion or 'working', that breaking down of the original that forms the essential act of transmutation, or incorporation. Such feeding on the earlier writer, Jonson implies, involves selection as well as appropriation. If Shakespeare is 'engrafted' into the mind, or part of the 'constitution', do not these phrases suggest glimpses of this deeper, more complex relation?

There is an interesting convergence between this way of seeing relatedness between authors and the psychoanalytic mode of seeing relatedness between people and the others who have been important to them. Psychoanalytic thought speaks of our 'identification' with others, but also of our 'incorporating' or 'introjecting' others into our psychic life. This is because psychoanalysis is theoretically committed to the view that all psychic processes are extrapolations, or sophistications, of very early experiences of the infant. These are of necessity primarily physical. As Freud put it, defining introjection and projection, '[e]xpressed in the language of the oldest – the oral – instinctual influences, the judgement is: "I should like to eat this", or "I should like to spit it out"; and, put more generally, "I should like to take this into myself and to keep that out." '[46] Psychoanalysis therefore proposes that the infant's earliest experience of consuming the mother, actually taking her in – taking in her milk – becomes elaborated in our later 'incorporation' of others.[47] An important component of the notion of incorporation is processing. The self takes in the other, but also, as when we eat, breaks it down, making it, in the process of incorporation, something else, part of the 'new' self's own substance.

The process of identification, as Winnicott emphasises, involves both absorption and attack. Mingled with the beneficent drinking in of the mother is the phenomena, which he sometimes describes as 'excitement', and sometimes as 'the primitive love impulse'[48] which can manifest itself (to the mother, and to adult eyes) as aggression and sadistic violence. This too forms a basis on which relations to other people are established. But 'destruction' (the global term psychoanalysts give to this rather complex process) of the other person, as Winnicott argues, is especially necessary for the process of absorption of the other to take place. Hatred, envy, contempt and other hostile emotions play important roles (one might compare them to the bile, the digestive juices). But the end result is that a person absorbs or assimilates the other. In his last important paper, as we have seen, it frees one from that which earlier psychoanalysis had taken as constituting human subjectivity, 'relating through identifications'.[49]

This model then offers a more complex analogy for thinking about the relation between authors than does the idea of influence. Influence is like milk, taken in and absorbed, unproblematically. Alternatively, one can think of the other writer as solid food, offering much more resistance to incorporation, requiring much more psychological and creative labour to incorporate. A contrast to this process is idealisation, in which one retains a deep psychological tie to the other person, object or body of work. This may well manifest itself in admiration and 'love', and often gives rise to pain if the idealised object is tampered with or treated lightly. These are obviously no more than ideas, suggestions about a difficult to define process that has many levels and may differ greatly from author to author. In literary-critical terms, a successful adaptation will manifest itself as much in treating the source 'cavalierly', as *Clueless* treats *Emma*, as in fidelity or obedience to the earlier text's internal image. The end result will not be imitation or mimicking of the original, but a new independent work of art that can stand comparison, which perhaps prompts in readers a sense of deep similitude or affinity, but which rarely resembles the original in any obvious way.

Would it be going too far to suggest that Jane Austen understood something of this? The reviewer of *Pride and Prejudice* for the *Critical Review* in March 1813 remarked that Elizabeth Bennet 'takes great delight in playing *the Beatrice* upon' Darcy.[50] He thus saw immediately that the dialogues between the two resemble the contests of wit – the way that a word or trope is caught and tossed back to the original speaker in reworked or elaborated form[51] – between the heroine of *Much*

Ado About Nothing and Benedick (though these were no doubt also mediated to Jane Austen through Congreve, Sheridan and other dramatists). An example occurs very early in their acquaintance. In company with Darcy and Bingley, Mrs Bennet is boasting that Jane was so pretty at fifteen that 'a gentleman' wrote some verses on her. ' "And so ended his affection," said Elizabeth impatiently. "There has been many a one, I fancy, overcome in the same way. I wonder who first discovered the efficacy of poetry in driving away love!" ' Darcy replies quickly, 'I have been used to consider poetry as the *food* of love', and Elizabeth returns '[o]f a fine, stout, healthy love it may . . .. But . . . I am convinced that one good sonnet will starve it entirely away' (*Pride and Prejudice*, p. 44). The dialogue is used to suggest how the participants have rather more in common with each other than they know. The material of their exchange alludes to the famous opening lines of *Twelfth Night*. When Elizabeth says 'I wonder who first discovered . . .?' she is putting lightly a historical or cultural question and it is this hint that Darcy is able to respond to with his play on Shakespeare's line. He in fact feeds her this line so that – at his rather tense moment in front of her relations – she can go on to cap her earlier comment. But it's also notable that Elizabeth's remark expresses a refreshing scepticism about the relation of true feeling to literary, or received expression. So whilst the exchange is 'feeding off' both of Shakespeare's comedies, it is simultaneously questioning whether rehearsing the language of another can ever reliably express true feeling. As Marianne Novy comments '[w]hile Austen is making fun of cultural uses of Shakespearean quotations, she is also employing a technique rather like his own: both of them include and parody ideas of love associated with literary convention.'[52]

To use another Winnicottian formulation one might say that Darcy and Elizabeth are playing together in the presence of Shakespeare.[53] That is to say their freedom (or perhaps it is only Elizabeth's freedom?) to play with Shakespeare is attained through Shakespeare but is in no way dependent on him. The passage is offering a kind of metacritical commentary on what it is performing, suggesting the idea of literature (or at any rate of writing) as nourishment of one's feelings, and critiquing the notion of feelings needing the bolstering or mediation of writing. Jane Austen's relation to Shakespeare seems often to involve simultaneously resumption and mockery or scepticism, trashing, even – that 'destruction of the object' that Winnicott saw as a vital step towards psychological (and, let us say, authorial) independence.

Austen then can be said not just to borrow from Shakespeare but to actively work quotations from his plays into a considered design of her own. At other times she expresses impatience with his currency, or possibly rebellion against his overbearing reputation, and the psychoanalytic theory I am drawing on offers an explanation of how such insouciance might be grounds for attributing to her, not indifference to his plays, but a deep absorption of them. But if one models the relation of a writer to her sustaining predecessor not on influence, on drinking in, but on eating, on incorporation, then one is led to a critical dilemma. In the nature of things evidence of such incorporation is not to be found on the surface, not to be marked by verbal resemblances, echoes or allusions. It is not a relation of obvious indebtedness, since that would be a sign of a still-unbroken bond of dependency. Winnicott's point about the infant truly digesting, truly taking in, the object, was not only that the infant can treat the mother cavalierly, it is that the cavalier treatment is an index of the infant having truly internalised the mother. An observer may detect the achievement of this psychological milestone by the freedom which the infant assumes in the mother's presence. In the adult this benefit of ordinary 'good enough' mothering shows up only in one's freedom from the more crippling inhibitions and feelings of inadequacy and unreality. In the literary version of assimilation it may be as difficult to detect.

Martin Price introduced an anthology in 1967 with the remark: 'There is no term that recurs more often in recent Dickens criticism than "Shakespearean", for the comparison is an almost inevitable way of defining some of Dickens's powers: his effortless invention, his brilliant play of language, the scope and density of his imagined world.'[54] If the same comparison has been so consistently applied to Jane Austen the critics who employ it must certainly have other qualities in mind, qualities in their author that are by no means as obviously in evidence. In the final part of this chapter I suggest that there are ways in which the influence of Shakespeare's characteristic dramatic structures might be discerned in Austen's work, but I do not mean to imply that Austen is the only novelist in English (or indeed in other languages) who might be said to resemble Shakespeare in this way. It could almost be said that the Shakespearean way of constructing a dramatic argument is so naturalised into our culture that we take it for granted.

Yet when Macaulay aligned Fanny Burney's novels with Jonson's comedies of the humours, and Austen with Shakespeare, he was putting his finger on something important, though he could see it only in terms of the creation of 'character'. In Burney's novels, he wrote, we find 'striking groups of eccentric characters, each governed by his own peculiar whim, each talking his own peculiar jargon, and each bringing out by opposition the oddities of all the rest'. In Shakespeare's characters, by contrast, he thought, 'no single feature is extravagantly overcharged'.[55] The effect of individuality in Austen is similarly achieved by some form of convergence or affinity rather than 'opposition', he implies, but Macaulay does not explore this consequence of his terms. I suggest that it is the multiplication of lines of connection between figures which gives the sense of an integrated 'world' in Shakespeare's plays and Austen's novels, whilst simultaneously generating the sense of moral drama; that successfully gives the effect of verisimilitude, whilst at the same time bringing the pleasures of a tightly organised psychological or moral argument, and that this may be one sign of how deeply Jane Austen has internalised her reading of Shakespeare.

Shakespearean criticism has often recognised that characteristic feature of his work which Hazlitt in 1817, describing the dramatic structure of *Cymbeline*, called 'the use he makes of the principle of analogy'[56] and A. P. Rossiter called 'beautifully complicated parallelisms'.[57] More recently G. K. Hunter has described the characteristic 'creation of meaning by antithetical structuring'[58] in the romantic comedies and Graham Bradshaw has demonstrated his 'dramatic "rhyming"'.[59] As Bradshaw points out, 'it is by now a critical commonplace to observe that *Hamlet* presents the differing responses of three sons and a daughter to the loss of their fathers, so that our reactions to Fortinbras, Laertes, or Ophelia figure in our thinking about Hamlet' (*Misrepresentations*, p. 64). Bradshaw goes on to demonstrate that it is often the case that the resemblance, the 'rhyming', is ' "off" in some dramatically pointed or provoking way: there is enough of a resemblance to set us thinking about differences, which may be far more important' (*ibid.*). This may well be a development out of the early Shakespearean use of the subplot to parallel or echo the main plot, but Bradshaw's argument is that effects of 'rhyming' are more tightly woven into the dramatic fabric than this suggests, that odd, provocative effects are generated not only through resemblances of situation or plot, but in co-incidences of phrasing and metaphor. He suggests that Shakespeare's 'variational development' resembles Beethoven's late sonatas, in which 'the exploratory impulse to vary and transform combines with the urge to integrate' (*Misrepresentations*, p. 76).

In *Much Ado About Nothing*, Beatrice compares 'wooing, wedding and repenting' to 'a Scotch jig, a measure and a cinquepace', all of them

dances.[60] 'But they are such very different things!' exclaims Catherine
Morland when Henry Tilney borrows the comparison: 'People that
marry can never part, but must go and keep house together. People that
dance, only stand opposite each other in a long room for half an hour'
(*Northanger Abbey*, p. 77). There is no disputing the truth of this, but it is
obvious that the courtship romances that constitute the basic plot of
Jane Austen's novels do resemble as well as include the balls and dances
that feature in them. Like a ball or Assembly, Austen's novels are often
limited to the gentry of a neighbourhood, and, as in a dance, a certain
amount of stylised movement takes place, and the furtherance of social
as well as erotic relations is the underlying goal. One might explore this
metaphor further: as in the kind of dance with which Austen was
familiar, a succession of possible erotic partners is encountered; as in the
dance, successive partners ask to be compared with each other. The
trope of the ball suggests that whilst the focus of the novels is on one
particular couple, what is being simultaneously alluded to, or indicated,
is the possibility of other partners, and other affiliations. Other dancers
are performing analogously to the main figures in another part of the
room, or text. To alter the metaphor, the result resembles the 'realism'
we associate with perspective: the heroine is in the foreground, but she is
represented against similar figures, who move in different planes of the
background, their presence there giving an effect of depth.[61]

It is this effect of interconnection among individualised figures which
resembles the inner structure of Shakespeare's plays, and especially his
comedies. It may explain in part the 'dramatic' quality her early critics
so often emphasised. But the dance is, after all, only a rudimentary
metaphor to describe the representational mode of these novels. Another way of approaching this is to note how Austen persistently invites
her reader not to enjoy eccentricity, the extreme or odd, as in Burney,
but to perceive or acknowledge similarities within difference. Just as
Shakespeare (to use obvious examples) invites comparisons between
Banquo and Macbeth's responses to the witches' prophesies, so *Pride and
Prejudice* asks the reader to compare Elizabeth Bennet's response to Mr
Collins's proposal with Charlotte's, and to compare Wickham's with
Colonel Fitzwilliam's behaviour when it comes to the question of
finance and marriage.[62] The employment of allusions and cross refer-
ences between characters, rather than sharp contrasts, becomes a
crucial part of the three novels written after Jane Austen moved to
Chawton Cottage in 1809. Consider how Fanny Price as virtual orphan
and ward is rhymed by Mary and Henry Crawford as orphans and

wards, how the influence of one adopted uncle is paralleled with the influence of another, how the notion of fraternal love is worked through the Crawfords, through Fanny and William and through Fanny and Edmund. Emma's dependence on the whims of her hypochondriac father is duplicated or rather 'rhymed' with Frank Churchill's dependence on the whims of his hypochondriac adoptive mother, and his inventive mischief – serving an erotic purpose – is cousin to Emma's mischief, where the underlying impulses are less obvious. If *Hamlet* presents a range of different reactions to loss, consider the varieties of mourning and melancholia that are represented and 'rhymed' throughout *Persuasion*. Structurally, the effect is more like a complex of references and allusions, as in a musical composition, rather than a set of clearly calibrated comparisons. When readers speak so familiarly of 'Jane Austen's world' one of the things they may be alluding to is this impression of coherence which exists at the same time as the effect of distinctness and individuality in her characters. Yet such effects of cross-referencing and comparison, it must be confessed, are common in literature and art.

It may be possible, then, to claim that Jane Austen really 'knew' her Shakespeare. What is striking in that passage in *Persuasion* which Simpson and other critics agree reminds one of Viola's oblique confession to Orsino in *Twelfth Night* is that, into a context or situation that inevitably recalls Shakespeare, there is inserted a tiny mark of repudiation or rivalry. When Anne Elliot cries 'If you please, no reference to examples in books. Men have had every advantage of us in telling their own story' (*Persuasion*, p. 234) Austen is perhaps, as in *Pride and Prejudice*, shrugging off the indebtedness that she is simultaneously enacting, declaring her rivalry of the master she cannot but also acknowledge. But such a construction of the matter, as I have argued in Chapter 2, would recognise only part of the truth. Jane Austen could treat Shakespeare casually, yet at the same time use quotations from him to specfic effect in her novels, because she had in fact assimilated his work in a more thorough and complete way, a way which enabled her to be independent. She may be deeply indebted to Shakespeare, not for phrases and characters, but for the principle of organisation of her novels, for her way of conceiving of dramatic conflict, and her capacity, through generating moral and psychological sets of affinities between her characters, to provide a sense of a homogeneous world. These features, I suggest, may lie (obscurely, perhaps) behind the association or merging of these two writers in the cultural imagination. In the next chapter, however, I suggest a more specific way in which Austen's work achieves comparable effects to Shakespeare's. Her representation of the inner life is crucial to that intimate contact readers feel with her work. At the same time it provides a major challenge to the filmmaker who seeks to recreate her art.

CHAPTER 4

From drama, to novel, to film: inwardness in Mansfield Park and Persuasion

The advantage of the cinema over the theatre is not that you can
even have horses, but that you can stare closer into a man's eyes.
Grigory Kozintsev, *'King Lear', the Space of Tragedy*[1]

The example of Frances Burney, though, was of more immediate
importance to Jane Austen than Shakespeare. There is a scene in
Burney's third novel *Camilla* in which the youthful heroine learns that
her beautiful but trivial cousin Indiana is engaged to Edgar Mandlebert,
the young man whom at the end of the novel, after many misunder-
standings, she is eventually to marry. What she overhears brings with it
'a consciousness too strong for any further self-disguise', the revelation
that she herself is in love with him. 'The sound alone of the union struck
as a dagger at her heart', Burney writes, 'and told her, incontrovertibly,
who was its master'. Camilla, as is the habit of Burney's heroines,
registers the impact of this revelation on her body, in this case as illness.
'Her sensations were now most painful: she grew pale, she became sick.'
'Strangely disordered,' but 'no longer self-deceived', she staggers back
to the carriage where she laments, 'in a new burst of sorrow, her
unhappy fate, and unpropitious attachment'. But Camilla is a good girl
and it is not long before she stops weeping and pulls herself together.
'Her regret was succeeded by a summons upon propriety.' Remembering the lessons of her parents, 'she determined to struggle without
cessation for the conquest of a partiality she deemed it treachery to
indulge'. She obediently resolves to avoid Edgar's company hence-
forth.[2]

Jane Austen was one of the subscribers to *Camilla*, published in 1796,
and recorded in her copy a not altogether flattering comment on the
novel.[3] There is some similarity however between Camilla's situation
and a striking moment in *Mansfield Park* when young Fanny Price is left
to deal with the just delivered news that her cousin Edmund intends to

marry Mary Crawford. In confiding in her, Edmund has no inkling of her own feelings. He leaves her, thinking that she will be pleased at his decision. ' "I would not have the shadow of a coolness arise", he repeated, his voice sinking a little, "between the two dearest objects I have on earth." ' Fanny's response to this visit is given in a passage of free indirect speech:

> He was gone as he spoke; and Fanny remained to tranquillise herself as she could. She was one of his two dearest – that must support her. But the other! – the first! She had never heard him speak so openly before, and though it told her no more than what she had long perceived, it was a stab; – for it told of his own convictions and views. They were decided. He would marry Miss Craw-ford. It was a stab, in spite of every long-standing expectation; and she was obliged to repeat again and again that she was one of his two dearest, before the words gave her any sensation. Could she believe Miss Crawford to deserve him, it would be – Oh! how different would it be – how far more tolerable! But he was deceived in her; he gave her merits which she had not; her faults were what they had ever been, but he saw them no longer. Till she had shed many tears over this deception, Fanny could not subdue her agitation. (*Mansfield Park*, p. 264)

Both young women, Camilla Tyrold and Fanny Price, receive their news as a violating blow, both struggle with their pain and distress, and resolve to renounce the object of their affections. The earlier author's notation of strong emotion draws its vocabulary, its system of significa-tion, from the pictorial arts and from the theatre. Emotions are readable by their bodily signs. Blushes, deep sighs, husky voice, stammerings and flights from the room characterise Camilla's extremities of feeling. In many episodes of *Mansfield Park*, Fanny, too, is prone to experience emotional stress as physical debility, headaches, faintness. But this is not the case here. One could not say that in this passage her distress is represented either as wholly a matter of feelings, nor wholly of thoughts, but the effect is certainly to make the sympathetic reader experience her condition with some immediacy, and to induce an effect of intimacy.

Jane Austen's position in the history of the novel is due, in part, to her mastery of techniques for the representation of inner life, or interior consciousness. This part of her work can be plausibly compared, I suggest, with Shakespeare's soliloquies, and not only because each differs so remarkably from the dominant mode of the forms, drama and novel respectively, from which they emerged. Other writers, Richardson and Burney among them, obviously helped Jane Austen to give an impression of immediate life, but there are aspects of her achievement that make Shakespeare's presentation of the intimate lives of his characters seem the model – distant, but not the less powerful for that – for what she does in the novel. But in focusing on this specific example of her affinity to Shakespeare, and in possibly implying something more concrete – something in the nature of assimilation and recreation – one needs to note that it crosses three lines: media, genre and gender. Jane Austen writes fiction, directed mostly to the solitary reader, not plays for an audience. She writes novels whose framework is satiric and comic, not the tragedies and 'problem plays' in which Shakespeare most famously represented his protagonists' inner struggles (though her depiction of inner life brings with it some darkening of tone). And she represented the private conflicts of women, not of men: an implicitly if perhaps unconsciously feminist agenda which, according them moral stature, nevertheless tends to shape her characters' inner strivings towards submission to circumstance rather than towards choice and action.

These crossings make Austen's relation to Shakespeare a suggestive, if loose, model for the filmmaker's relation to her own novels. Each translation or imitation takes place in a different medium, with different materials. They involve a comparable displacement, in which quite new technical means are brought into play. The mode of free indirect speech is unlike the mode of the soliloquy; the cinema's system of signification is quite unlike the novel's. Thus I am not suggesting that Austen 'rewrites' Shakespeare, or that she can be said to have had Shakespeare in mind when she conceives her characters to have inner lives. One might rather say that she had forgotten Shakespeare than that she remembered him. From a certain point of view all I am doing is pointing out a resemblance between an artist who in the theatre gives an unprecedented effect of intimate connection with an individual selfhood (and thereby perhaps made his audience able to experience themselves as having interior lives) and an artist who achieved a comparable result in the novel. But by following the fate of interiority from Shakespeare to Austen and thence back into the newly dramatic but actually quite distinct medium of the film, I hope to raise a central issue that confronts any filmmaker working in the orbit of Austen's achievement.

Jane Austen, by general consent, achieves in *Mansfield Park* means by which inner life can be represented as if it were a continuous inner speech. Marilyn Butler writes, for example, that, in the second volume of the novel, 'Fanny's free indirect speech becomes the vehicle of the narrative, and the special quality of her mind colours, or dominates the story.'[4] Interestingly, Austen refers at least twice in *Mansfield Park* to Fanny's 'soliloquies'. One of them occurs when Fanny has just returned to her room to find, for the first time, that a fire has been laid. She is overwhelmed by the kindness of the uncle who has just previously been accusing her of ingratitude, and Austen writes: ' "I must be a brute indeed, if I can be really ungrateful!" said she in soliloquy; "Heaven defend me from being ungrateful!" ' (*Mansfield Park*, p. 322–23). Another occurs when Fanny, alone and melancholy in Portsmouth, receives a disappointing letter from Edmund. ' "I never will – no, I certainly never will wish for a letter again," was Fanny's secret declaration, as she finished this. "What do they bring but disappointment and sorrow?" ' There follows an extended passage, in inverted commas, and including the phrase 'said she', which ends with the narrator's comment that '[s]uch sensations, however, were too near a kin to resentment to be long guiding Fanny's soliloquies' (*Mansfield Park*, pp. 424–25).

Does Austen really mean that Fanny makes such a long speech aloud? Despite the use of this word, it would be difficult to think of these passages as in any sense 'Shakespearean'. And there are many similar examples in Jane Austen. One is the critical moment when Elizabeth Bennet re-reads Darcy's letter in Chapter 8 of the second volume of *Pride and Prejudice*. Moments occur here of old-fashioned rhetoric: 'Astonishment, apprehension, and even horror, oppressed her', a sentence describing a character's emotions which a dozen eighteenth-century novelists besides Burney might have written, and been proud to write. But earlier in the same sequence, the formal Burneyan cadences that represent Elizabeth's emotions – 'With amazement did she first understand that he thought an apology to be in his power . . . With a strong prejudice against everything he might say, she began his account' (*Pride and Prejudice*, p. 204) – culminate in a different moment. 'He expressed no regret for what he had done which satisfied her; his style was not penitent, but haughty. It was all pride and insolence.' For a second the reader is allowed to fancy that she or he hears Elizabeth's inner voice suspiciously defaulting to its habitual prejudice against Mr Darcy.

But what Jane Austen largely does in fact is represent Elizabeth thinking over the letter's propositions, rationally and consciously searching her memory, and weighing possibilities.[5] Then, separately, she represents Elizabeth's feelings of chagrin and self-reproach as a dramatic speech, or what Dorrit Cohn distinguishes as 'quoted monologue'.[6] ' "How despicably have I acted!" she cried – "I, who have prided myself on my discernment! – I, who have valued myself on my abilities!"' (*Pride and Prejudice*, p. 208). Even if this is not what Elizabeth actually says aloud, it has all the confidence of a clearly felt inner conviction that can be immediately expressed in words. The similarly extrovert Emma Woodhouse has many cheekily 'secret' thoughts too but these are secrets from the world, not from Emma herself, and so appropriately represented in inverted commas, as inner 'speeches' too. But there are also self-communing moments in *Emma* when the character is less clearly in possession of her own impulses and motives.

Austen was to move away from the 'soliloquising' mode in which a character in effect retrospectively sums up their condition. In her last three novels, those both begun and completed at Chawton after 1809, there is a development of techniques which represent struggles between incipient thoughts and feelings – a development that (to anticipate a little) parallels the changes which, as a number of recent critics have emphasised, Shakespeare's verse underwent in the 1590s. The freedom of free indirect speech consists in the fluidity with which the consciousness of a character can be melded into or overlayed by the commentary – either explicit or expressed as irony – of the narrator. One might appropriate the notion of 'transitional space' in fact to free indirect speech, for the character's thinking is held within a narrative 'space' which allows the character to articulate the situation as they imagine it, at the same time as the encompassing tone and commentary – sometimes fused with the character – dispassionately sites it within reality. (Neither 'character' nor 'narrator' has actual existence: one of these convenient critical fictions is always dissolving into the other convenient critical fiction: and sometimes these airy nothings 'speak' in unison.) The surrounding narrative can shift from the presentness of certain moments to summary: it is not committed to the same time frame as the thoughts which it reproduces. This in part counters the tendency for the writing to seem theatrical or declamatory, as in the *Pride and Prejudice* chapter. In the passage from *Mansfield Park*, the slightly astringent note of the commentary, for example, – 'Fanny remained to tranquillise herself as she could' – wryly glances at Edmund's obtuseness, and intimates an observer, a narrator.

The next paragraph of *Mansfield Park* is given more emphatically over to the transcription of Fanny's inner thoughts. Like Camilla, and like a dozen 'conduct book' heroines, Fanny exerts herself:

It was her intention, as she felt it to be her duty, to try to overcome all that was excessive, all that bordered on selfishness in her affection for Edmund. To call or to fancy it a loss, a disappointment, would be a presumption; for which she had not words strong enough to satisfy her own humility. To think of him as Miss Crawford might be justified in thinking, would in her be insanity. To her, he could be nothing under any circumstances – nothing dearer than a friend. Why did such an idea occur to her even enough to be reprobated and forbidden? It ought not to have touched on the confines of her imagination. (*Mansfield Park*, pp. 264–65)

This paragraph continues the inner agitation so far represented, but now moves towards Fanny's assertion of her will. Different impulses or agencies of the self are battling for dominance. Moreover the sequence of sentences – the shift from one articulated thought to another – intimates an inner process that is not itself articulated. One might plausibly suggest that only Shakespeare among dramatists offers an analogous effect, and that Austen's novelistic technique of free indirect speech harvests what he had achieved in the soliloquy and elsewhere and combines it with narrational commentary to produce a novelistic recreation of his characteristic achievement.

Shakespeare's soliloquies are, of course, very varied in nature and function.[7] Even in his mature works, as Daniel Seltzer indicates in a well-known essay on Shakespeare's development, they sometimes merely offer self-description.[8] In *The Tempest*, for example, Prospero declares that 'Though with their high wrongs I am struck to th' quick, / Yet with my nobler reason 'gainst my fury / Do I take part . . .' (V, i, 24–26). This is the equivalent, loosely speaking, of 'she determined to struggle without cessation for the conquest of a partiality she deemed it treachery to indulge'. The much anthologised 'Farewell, a long farewell' of Cardinal Wolsey in *Henry VIII*, is another example. The actor, as Seltzer puts it, '(in full fusion with the "character") seems somehow to stand a little to oneside of himself, and to describe what is going on inside him'.[9] The critic contrasts this with what he describes as the specifically Shakespearean communicative projection of interior life, which he links, importantly, with a moment by moment representation of the character's thinking. This was not something that Shakespeare found it easy to arrive at, and the early tragedies, he claims, do not contain it. 'Titus, Romeo, and Juliet may become more movingly adept at *describing* the emotional weight of what they feel, but there are no lines in either text which seem to spring, moment by moment, line by line, in precise counter-point to real time, from inwardly felt change, from true human growth.'[10] In *Richard II*, though, there are passages in the soliloquies that convince us that the character, at the moment when he is speaking, is moving forward, developing emotionally, his selfhood evolving in real time – an experience shared by playwright, actor and audience alike. 'Richard II achieves what he knows and feels exactly at the moment we understand, feelingly, that he knows and feels it; there is no descriptive element, no after-the-fact analysis.'[11]

One effect of this, notoriously, is that the soliloquies can be 'difficult'. The shifts of feeling, the links between articulated moments sometimes seem irrecoverable, and Shakespeare's identification with the speaker so intense that he is so entangled with unwieldy sentiments, as Johnson put it, that he abandons them to the reader to sort out.[12] A touch of this difficulty is present in the first soliloquy of Helena in *All's Well That Ends Well*, which, for several reasons, will be a useful representative of Shakespeare's characteristic mode. This speech invests a woman, treated with condescension by all the characters in the preceding scene, with emotional and dramatic dominance. Helena is a physician's daughter, an orphan of lower social status, who is secretly in love with the Countess's son, Bertram. The opening scene of the play sees Bertram set off for the wars, and after he has left the stage, she responds to the courtier Lafew's injunction to maintain the credit of her dead father:

> O were that all! I think not on my father,
> And these great tears grace his remembrance more
> Than those I shed for him. What was he like?
> I have forgot him. My imagination
> Carries no favour in't but Bertram's.
> I am undone. There's no living, none,
> If Bertram be away. 'Twere all one
> That I should love a bright particular star
> And think to wed it, he is so above me.
> In his bright radiance and collateral light
> Must I be comforted, not in his sphere.   (I, i, 78–88)

The reader or audience cannot know at first of whom she is speaking when Helena says 'his remembrance'. There is a momentary confusion between one and the other internal object. The effect is to take one immediately into the inner world of Helena's emotions. Thus the speech is not merely an announcement, or declaration, of feeling – though that for the audience may be its primary dramatic purpose. In the next lines Helena is simultaneously expressing her love for Bertram and expressing her dismay at it as desperately absurd or transgressive, seeking to quell it, to bring it into proportion. The abrupt and seemingly irrational transitions between one sentence and another suggest this agitation and an inner implicit continuity. This creates the typically 'Shakespearean' effect: the expression of thoughts or emotions as they arise, without concern for the coherence or smoothing out that retrospective presentation – what Seltzer calls 'description' – would bestow on them.

Fanny's situation is not unlike Helena's. Both are orphans, or orphan-like, wards in a wealthy household, desperately and secretly in love with a son of the house: and both sons, oblivious to the women's passion, are called Bertram. (One might then say that Austen is 'rewriting' *All's Well* – a play about the calibration between social class and moral worth – and go on to show how Austen's conservatism and commitment to realism led her to repudiate the proto-feminist enterprise of Helena which made her so unpopular a heroine in the nineteenth century, and reinscribe her own heroine's determined passion in a very different mode.[13]) But it is not for such reasons that I have drawn attention to Helena's speech. Her soliloquy and the representation of Fanny's inner life have several qualities in common. The expression of their feeling spills out in private, after an emotionally challenging social event has just occurred. The Shakespearean monologue, delivered often after others have left the stage, discloses that the character has a secret life quite at odds with that which social interaction permits. 'I have that within which passeth show', says Hamlet ambiguously, edgily, to the queen: the soliloquy which follows ('O that this too too solid flesh would melt') derives its impact, like Helena's, partly from the contrast between the character's style and demeanour in the social world and the turbulent inner, secret or passionate self now displayed. A perhaps more important similarity is in the means whereby this inner turbulence is communicated.

In his famous diatribe against Shakespeare's 'unnaturalness', Tolstoy relented for a moment and declared that 'good actors' could, nevertheless, 'evoke' 'sympathy' with characters. 'Shakespeare, himself an actor, and an intelligent man, knew how to express by the means, not only of speech, but of exclamation, gesture, and the repetition of words, states of mind and developments or changes of feeling taking place in the persons represented.' Jonathan Bate comments that 'Tolstoy pinpoints this peculiar art with great precision':

in many instances, Shakespeare's characters, instead of speaking, merely make an exclamation, or weep, or in the middle of a monologue, by means of gestures, demonstrate the pain of their position (just as Lear asks someone to unbutton him) or in moments of great agitation, repeat a question several times, or several times demand the repetition of a word which has particularly struck them, as do Othello, Macduff, Cleopatra, and others.

'Shakespeare', Bate declares, 'is most Shakespeare not when some character is philosophizing or talking politics, but when Lear says "Pray you undo this button" or Macduff hears Ross's "Wife, children, servants, all / That could be found" and cannot get the word "all" out of his head: "All my pretty ones? / Did you say all? O hell-kite! All?" The peculiar immediacy of the plays comes from such details as these.'[14] A classic, an unforgettable example of the distracted repetition of a heard phrase that Tolstoy noted would be that first soliloquy of Hamlet, with its tortured playing upon the idea that his father has been 'but two months dead'. An earlier, cruder, example, is Juliet's response to the Nurse's news of Romeo's killing of Tybalt:

> All this is comfort. Wherefore weep I then?
> Some word there was, worser than Tybalt's death,
> That murdered me. I would forget it fain,
> But O, it presses to my memory
> Like damnèd guilty deeds to sinners' minds!
> 'Tybalt is dead, and Romeo banishèd'
> That 'banishèd', that one word 'banishèd' . . .
>
> (*Romeo and Juliet*, III, ii, 107–13)

Austen's representation of Fanny's inner speech suggests a certain affinity with these Shakespearean effects. There is little resemblance of situation (thus cutting out the idea of imitation or reminiscence). Nor is the particular feeling referable to any Shakespearean model: the sudden woundingness of learning that one is not the preferred lover, exacerbated if anything by the sisterly role to which one is simultaneously assigned. The language here too is unlike Shakespeare's, and is certainly not entangled with metaphors. 'My imagination / Carries no favour in't but Bertram's', Helena confesses. Yet she is not scared of her 'imagination' as Fanny Price – like her creator, a reader of Johnson's essays – is. As I have argued, if Jane Austen has incorporated Shakespeare, the signs of that ingestion will not be readily legible.

Yet the character is certainly struggling with dreadful news, and seeking to master the turbulent and disturbing feelings it arouses in her. Like Juliet, or like Macduff's struggles with the word 'all', or Hamlet with the ghost's injunction 'Remember me', her emotions fasten themselves on words that have just been delivered. As in these Shakespearean instances, the phrase 'the two dearest' in which lies the most cruel pain, is reiterated in her consciousness, its power to sting being registered in this repetition, until the hurt is worn down. When in the final reprise Fanny tells herself that she could be 'nothing dearer than a friend' she is still forcing herself to bear the brunt of this phrase, using it against herself in an attempt to quash her desires utterly.

From Shakespeare, and possibly through the novelists of sensibility, Austen learned the expressive power of interruptions to normal syntax.[15] Outbursts of feeling that are not to be contained by the logistics of sentence structure punctuate Fanny's thoughts. 'But two months dead – nay not so much, not two,' says Hamlet. 'It would be – Oh, how different would it be', thinks Fanny. But it is not only these back-tracking moments that suggest a quasi-Shakespearean quality to this registration of consciousness. In *Sense and Sensibility* Willoughby says that 'Every line, every word' of Marianne's letters was ' – in the hackneyed metaphor which their dear writer, were she here, would forbid – a dagger to my heart' (p. 325). The metaphor is revived when what is registered is not the instrument, but its effect, and the effect is animated in the jolting repetition: 'it was a stab'. The phrasing suggests how Fanny experiences Edmund's unconscious unkindness as intentional, evil striking us, as Emmanuel Levinas puts it, 'as if there were an aim underlying the bad destiny that pursues me'.[16] Fanny, reverting to the primordial sense of what evil is, cannot but conceive it as physical. Moreover, this is only one of several subtle ways the passage conveys the sense that Fanny is experiencing this attack as a rupture within, not just her consciousness or her body, but her very being.

Most of the passage I have quoted consists of the character's internal speech, imagined to take place simultaneously with the reader reading. But moving from what Dorrit Cohn has called 'narrated monologue' to what he calls 'psycho-narration', the passage includes moments of brief authorial summary.[17] 'She was obliged to repeat again and again that she was one of his two dearest, before the words gave her any sensation.' This – which has no equivalent in the soliloquy – acknowledges what William James called 'other mind stuff', the non-verbal quality of certain inner experiences:[18] here something corresponding to that condition we call being stunned, or shocked, that cannot be contained by, or focused in, the character's own articulation. Later in the passage, language again fails: 'To call or fancy it a loss, a disappointment, would be a presumption; for which she had not words enough to satisfy her own humility.' 'Words', and the will that supports or is expressed in them, are in a different territory or sphere of the self from emotional pain; a gap between what can be said, what consciousness can impose, and what experience is, opens up and reflects that laceration in the fabric of ongoing existence that Fanny experiences. In this way the passage brings the reader close to the character – allows us to 'share' her secret, intimate experience as we never can in real life – and simultaneously suggests how much more there might be about Fanny's whole experience than registration of her formulated thought itself would convey. 'It ought not to have touched on the confines of her imagination.' This means, roughly, 'it ought not to have entered her head'. Yet 'touched' suggests how fragile is the defence Fanny has created, her apprehension that the slightest incursion of desire might spread ruin everywhere. 'The confines of her imagination' is an obscure phrase: the imagination as a bounded space, as a prison, a purgatory?[19] If so, it disturbingly suggests how Fanny in some secret recess of her being acknowledges that her self-fortification is self-destructive. As with many of Shakespeare's characters, the more knowledge we glean of her, the less exhaustive this knowledge seems.

Frank Kermode has demonstrated how the 'bookish rhetorical display'[20] Shakespeare learned from his predecessors became infused with dramatic energy during the plays of the late 1590s, so that gracious commentary becomes, as in *Coriolanus*, 'the representation of excited, anxious thought; the weighing of confused possibilities and dubious motives'.[21] Something analogous occurs as Jane Austen takes up the rhetorical parallels and formal structures of Johnson's and Burney's prose here and gives them expressive life. 'To try to overcome all that was excessive . . . To call or fancy it a loss, a disappointment . . . To think of him as Miss Crawford might be justified in thinking . . .' The sentences have a similar structure, and they might seem at first to denote a rather abstract or detached representation of Fanny's feelings. But this is not a strategy of the writer but rather of the mind in a stressful situation that the author has understood and is representing. In this paragraph Fanny thinks in the rhythmical equivalent of clenched determination through the reiterated abstract and apparently impersonal style of the phrasing (for looking at oneself from the outside may be a way of gaining stability, a control over one's emotion). Yet as she tries to hold onto the 'rational' perspective that the syntactical structure represents, it collapses back on itself. 'To her, he could be nothing under any circumstances – nothing dearer than a friend.' The notion that Edmund might love her – she might marry him – is never articulated, but powerfully implicit as the negative of the propositions that so roundly condemn it. 'Why did such an idea occur to her even enough to be reprobated and forbidden?' The idea has not 'occurred' in what has been given to the reader: it has been present only in the interstices of the articulated or formulated thoughts. When Fanny, conscientiously trying to be fair, uses the phrase 'this deception', it sounds as if Mary is the deceiver, not Edmund the deceived: and thus her antagonism towards her rival leaps out. Like the gaps or jumps in the train of ideas of Shakespeare's characters, such moments make us aware, in Seltzer's words, of 'the felt existence of an inner life from which action and motivation both spring'.

I am giving Austen's language here so much intense attention partly because one effect of the filmic representations of her novels is to suspend our understanding that Jane Austen is a great novelist, not just a great creator of characters, or 'dramatist', as the nineteenth-century critics were inclined to put it. It is tempting for commentators who link novels and the films based on them to focus on incident and rendering of character, because these are the common denominators of the two forms. One can readily point to omissions and elisions and differences of stress, or make substantive comparisons across the artefacts, as I have partly done in reading *Metropolitan* in Chapter 2. But such a criticism remembers novels only as dramatic structures, and thus surrenders in its first gesture the very ground that is at issue here. For the two forms, novel and cinema, are not commensurate, certainly no less incommensurate than Austen's novels and Shakespearean tragedy. Their systems of representation are quite different. If film were to reproduce that interiority, which, as I have argued, both Austen and Shakespeare succeed in communicating to their different audiences, it must adopt its own distinct means. The study of recreation is then in part the study of how that disjunction between means may be resolved or sublated.

The presentation of the inner life is more pivotal even in *Persuasion* than in either *Mansfield Park* or *Emma*. 'It is *Persuasion* that offers the fullest and most important use of free indirect speech in Jane Austen's work', Norman Page stresses. 'We are given an insight into Anne's consciousness that is the fictional equivalent of the dramatic soliloquy.'[22] Opening with its focus upon Sir Walter Elliot and his elder daughter Elizabeth, *Persuasion* depends upon Anne Elliot becoming only gradually disclosed as the novel's emotional centre. The structure of the novel's first chapters metonymically reproduces Anne's position within the family. Whilst other characters speak, often at length, Anne's interventions and comments are merely reported, recessed into the text. The narrator's exclamation at the end of Chapter 4, 'How eloquent could Anne Elliot have been!' thus has something of the effect of Hamlet's 'I have that within which passeth show', presaging an interiority that cannot be expressed within the social world and is to be disclosed only in the subsequent rendering of private experience. 'From the moment Anne's sad and isolated consciousness takes centre stage in the novel', as Linda Bree puts it, 'the narrative proceeds through the filter of her subjective mind', so that, 'in fact, the only close relationship Anne Elliot has is with the reader'.[23]

When Austen describes Anne Elliot's first re-encounter with Wentworth some of the effects of Fanny's shock at Edmund's announcement are recapitulated:

In two minutes after Charles's preparation, the others appeared; they were in the drawing-room. Her eye half met Captain Wentworth's; a bow, a curtsey passed; she heard his voice – he talked to Mary, said all that was right; said something to the Miss Musgroves, enough to mark an easy footing: the room seemed full – full of persons and voices – but a few minutes ended it. Charles shewed himself at the window, all was ready, their visitor had bowed and was gone; the Miss Musgroves were gone too, suddenly resolving to walk to the end of the village with the sportsmen: the room was cleared, and Anne might finish her breakfast as she could. (*Persuasion*, pp. 59–60)

This passage is celebrated because of the deftness of the means by which Anne's inner agitation is represented, 'the little flutter given to the sentence'[24] by the simple repetitions of 'said' and of 'full' which catch her inability to focus, to concentrate, the momentary suspension of rational perception; the disordered, bumpy rhythms mimicking quick breathing and pounding heart. In the scene that follows Anne is not literally alone, but her thoughts are given as a loose version of the soliloquy. ' "It is over! it is over!" she repeated to herself again, and again, in nervous gratitude. "The worst is over!" ' – the burst of feeling is captured in a series of inner exclamations, punctuated and intercut by repeated attempts to moderate them from other resources of the self, to 'reason with herself'. When Mary carelessly forwards the information that Wentworth has said: 'You were so altered he should not have known you again', there is a similar reworking of the emotional pattern in *Mansfield Park*, and in Shakespeare: the hurtful word 'altered' is reiterated in Anne's inner speech just as Macduff's 'All?' and Fanny's 'two dearest' had been, and with a final stoic (perhaps self punishing) resolution to face up to its truth.

Persuasion, then, is a novel in which the heroine's inner life is shared only with the reader. What happens when such a novel, which is carefully built around its heroine's silent attentiveness, in which public dialogue is understood and coloured by notation of the heroine's reactions, is 'adapted', converted into a form whose resources or conventions do not allow these to be represented directly at all? The soliloquy and free indirect speech are both technical devices through which the inner life (that is, the secret thoughts and conflicting psychological impulses) of subjects can be displayed. But the film form largely eschews soliloquy and relies upon very different means by which inner life can be attributed to characters. To attempt a film version of *Persuasion* is almost to nullify and erase the very thing that makes the novel a singular fictional enterprise. Imagine a *Hamlet* without the soliloquies. This it seems is the impossible attempt that is involved in making a film of *Persuasion* without the device of free indirect speech.

One of the most challenging commentaries on this aspect of film remains Virginia Woolf's essay 'The Cinema', written over seventy years ago. Woolf commented explicitly on the film's difficulty in presenting the thoughts and consciousness of characters. She makes fun of a version of Tolstoy's *Anna Karenina* – presumably a silent version which she had seen.[25] 'The eye says "Here is Anna Karenina". A voluptuous lady in black velvet wearing pearls comes before us. But the brain says, "That is no more Anna Karenina than it is Queen Victoria." For the brain knows Anna almost entirely by the inside of her mind – her charm, her passion, her despair. All the emphasis is laid by the cinema upon her teeth, her pearls and her velvet.' Woolf concludes that the cinema has a parasitic, rapacious relation to the most famous novels of the world, spelling them out 'in words of one syllable, written, too, in the scrawl of an illiterate schoolboy.'[26] The point bears reiteration, in Judith Mayne's words: 'Many film adaptations have been little more than illustrated comic-book versions of the classics.'[27] Yet criticism like Woolf's, as Mayne points out, presents the novel as the master system which the later work cannot ever approach. That the semiotic system of the cinema is necessarily simpler, cruder, and works with a much less complex vocabulary than the language of the novel, however, is a premise which certainly might be challenged.

The 1971 television version of *Persuasion* deals with the problem of Anne's interior life very directly. Instead of Anne's centrality to the text being gradually admitted, as in the novel, she is a forthright speaker from its very first scene. Whatever she may be socially, Anne is thus seen as a figure with the same level of representational status as the other members of her family. Little is done to suggest a distinctive depth to Anne's consciousness, though the facts about her past are efficiently presented in dialogues with Lady Russell. The novel's gradually evolving sense of an intelligent inner life which is in complete contrast to Anne's assignment to the role of old maid by her family and the Musgroves, is quite lacking. On the other hand, this serial's representation of Anne as a graceful, socially capable person, who finds much amusement in the foibles of her acquaintances, can certainly be found in the novel, where Anne's private 'smiling' to herself at their idiosyncrasies is perhaps a little too often repeated. But the scriptwriter has not found the means by which the interplay between her thoughts, memories and desires and the encompassing social world can be reproduced.

Instead the film falls back upon stage convention. The scene of Anne and Wentworth's first meeting is at first shot from the standpoint of a camera which takes in the whole room, Wentworth bowing slightly across the distance, and Anne giving an answering curtsy. Then the focus is on Anne's face, whilst dialogue between Mary and Wentworth continues. After the party has left, though, the camera follows Anne as she moves towards a sofa, reaches out to it, and holds her in a head-and-shoulders shot as she sits down and addresses the viewer as an audience. 'It is over! it is over!' she declares, speaking the words out aloud. 'The worst is over! I have seen him again after eight years. It is almost a third of my own life. It seems little more than nothing.' The abridgment of the text elides that struggle between different impulses which creates the effect of an inner self in the novel. Similarly, on the autumnal walk to Winthrop, where in the novel Anne walks alone, disconsolately recalling fragments of poetry to herself (vol. 1, Chapter 10) in the film, Anne's melancholy is signalled by her declamation aloud of a passage from Thomson's *Autumn*, (to the delight and approval of Henrietta Musgrove!). The same clumsiness is apparent when after Anne's reading aloud of Wentworth's proposal letter, she declaims, 'Frederick! Frederick! Frederick!' In other words, this early adaptation translates novelistic effects, not into cinematic ones, but into something akin to melodrama.

By contrast the 1995 version of the novel scripted by Nick Dear and directed by Roger Michell often succeeds in finding substitutive means by which Anne's inner life can be represented which do not parallel the novel, but have, it might be argued, equivalent structural status and dynamic force.[28] This is done not by elucidating the intricacies of Anne's feelings, but by registering her grief in a variety of ways – a grief, or mourning, that the film in its opening scenes elides into melancholia. Anne in the Kellynch scenes has little of the self-possession and maturity which characterise the figure in the novel. Indeed, she is in danger, in such a sequence as her journey to Uppercross in the farmer's cart, of appearing as a victim – another chattel, jolted along with the duck and the trunk, her face bleakly registering the utter desolation of her accumulated losses as the last glimpses of Kellynch are seen from her point of view, vanishing behind the trees.

This Anne is a traumatised figure, barely able to speak above a whisper, shaking at the mention of Wentworth's name. This certainly seems to register something crucial in the text, for it can be plausibly suggested that Anne Elliot is a figure of uncompleted mourning. In an article which appeared the same year the film was released, the theme of 'Mourning and Melancholia in *Persuasion*' was in fact compellingly explored. Elizabeth Dalton argued that 'the most striking feature of Anne's response' to Wentworth's return on the scene 'is her resistance to it' and that her condition exemplifies what Freud described as the 'introjection' of the lost object into the ego, 'where a sort of phantasmal relationship is maintained through suffering'.[29] In some ways Anne's 'obstinacy in thus clinging to the past', as another critic puts it, is close to 'a destructive form of sublimation'[30] in which she sustains her love for Wentworth not by marrying him but by suffering for him. 'This willingness to suffer may be not only the effect, but the cause of her loss of Wentworth', Dalton proposes, suggesting that it originates in a formative earlier experience. The scene in which Anne accompanies the others' dancing on the piano offers support for this suggestion:

> She played a great deal better than either of the Miss Musgroves; but having no voice, no knowledge of the harp, and no fond parents to sit by and fancy themselves delighted, her performance was little thought of, only out of civility, or to refresh the others, as she was well aware. She knew that when she played she was giving pleasure only to herself; but this was no new sensation: excepting one short period of her life, she had never, since the age of fourteen, never since the loss of her dear mother, known the happiness of being listened to, or encouraged by any just appreciation or real taste. (*Persuasion*, p. 47)

Anne's attempt to feel positively about the Musgroves is blended into and overlain by her depression and loneliness; the word 'fond' (meaning foolish or kind?) typical of the writing's plaiting together of different strands of response. The chords are lightly touched, but the association of Wentworth and the mother in this passage suggests how the second loss, so painful it can scarcely be more than glanced at here, recapitulates the earlier and more profound loss of the parent, which reverberates ('never . . . never') in the novel even more poignantly. Dalton notes that a death at the age of fourteen might lead to feelings of guilt, 'as if somehow the child's feelings had brought about this dreadful result. Perhaps Anne's habitual self-denial, [so manifest in this extract] including her original renunciation of Wentworth, is a sort of atonement: with her mother dead, has the daughter any right to freedom or pleasure?'

Speculations of this kind will strike some readers as unwarranted, an unnecessary excursion into fanciful psychologising. Yet such intimations of the character's emotional prehistory are precisely what Austen can convey in the subtle rhythms, the minute delays and muted inflections of this writing. This is *Persuasion*'s particular version of interiority. Here Austen has developed a prose that invites the reader, both consciously and unconsciously, to intuit the psychology of this character, to amplify their understanding in whatever terminology they have available, or through their own aquaintance with grief. The suggestions here connect too with the unresolved ambivalence of Anne's relation to her 'mother-substitute', Lady Russell.

Only by clumsy means might a film recapitulate or allude to Anne's psychological past. But through its focus on Anne as a still grieving being the film can give its narrative a centre. It uses strategies to convey the inner life of melancholy that are quite different from the technique of the novel, and thus manages that translation into a different form of expression that paradoxically, as Jessica Benjamin declares, denotes the congruence of inner experience.[31] These means are those anticipated by Virginia Woolf in her discussion of film. After mocking the current cinema's crude equivalents for novelistic emotion ('A kiss is love. A broken cup is jealousy. A grin is happiness') she goes on to ask what would happen if the film 'ceased to be a parasite, how would it walk erect?' A different vocabulary of visual effects might convey thought more potently than words. 'If a shadow at a certain moment can suggest so much more than the actual gestures and words of men and women in a state of fear, it seems plain that the cinema has within its grasp innumerable symbols for emotions that have so far failed to find expression,' she declares:

If so much of our thinking and feeling is connected with seeing, some residue of visual emotion which is of no use to either painter or to poet may still await the cinema. That such symbols will be quite unlike the real objects which we see before us seems highly probable. Something abstract, something which moves with controlled and conscious art, something which calls for the very slightest help from words or music to make itself intelligible, yet justly uses them subserviently – of such movements and abstractions the films may in time to come be composed.[32]

The silent gliding of the camera within a shot, and the way different shots are edited or orchestrated into a sequence has a similar power to play upon the viewer's unconscious or uncodifed responses that cadence has in poetry. In this film of *Persuasion* Anne's grief is conveyed in a variety of ways that have no ostensible connection with her 'character'.

Perhaps the most interesting is the sequence following her father and sister's departure from Kellynch. Anne is presented in a series of scenes in which the furniture in the public rooms of the house is being shrouded in white drapes. A strict (or literal-minded) reader of the novel might fidget about this: aren't the Crofts about to take possession, and aren't they to have the freedom of the house they have rented? Disregarding such quibbles, the film concentrates on ways of representing the end of an era. A stony-faced footman throws a cloth over a statue. Whilst the servants drape sheets over the chairs and tables, Anne, in a white dress, is seen anxiously crossing the library with a list in her hand. In the next scene she and a servant are dusting and packing away books. In the semi-darkness, lit by candles, Anne comes across a copy of the navy list, with a paper boat folded inside it. She glances across to see if the servant has noticed, and then looks away. No words are spoken. The candle throws a golden light on the pages. The scene eloquently, but without eloquence, represents the idea that Anne has an intense inner past history (the boat, itself folded out of a letter, is found tucked within the pages of the book), and simultaneously that she has no one with whom to speak. A close-up shows Anne's face looking out of the shot, whilst the voice of Lady Russell forms a bridge or lead-in to the next sequence, ironically manifesting this absence: 'For eight years, you have been too little from home, too little seen . . .' Now the camera takes in a large room, perhaps the main parlour, its furniture almost all shrouded in white. Panning to the left the camera finds Anne and Lady Russell talking within this desolate setting, whilst Lady Russell's speech con-tinues '. . . and your spirits have never been high since your – disap-pointment'.

'Something abstract, something that moves with controlled and con-scious art' is certainly present in these scenes. Through the motif of whiteness, the viewer is led to associate Anne with the draped furniture. The thought-association cannot be conscious, but putting furniture under dust-wraps suggests not only desolation, the house deserted, but life suspended, just as Anne's hopes have been put under wraps for the past years. On one level it signals mourning, finality, the loss of the home she has been used to, the closing of an epoch. On another, it suggests this suspension or repression: a period of time spent in waiting, and thus intimates something melancholy but not utterly without hope. Above all it signals the film and the novel's preoccupation with time.

Appropriately then, it is amid the draped furniture that Anne attempts to tell Lady Russell of her regrets about the past decision to break off the engagement. This is a scene which has no equivalent in the novel, where '[T]hey knew not each other's opinion, either its constancy or its change . . . for the subject was never alluded to' (p. 29), but Dear's script derives from the passage of free indirect discourse in Chapter 4. Having led up to this conversation by the sequence of scenes in which Anne has been the silent participant, her breaking silence has something of the force of 'How eloquent could Anne Elliot have been!' 'Lady Russell, – I have never said this – ' she begins. Lady Russell, though sympathetic, will not listen, but Anne, speaking with painful earnestness, presses on. Reaching for a book, Lady Russell turns the conversation to 'these Romantics'. In a replication of the novel's characteristic strategy, Anne scarcely replies now, yielding to Lady Russell's wish not to go into the past, not to talk of it. The camera focuses on her as she looks sadly, thoughtfully, perhaps resignedly, sideways, away from the camera. Everything that is not spoken therefore is invested by the viewer in her face.

Film is a means by which the emotions of the spectator are elicited by a great variety of sensory modes. Anne's face in fact is a key signifier for this film. The actor's features are not mobile, animated or obviously expressive (contrasting with Lady Russell and Mrs Croft). Instead her pale countenance, though focused on, is represented as blank, her whiteness literally a *tabula rasa*, her thoughts left to be intuited by the viewer in an act of identification. These thoughts or emotions are in effect located elsewhere in the film, generated by its lighting, by the movement of the camera, by the music, by that mise en scène which invests Kellynch with darkness and shadows and flickering but bright candlelight. The face, often lit from the side, looking away out of the shot, becomes a site saturated with feelings distributed throughout the filmic text. Out of this sensory information the viewer here generates what he or she might call a knowledge of Anne's 'character'. This is very different from that knowledge of her thoughts or consciousness that the trained reader reads off the page, but structurally it occupies the same place. Anne's drawn, blanched face, mysteriously or enigmatically blank, is a site or screen onto which the viewer is invited to inscribe a history which is never articulated. Thus the film conveys by quite different means, that impression of direct contact with another being's inner life which one finds in both Austen and Shakespeare.

Other decisions about the representation of interiority have been made in Patricia Rozema's film of *Mansfield Park* (1999).[33] In this respect, as in others, this film conspicuously repudiates Austen's great achievement, in the very gesture of its own assimilation. Private selfhood is acknowledged in this film, through Fanny's soliloquies, but at the same moment interior depth is abolished. As we have seen, direct transcription of Fanny's thoughts in the novel is blended into commentary. Where Fanny is concerned, the text is characterised and defined by the interlacing of distinct consciousnesses and tones; hers, youthful, sensitive – over-sensitive – and an older, sometimes caustic, and usually wryly experienced voice which one attributes to the narrator. This drier style infiltrates the presentation of the several other consciousnesses that the novel investigates, so that, as Flaubert was to put it, the author is 'everywhere felt, but never seen'.[34] It infuses Sir Thomas's mind, for instance, when he 'kindly' leaves Fanny to cry in peace 'conceiving perhaps that the deserted chair of each young man might exercise her tender enthusiasm, and that the remaining cold pork bones in William's plate might but divide her feelings with the broken egg-shells in Mr Crawford's' (p. 282) – one of the myriad touches which suggest how far the narrator's characteristic view of events differs from her nervous young heroine's.

Claudia Johnson, reviewing the film, claimed that 'it gives us what many of us love about Austen in the first place, what other movies never deliver: Austen's presence as a narrator'.[35] Fanny Price here by no means corresponds to the narrator (or narrator-function) in the novel. Fanny as character and Austen as commentator on the action are conflated. Speaking directly to the camera, and implicitly to her sister Susan in Portsmouth, a cheerful, upbeat Fanny Price provides continuity, quotes passages from her writing, and occasionally expresses her own feelings aloud. Austen's narrator permeates the reader's experience; when this Fanny Price acts as commentator she is spatially and conceptually segregated from the action, a reliable authority and reference point. Her remarks on Maria's marriage, for example, borrowed from Austen's most caustic narration, are visually confirmed by the sequence that precedes them. Yet *Clueless*, as I have noted, demonstrates how voice-over can flow into and out of the action, simultaneously representing the heroine's own consciousness and touching her with irony.

There are many other reasons for regarding *Mansfield Park* as a great novel besides its rendering of Fanny's inner life. But it is clear that her subjectivity, her conscience, is the primary focus of the narrative. In *Mansfield Park*, as Jan Fergus puts it, Austen creates a heroine 'whose complicated "distress" is legitimate and genuine, not spurious as it is in the sentimental novel'. Fanny's 'extreme capacity for feeling' is thus central to the sympathetic reader's experience.[36] In the film Fanny's inner life is articulated through a series of fragments drawn from letters and from Austen's youthful skits, from 'Jack and Alice', 'Love and Freindship' and the 'History of England'. These writings, completed when Austen was fourteen or so, are by and large parodies of the sentimental novel and the cult of sensibility.[37] They are notable for their 'grossly ironic treatment of heterosexual romance',[38] conceived in a spirit of youthful mockery of 'feeling'. Yet phrases from these texts, often spoken aloud, in the manner of the soliloquy, are made to carry the burden of Fanny Price's inner life. By representing Fanny in fragments taken only from burlesque, the film refuses to engage with the possibility that Austen in *Mansfield Park* has matured beyond the phase of youthful defensiveness, and is now concerned with intimate, powerful, conflicted and painful feelings on almost every page. Thus whilst the film celebrates its heroine's private affective life, alone in her room, writing, apart from the family, it nullifies and repudiates the depth of that affective life in the same gesture that invents Fanny as a writer. We never stare closely into Fanny's eyes.[39]

Shakespeare, wrote Milton, in lines that were echoed throughout the eighteenth century, 'warbled his native wood-notes wild'.[40] Jane Austen, Henry James declared in the nineteenth, was 'instinctive and charming' like 'the thrush who tells his story from the garden bough', but not systematic nor a proper model for subsequent novelists.[41] Both these practitioners of art might be paying a back-handed compliment to the fluidity and opportunism (so to speak) with which both Shakespeare and Austen took their chances with the rendering of consciousness – catching it on the wing – trying out different techniques, sometimes representing inner thoughts as formal dramatic speech, sometimes, even in the midst of their greatest work, falling back into older modes, sometimes achieving a wonderful impression of inwardness and psychological life. As the remarks of Milton and James imply, what we percieve as 'natural' in the realm of human psychology is their creation.

George Henry Lewes, comparing Austen and Scott with Shakespeare in 1847, and noting that Scott's borrowings were far more obvious than Austen's, yet wrote that he 'had not that singular faculty of penetrating into the most secret recesses of the heart, and of showing us a character in its inward and outward workings'[42] that Shakespeare and, by implication, Jane Austen possessed. This is more true of the later novels than of the earlier, as my presentation has implied, and in turning to *Pride and Prejudice* in the next chapter I will be looking at both its 'outward' and its 'inward' workings. At the end of this novel, Darcy's sister is taken aback by the 'liberties' Elizabeth takes with her husband (*Pride and Prejudice*, p. 388). The relationship Elizabeth finally achieves with Darcy might well be said to parallel the relation between Jane Austen and Shakespeare.[43]

CHAPTER 5

Pride and Prejudice, *love and recognition*

Morality in the novel is the trembling instability of the balance.
D. H. Lawrence, 'Morality and the Novel'[1]

The 'great subjects' of *Pride and Prejudice*, as Lilian Robinson put it, are 'class, love, money and marriage'.[2] The producer of the successful BBC television version of the novel first shown in 1995 declares too that 'though it's about many things, it's principally about sex, and it's about money: those are the driving motives of the plot'.[3] This film, which I shall refer to later in this chapter, very convincingly represents the sexual attraction that impels Fitzwilliam Darcy towards Elizabeth Bennet, and also contrives to suggest that Elizabeth is unconsciously attracted towards him.[4] The critical tradition has generally insisted however that there is another thread to the plot that is equally, if not more, crucial, a thread one might briefly call epistemology.[5] The novel is 'most importantly', wrote Tony Tanner, for example, 'about prejudging and rejudging. It is a drama of recognition – re-cognition, that act by which the mind can look again at a thing and if necessary make revisions and amendments until it sees the thing as it really is.'[6] Such readings, in which Elizabeth, in Marilyn Butler's words, arrives at 'true criticism of the self via correct, humbling assessment of another'[7] are plentiful, but come uncomfortably close to the 'girl being taught a lesson' syndrome pilloried by Sedgwick, and risk suggesting that Elizabeth accepts Darcy the second time round solely because he is so kind to his servants and so decent to the Gardiners (or, on the other hand, because of the magnificent grounds of Pemberley!). Nevertheless the novel does rather insistently call the reader's attention to the difficulty and importance of 'knowing' another person's character. In this chapter, I offer a reading of *Pride and Prejudice* that fuses the novel's undoubted interest in epistemology with its equally obvious appeal as a story about love. I've tried to recreate this familiar text in new terms. Reading the novel requires, I will argue, that we give both 'recognition' and 'love' enhanced, richer meanings.

As in the common English idiom 'I see!' meaning 'I understand!' knowing and the visual are interwoven in *Pride and Prejudice*. To understand someone by observing them closely plays an important part in the novel's plot, since it is by misreading Jane Bennet's countenance and demeanour that Darcy makes his worst error. Complementing the early action in which Darcy looks at Elizabeth and Elizabeth tries to gauge the meaning of his gaze is a series of exchanges in which the link is explicitly made between observing someone and possessing a knowledge of them. Often this is further figured as 'taking' a picture. A character is a portrait in which, for instance, 'implacable resentment *is* a shade' (p. 58). 'I have always seen a great similarity in the turn of our minds', says Elizabeth, teasingly, at the Netherfield ball: to which Darcy responds that her comments offer no 'striking resemblance' of her own character. 'How near it may be to *mine*, I cannot pretend to say – *You* think it a faithful portrait undoubtedly', he then remarks (p. 91). 'I could wish, Miss Bennet, that you were not to sketch my character at the present moment', he soon decides: 'But if I do not take your likeness now, I may never have another opportunity' she replies (p. 94). Attempting to 'illustrate' Darcy's character, she finds she does not get on at all.

Another twist is given to this thread of the novel when it becomes clear that 'taking a likeness' is very often indistinguishable from giving or making one. 'First impressions', the novel's original title, suggests this Janus-like quality: not only what you 'impress' upon me as your character or reality (you being the agent), but also what I impress upon you through my own prejudices and expectations. All too often what happens when people respond to others in this novel is more nearly akin to what psychologists as early as David Hume would call 'projection', not taking, but putting into, the attribution to others of what we feel or desire ourselves. This is specifically noted when the newly married Lydia and Wickham are due to come on to Longbourn. 'Their arrival was dreaded by the elder Miss Bennets; and Jane more especially, who gave Lydia the feelings which would have attended herself, had *she* been the culprit, was wretched in the thought of what her sister must endure' (p. 315). Elizabeth earlier has imagined how 'miserable' Lydia will be 'when she first sees my aunt' (p. 305): both projections amusingly at odds with Lydia's own aplomb when she eventually arrives on the scene. More critically, when Charlotte declares that '[h]appiness in marriage is entirely a matter of chance', Elizabeth assumes that this is being put forward in the same spirit in which she herself delights in sometimes professing opinions she does not hold (p. 23). And when Elizabeth says that Darcy 'has a very satirical eye' (p. 24) her interpretation of the meaning of his gaze owes more, it becomes clear, to her own temperament and expectations than it does to his.

A more insidious form of projection consists not just in attributing one's own feelings to another, but giving them one's own desires. This comes closer to the heart of the novel's investigation of what it means to really know someone. 'It is a truth universally acknowledged, that a single man in possession of a good fortune, must be in want of a wife.' This is the narrator assuming a voice in order to expose how widespread is the attribution to others of what we ourselves wish. The Mrs Bennets of this world bestow their own desires on the young men who are their object. 'Is that his design in settling here?' (p. 4): Mr Bennet's reply crisply exposes the absurdity of what Rachel Brownstein calls this 'gossip's fantasy', but it is inveterate.[8] Conflating another's interests with one's own desires is so endemic that Austen seems to feel it requires no complicated irony: Charlotte Lucas, for example, in her 'kind schemes for Elizabeth' at Hunsford lets her own ambitions for her husband's preferment displace her initial focus on her friend (p. 181). When, in an unusual moment, Lady Catherine actually perceives that Darcy is low-spirited (after the rejection of his proposal by Elizabeth) she has no difficulty in attributing it to his unwillingness to leave Rosings, thus substituting her own desires for the marriage with Miss Anne, for his (p. 210).[9]

Several figures exist at the extreme end of a spectrum in the novel, as if their presence were there merely to mark the point of inveterate projection. For Mr Collins, if one attractive and marriageable young woman is not available, then another will fit the bill just as well ('it was soon done – done while Mrs Bennet was stirring the fire' (p. 71)). The young women he courts have no real existence for him: what matters is how they suit his schemes. (Just as for Lydia, one redcoat is very much like another: 'her affections [were] continually fluctuating, but never without an object' (p. 280)). Without reflection, Collins attributes to poor young women what Mrs Bennet attributes to rich young men: desire for what he wants. He has no inkling that others have lives and motives independent of himself (his attachment to her must be 'imaginary', as Elizabeth succinctly remarks), and his proposal turns on what Elizabeth will contribute to his happiness, not he to hers. And because neither she, nor anyone else, exists for him, he is incapable of change. Taking up the novel's own pictorial metaphor, it seems natural to say that he is both aesthetically and morally a 'caricature'.[10]

At the other end of the continuum is such a self-scrutinising figure as Darcy, and this aspect of his nature is examined through his friendship with Bingley. The relation of Elizabeth and Mrs Gardiner, as Claudia Johnson points out, is a model of 'rational friendship, where domination plays no part'.[11] On the other hand, Bingley's persuasibility and Darcy's intellectual superiority disturb the balance of their relationship, and make it possible for Darcy to treat Bingley as a surrogate, proxy or experimental self. It is suggested that his plans for his sister and Bingley influence his endeavour to separate his friend from Miss Bennet 'without meaning' that they should (p. 270). But one might go further: not all of Darcy's cautions about judging objectively can guard him from using Bingley as part of his own internal system of defence – making Bingley's separation from Jane Bennet do duty for his own wish to break free from Elizabeth. 'Towards *him* I have been kinder than towards myself' (p. 191): the maladroitness of this remark in the proposal scene betrays the confusion into which he has been led. Hence, as he recognises, he finds himself seduced by 'unworthy' motives, since he obeys his unconscious wishes rather than his own principles in keeping the knowledge of Jane's being in London from Bingley.

Pride and Prejudice, then, is certainly about knowing, knowing oneself and other people, as well as about money and sex. 'Till this moment, I never knew myself.' (p. 208): in the BBC film, the painful process through which Elizabeth Bennet comes to understand that she has been mistaken about Darcy is given very short shrift – thrown away in a bedroom scene in which Jane and Elizabeth pour into each other's bosom the balm of sisterly consolation – but it fills a critical chapter in the novel, as everyone acknowledges. At the same time, this is only half the story. Accounts that represent Elizabeth merely as a thinking being, rather than as a selfhood, a locus of subjective experience, both conscious and unconscious, tend to leave out a whole dimension of the readerly experience of the novel – the perennial fascination of what is actually going on in those dialogues between Darcy and Elizabeth. Moreover, 'knowing' in the novel, I suggest, is very intimately bound up with its understanding of what it is to love someone. The novel is certainly about love, even if it is no more exclusively about the romantic love that consumes the other in its own yearnings than it is about 'sex' as an appetite. But the fundamental weakness of such readings is that their conception of what it is to 'know' another person is psychologically naive.

Such an account of Darcy's motives as I have given above would be open to the familiar criticism that one is 'psychoanalysing' the characters as if they were 'real' people. An objection like this rests upon rather unreflective notions about the reality of actual people. When one says that other people are 'real' one is not referring to their physical presence near or around one. Their 'reality' refers to the degree to which they are present *to* us, and thus must refer to the degree they become real in our thoughts and imaginations. The kind of novel Jane Austen writes depends upon the reader identifying in turn and sometimes virtually simultaneously with several characters. But the 'caricatures' in *Pride and Prejudice* – Collins, Mrs Bennet, Lady Catherine, Lydia – have no meaningful interaction with the outside world of others' feelings, and thus are stuck in a set of repetitive behavioural styles. They correspond, I suggest, to the presence of some 'real' people in our mental landscape. Such people (politicians, celebrities, for example, but also acquaintances) occupy a space in the inner theatre like that of the caricature, for in the economy of our psychological lives we cannot spare the energy to lend them an inner being. Instead they serve as objects: objects onto which we may project, or into which we may invest, atavistic propensities of our own. We may think of them as wholly bad, or as buffoons, or admire them as heroes and heroines. We make do, in other words, with partial and stereotyped notions of others. The novel is populated with some figures who have only one gesture (Sir William Lucas) or a limited repertoire of personality traits (Bingley), who thus correspond to the far off and nearer figures in the inner world, and with others who come closer to that full, complex emotional life we usually ascribe to ourselves. It is one of its pleasures that Mr Bennet, whom we are in the habit of understanding in one mode, emerges, as when he speaks to Elizabeth about marriage, as a person in another.[12] But in ordinary life almost all of our internal representations of others are partial, prejudiced, incomplete. Few, very few, actual people, one ventures to assert, are present to us as 'real', their feelings and motives as fully and unequivocally known to us as those of the protagonist of a novel, as an Elizabeth Bennet.

The novel's representation of people, then, corresponds to modalities of the psychological life, in which others are present to us largely as what psychoanalysis calls 'internal objects'. Winnicott's last, and influential paper, 'The Use of an Object and Relating through Identifications' which I have discussed in Chapter 2, looks at the possibilities of escape from this mode.[13] 'The Use of an Object' describes how the analyst is present to the patient almost wholly as a partial being – as someone who can stand in for, or represent others. The analyst is 'related' to through 'identifications', those modes of being with others which throw, so to speak, the cloak of one's own desires and needs over the other person and respond to him or her in this psychological costume. Because the patient never makes contact with the analyst as a real other being, he or she operates in an 'omnipotent', self-enclosed, domain. However, Winnicott suggested, there are moments in the treatment when the analyst must withstand negative or hate-filled attacks from the patient, and when this happens something crucial can take place. In the intimacy of the psychoanalytic contact, as in the closeness of the family – 'Tease him – laugh at him. – Intimate as you are, you must know how it is to be done' (p. 57) – a patient learns what are the analyst's weak spots. Such attacks can be difficult to field. (As Winnicott remarks in a characteristic footnote, 'when the analyst knows the patient carries a revolver then, it seems to me, this work cannot be done'![14]) But if the analyst survives this 'destruction', does not succumb to the patient's mood or retaliate, does not feel resentment or hatred, he or she becomes established as an independently existing being, both steadying and exhilarating because he or she truly exists.

The later analyst and social critic, Jessica Benjamin, develops these thoughts of Winnicott's, taking them beyond the consulting room to a general theory of human relations. Benjamin's work in *Like Subjects, Love Objects* (1995) and *Shadow of the Other* (1998) as with her earlier *The Bonds of Love* (1988),[15] has been focused, perhaps more explicitly than any earlier psychoanalytic thinker, on the phenomena of human relations we call love. Winnicott saw 'relating through identifications' and the 'use of an object' as successive developmental stages in the drama of human affections: for Benjamin they are more like positions, simultaneous and intermittent potentialites of the psyche, and this perception enables her to extend his thinking more explicitly into the realm of ethics.

The traditional focus of psychoanalysis on the processes occurring within the individual psyche can certainly throw some light on *Pride and Prejudice*. Its understanding of projection, in which 'the subject attributes tendencies, desires etc., to others that he refuses to recognise in himself' is an example.[16] This might suggest why Elizabeth makes no progress in her avowed design of understanding Darcy, of painting a portrait or taking a sketch of his nature. Her declared aim is always being undercut and subverted by her unconscious wishes. One might say that Elizabeth denies Darcy's subjectivity at the same time as she professes to invite it to speak. Elizabeth disowns parts of herself and bestows them instead on Darcy. For it is plain that Elizabeth, who is 'determined to dislike' Darcy (as she tells Charlotte, in half-jest), herself enacts just that 'implacable resentment' she attributes to him – building on that first insult and making everything else she hears from or about him, feed into this original orientation. In a series of encounters Elizabeth attributes to Darcy the very emotions that are driving her – pride and prejudice among them.[17] Her anger at his words about her family's behaviour enables her to forget or displace her own sense of shame, or rather it converts that shame into anger against him. Her hatred of her mother, for example, which Darcy's presence makes her experience most keenly, is naturally projected onto him. Thus this 'Mr Darcy' is for Elizabeth not someone who is perceived in his own right (so to speak) but someone who plays a role in her psychological life, as receptacle of her own projections and needs.

And to an extent less illuminated by the text, it seems the same is true of Darcy's relation to Elizabeth. In a different way, he attributes his own desires to her, so that up to the proposal, as he later confesses, he believes that she wishes for, and is even 'expecting his addresses' (p. 369). Just as it was taken for granted that a young man in possession of a fortune would seek a wife, Darcy assumes that a young lady in want of a fortune would accept a husband with one: but this is not all. As Elizabeth realises, listening to him in the proposal scene, she has no real presence to him: he is, in effect, though speaking in her company, conducting an inner dialogue with himself. His passion for her contains no element of perception of her as an independently existing being (hence, as in the formality of his proposal address, what Johnson calls its 'appalling resemblance'[18] to Mr Collins's).

It is such processes – the way that selves make use of other selves, fantasising about them, incorporating them into their own psychic life – that psychoanalysis classically studied and illuminated. It is as if the self radiates out, and the phenomena of the external world, other people, were only visible in its own light. But through psychoanalysis's intense focus on the individual in whom they are enacted, the discourse itself tended to reproduce precisely that solecism – the focus on the operations of the monadic individual psyche – in its own theoretical writings. It seemed to suggest that this is all that need be said about normal human relations, that others exist for a human subject wholly as receptacles and vehicles for their psychic needs, or as 'objects' for their impulses. Jessica Benjamin argues that this concentration on 'object relations' very largely does reflect the nature of human psychological life. But, she insists, there are moments when we get beyond this – when we see others as existing outside ourselves with their own 'equivalent centres of self' (a phrase from George Eliot she uses as an epigraph).[19] Drawing on Hegel's concept of the master–slave relation, she argues that, most of the time, our relationships with others are relations of 'domination', in which we make psychological (ab)use of them. Darcy is using Elizabeth in this way in his first proposal – he addresses her not as an individual being but, as Rachel Brownstein puts it, as just another girl with a vulgar mother.[20] He is in 'the bonds of love', so overwhelmed by 'the utmost force of passion' (p. 198) that he is in fact oblivious to the person he is addressing – a classic instance of love as domination.

This is the psychological state commonly called 'romantic' love. Romantic love is obsessed with the other person and idealises them, but does not perceive them as other to the self. On the contrary it merges self and other ('Nelly, I *am* Heathcliff!'[21]). It reproduces some aspects of the infant's earliest relation to the mother, in which the mother is only present to the infant, as a supplementary self, serving the immature ego's emotional needs. The patient in classical analysis makes use of the psychoanalyst in the same way, the analyst's neutral demeanour facilitating the patient's freedom to employ her for whatever psychological purposes he or she requires. But Benjamin argues, after Winnicott, that something beyond this must occur for the patient to truly develop. Benjamin calls this the moment of 'recognition'. This recognition that the other person is what she calls a 'like subject', just as much a fully human being as I am myself, this shift into the realm of the intersubjective, involves a momentous psychological, and epistemological, alteration. The 'love' of the 'outside other', as Benjamin puts it, 'is a continuation under more complex conditions of the infant's original fascination with and love of what is outside, her appreciation of difference and novelty'.[22]

'Recognition' is an obviously helpful term in the context of *Pride and Prejudice* because it chimes in with the novel's emphasis on the visual. To recognise someone in this larger, deeper sense, though, is not just to see him or her clearly, as an object might be seen, but simultaneously to love them and respect their own nature. Nor is it merely 'that act by which the mind can . . . make revisions and amendments until it sees the thing as it really is', as Tanner describes it.[23] An act of the whole being, not just of the mind, it names that capacity to respond to the other person not merely as a repository for one's own desires, hopes, fears, anxieties and dreams, but as a wholly different (and equivalently human) other person, a 'like subject'. But, as Benjamin repeatedly emphasises, this can never be a permanent or continuous capacity of the psyche: the moments in which one sees the other in their own light fall constantly under siege to the inveterate human propensity to shadow that other with one's own inner needs and hidden purposes. Recognition is momentarily plucked out of the continual common traffic of reciprocal domination.

Benjamin's concept suggests that Jane Austen thinks through the category of 'knowing' – knowing someone else – as an emotional, even erotic, as well as an epistemological ideal. Such a notion of recognition, then, takes in more than knowledge, philosophically understood:[24] and on the other hand it is rather different from our usual conception of 'understanding' another person. Benjamin makes reference to the French philosopher Emmanuel Levinas's concept of 'alterity', which clarifies the distinction. The two writers have in common a belief that acknowledgment of the other is at the heart of ethics. In Levinas's thinking an ethical relation to the other (the 'Altrui') is to their alterity, but this is not to be obtained through 'empathy' or the enveloping of others in our own sympathetic feeling, the route of 'understanding'.[25] Recognition of another in this sense is simply the dispersion of one's own self-understanding onto another. This mode is exemplified in the novel pre-eminently by Jane Bennet. But Jane's sympathy for others is not recognition of their difference from herself: on the contrary, it is guaranteed by her assimilation of everyone else to herself, qualified by her inability to acknowledge that others have radically different being from her own. If Elizabeth is to reach recognition of Darcy's otherness, and he of hers, it must be by a quite different path.

Jane Austen's comment that *Pride and Prejudice* is 'rather too light, and bright, and sparking' has received more attention than her remark that she has 'lopt & cropt' the manuscript.[26] Yet the two comments complement each other. *Pride and Prejudice* is a novel in which much is not told. What is not commented upon, amplified, or contextualised, is crucially important; interrruptions, breaks and what is witheld from our understanding often contribute decisively to the novel's intellectual and emotional excitement. Early in *Pride and Prejudice*, when Charlotte Lucas expresses her cynical opinion of marriage, Elizabeth replies: 'You make me laugh, Charlotte; but it is not sound. You know it is not sound, and

that you would never act this way yourself.' (p. 23). Their dialogue
ceases at this point. How Charlotte responds to this – whether she
replies, whether she smiles wryly, whether she raises her eyebrows – is
unknown, since the next paragraph turns immediately to another topic,
Mr Darcy's beginning to find Elizabeth 'an object of some interest'. The
effect is that the reader is left to take up Elizabeth's opinion as his or her
own, pockets as a piece of knowledge what has later to be painfully
repaid.

The pruning away of material – the absence of many indications of
facial expression, of guiding commentary from the narrator, even of
scene setting (so that, as is often remarked, Mr and Mrs Bennet's
opening dialogue might be written for the stage) – has critical consequences for the reading of Elizabeth and Darcy's dialogues leading up to
the proposal scene. In that scene, the changing expressions on Darcy's
face play an important role in the reader's understanding of the drama.
But in earlier exchanges almost the only facet of physical representation
recorded is that Darcy 'smiles' quite commonly before speaking. Except
for one instance at Hunsford (p. 179) what is not recorded is whether
Elizabeth notices these smiles, what effect they have on her, if and how
they disturb her fixed idea of him. This means that when it comes to the
interpretation of Mr Darcy, the reader is more or less on his or her own,
or guided by Elizabeth's responses.

'What most satisfies us in reading the dialogue in *Pride and Prejudice*',
wrote Reuben Brower, 'is Jane Austen's awareness that it is difficult to
know any complex person, that knowledge of a man like Darcy is an
interpretation and a construction, not a simple absolute'.[27] He was
commenting on such dialogues as that in which Elizabeth expresses
herself 'perfectly convinced that Mr Darcy has no defect. He owns it
himself without disguise', a challenge he takes up:

> 'No' – said Darcy, 'I have made no such pretension. I have faults enough, but
> they are not, I hope, of understanding. My temper I dare not vouch for. – It is I
> believe too little yielding – certainly too little for the convenience of the world. I
> cannot forget the follies and vices of others as soon as I ought, nor their offences
> against myself. My feelings are not puffed about with every attempt to move
> them. My temper would perhaps be called resentful. – My good opinion once
> lost is lost for ever.' (p. 58)

Disputing Marilyn Butler's description of Darcy's manner as 'though
stiff, careful, scrupulous, truthful',[28] an acute recent critic, Mary Waldron, calls these remarks 'pretentious and intended to inhibit discussion
which might put [Darcy] at a disadvantage'.[29] These readings are not

mutually exclusive, however. It is Elizabeth's hostile reply: '*That* is a failing indeed! . . . Implacable resentment *is* a shade in a character', that inhibits or shuts off the possibilities which are present in Darcy's speech. He is here both self-important, and struggling towards self-understanding; he is both defensive and striving for an unpractised openness. As with many human confessions it is the way this one is received that determines its intent and meaning. In this instance what Elizabeth hears in Darcy's speech fits in with her 'premeditated' or previous notions about him, and the reader, whose dominant allegiance is to her, tends to 'hear' Darcy's speech as she does. Darcy at this point in the novel is understood from within Elizabeth's consciousness.[30]

If Darcy's speech is claiming a confident and consistent self, it is at the same time made of repetitions and restressings that might suggest a much less integrated or sure person – an undertow Elizabeth is much too preoccupied to attend to. This is far from the only instance in which, one might argue, Darcy proffers more to Elizabeth than she is able to receive. It could be seen that he is continually offering possibilities of intimacy which she is too intent on her own performance of wit and vivacity, to pick up.[31] The reader will register more in Darcy's tone and address than Elizabeth does, but these bits of information, this aura about him, do not yet cohere into an imaginative whole, unlike its representation of her psychological life. If Elizabeth later 'remembers' Darcy 'boasting, one day, at Netherfield, of the implacability of his resentments' (p. 80), it is in what the neurologist Gerald Edelman calls the 'remembered present', by which he means the capacity of the mind, and specifically the memory, to reconfigure itself at the behest of immediate contingency.[32] Elizabeth's 'memory' of Darcy when she is with Wickham comes into being in order to meet her present psychological needs. Incapable of contacting Darcy's mind when he originally spoke the words, she recalls not them, but her own responses, what she made of them at the time. Austen's presentation of her 'memories' as arising to meet present circumstances is one way in which the figure of Elizabeth, distinguished from Darcy in this respect, is endowed with psychological continuity and apparent historical depth. When, at a critical point of the novel, Elizabeth 'remembers' outside her own past emotions, this common mode of psychological life is momentarily transcended.

Darcy, then, is capable of being read in quite different ways. One might call this a hologrammic narrative, a hologram being a picture which, observed from a different direction, reveals itself to contain a quite different representation. (Looked at as one moves up the escalator, a poster shows a face smiling: as one moves past, it is transformed into a snarl. What the picture shows depends, literally, on one's point of view.) In this novel, the absence of anything but minimal guidance from the narrator (and in particular the minimisation of authorial irony towards Elizabeth) induces the reader to 'see' Darcy as she does. The reader's response to this dialogue is left in suspense because it is broken off: ' "Do let us have a little music," cried Miss Bingley, tired of a conversation in which she had no share.'

The most intriguing exchange between Elizabeth and Darcy is at Rosings, over the piano. Once again the topic of conversation bears on what the novel itself is about: character and relations to others. Darcy declares that he is 'ill qualified to recommend' himself to strangers. Elizabeth draws Colonel Fitzwilliam into the dialogue and he declares that this is because Darcy 'will not give himself the trouble'.

> 'I certainly have not the talent which some people possess,' said Darcy, 'of conversing easily with those I have never seen before. I cannot catch their tone of conversation, or appear interested in their concerns, as I often see done.'
>
> 'My fingers,' said Elizabeth, do not move over this instrument in the masterly manner which I see so many women's do. They have not the same force or rapidity, and do not produce the same expression. But then I have always supposed it to be my own fault – because I would not take the trouble of practising. It is not that I do not believe *my* fingers as capable as any other woman's of superior execution.' (p. 175)

That she is intending to teach Darcy a lesson is obvious. But it is entirely ignored in his non-sequitur of a reply: 'Darcy smiled and said, "You are perfectly right. You have employed your time much better. No one admitted to the privilege of hearing you, can think any thing wanting. We neither of us perform to strangers." ' This extraordinary response remains unclarified because, once again, the dialogue is broken off: 'Here they were interrupted by Lady Catherine, who called out to know what they were talking of. Elizabeth immediately began playing again.' (p. 176). We can never know, for instance, whether she understands the compliment as ironically intended.

It is an extraordinary response because it ignores the challenge in Elizabeth's words (perhaps the first time Darcy has not risen to Elizabeth's bait), because of the lack of apparent connection between the sentences in his speech and because of the leap or assumption of affinity made in his last assertion, especially the oddly contradictory word 'perform'. Once again the speech resembles a hologram. Reading it one way, sympathetic to Darcy, one hears a man who is now able (or feels he is able) to speak to the real person beneath her taunting conversational style. He is taking his time and, despite Fitzwilliam's presence, paying her a great compliment. He says in effect 'You and I are alike: what you say before Fitzwilliam does not reflect your real self, which I understand.' When he says 'We neither of us perform to strangers', he is commenting on her having an inner life or self which is not reflected in her banter, claiming to be in touch with that private life. And (this reading would continue) he is right: Elizabeth does have an inner self which she conceals from many people in the novel.[33]

In the alternative reading, Darcy does not hear her comment as criticism because he is so much in love with her, and so full of himself. He hears in her words no irony, no satiric reference to himself, perhaps only an assertion of modesty. In ignoring both her and Fitzwilliam's criticisms he is once again demonstrating his standoffishness. When he says 'We neither of us perform to strangers', he is making a claim to affinity between them that is quite groundless, as must be perceived by all readers who know what Elizabeth in fact feels about him at this stage of the novel. He is simply articulating his desire, and his assumption emerges out of the present state of his psychological liaison with her, which is 'relating through identifications'. The hostile and the sympathetic readings exist simultaneously and depend – roughly speaking – on whether one reads from Elizabeth's or from Darcy's position. There is simply no way of knowing which of these ways of interpreting the exchange is the more exact: and because it is 'lopt', by interruption, the enigma persists. Augmenting it is the persistent puzzle of Darcy's smile.

This hologrammic switch from one to another point of view corresponds to differing dispositions of the self. Perhaps more exactly, the reader does not so much choose between these two interpretations as hold them in some kind of balance, one side intermittently weighing down the other. Attending to these scenes thus causes a reader to experience a simulacrum of the shift between domination and recognition that is our psychological experience of others. It is pertinent to note that Benjamin insists that recognition is not a stable position or capacity. 'Alienated forms of complementarity . . . in the best of circumstances alternate with recognition.'[34] The moment of recognition of the other is always giving way to repudiation or to some form of narcissistic identification or idealisation. When we read from Elizabeth's position we are ensconced in the psychological state in which the other is negated. But we do catch glimpses of the possibility of reading from outside her position in which Darcy appears differently. On the other side, the novel allows the reader quite plainly to see that Darcy himself, broadly speaking, 'sees' Elizabeth from inside his own needs and desires – that indeed is the central irony of the text at this point. The alternation between one and the other reading is the formal equivalent of what Benjamin calls the 'other's liability not to survive, the inevitable failure of recognition'.[35] It is as if the reader's response to these dialogues offers a mimesis of this central aspect of human relationships, in which the other is part of the self, the vehicle of the self's needs, its projections and identifications, whilst it offers the intimation of the other as quite different, outside the self.

The question is how we shift from relating through identifications to the appropriate 'use' (not abuse) of the other. If one is to argue that *Pride and Prejudice*, besides being a great love story, is a great story about love, one is inevitably drawn to the moment of the first proposal and its aftermath, for it is here that the possibility of this crucial change is intimated. If Winnicott's and Benjamin's theory is correct, it is essential that the love of Elizabeth and Darcy pass through the moment of 'destruction', dramatised in the proposal itself, in Darcy's subsequent letter and in Elizabeth's reaction to this. This occasion sees both participants treating the other as vehicles for their own inner needs – though one is governed by passion, the other by a more complex mixture of sexually stimulated identification with Wickham, loyalty to her family and thwarted narcissism. Darcy's proposal is not addressed to Elizabeth as an 'outside other'; her angry response is fuelled by her stored up feelings. Elizabeth's reply to Darcy is an attack – an attack on him that vents her own anger and resentments. It is meant to destroy his love for her. Its effect, as might be expected, is temporarily to fill him with the anger and bitterness she herself feels. Darcy's practised self-control (treated with some humour earlier in the novel), enables him, under the impact of her assault, to resist retaliating, to express his feelings merely in a few curt departing words. When Elizabeth speaks her rejection of his offer Darcy is confronted with her undeniable, unassimilable otherness – she is a being quite different from the object he has been carrying around in his inner fantasies and projects. But ultimately only through her rejection of him is Elizabeth instantiated as real to him; only through his letter is Darcy perceived as real by her.

It is useful here to compare the BBC film's presentation of this scene. Elizabeth is sitting down and the camera looks up at Darcy from below, as if from her point of view, as he stands delivering his speech. This keeps continuity with the focus on Elizabeth in the previous sequence in which Colonel Fitzwilliam reveals Darcy's role in breaking off Jane and Bingley's relation. One small but critically important difference from the chapter in the novel, though, is that there the beginning of Darcy's speech is presented directly or dramatically, but nothing else in the proposal is.[36] The reader of the novel does not read, or 'hear' what Darcy says to Elizabeth; instead what he says is summarised in reported speech. What is directly represented is Elizabeth's reaction to the speech – her rising anger as he goes on – not the words themselves. This technical feature conveys an important psychological truth: if Elizabeth is hardly present as a feeling creature to Darcy's mind at this moment, Darcy is hardly present to Elizabeth either. He is an inside, not an 'outside other'. The representation of his speech as heard by her shows that Darcy is an actor in her own psychic theatre.

Darcy's letter is a formal turning point in *Pride and Prejudice*, because for the first time he comes forward in an independent voice, unconstrained by the social occasion, cut free from those responses of Elizabeth that have coloured the reader's attention to him so far. His letter forces Elizabeth to recognise that he exists outside her assumptions about him. Whilst his inner life has been given a kind of notional presence earlier in the novel through brief (and perhaps rather coy) acknowledgments of his sexual feelings, now he becomes established as an entity with depth and complexity. The film's visual representation of him, dishevelled, shirt collar loosened, whilst he writes his letter overnight, is appropriate, for Darcy is entrusting Elizabeth with intimate facts he has kept from everyone else but his fellow guardian, even Bingley. Elizabeth is now invited to see him as a being whose psychological and moral life is constituted largely by his family, as she keenly feels her own to have been. Forced to attend continuously to the other's thought processes, Elizabeth is overwhelmed. The shift from one convention, third person narrative, to the other, the novel in letters, enacts the abrupt change that takes place in the reader's consciousness. In one account, Darcy's letter 'seizes the female reader and turns her into the object of its force and her own hatred'.[37] Some may indeed feel that their response has been highjacked, so decisive is the reversal of sympathy from Elizabeth to Darcy at this point. Relating through identifications now gives way, in mimicry, to something like incipient recognition.

Next day Darcy, after loitering in the park, hands Elizabeth the letter. The focus is on Elizabeth, as she reads his words, not being able to take them in: she reads the letter at first much as she has heard his proposal, in a mode of psychological refusal. Gradually, and painfully, she is forced to accept the plausibility, and then the likelihood, of what he says. The novelist, by presenting the letter without narrative framing in one chapter and then reviewing the letter through Elizabeth's consciousness in the next, takes the reader through that travail of reading and rereading, that cumulative assault on previous conviction that is Elizabeth's experience. Her chagrin and remorse culminate in an internal 'speech'. ' "How despicably have I acted!" she cried. – "I, who have prided myself on my discernment! – I, who have valued myself on my abilities! . . . How humiliating is this discovery! – Yet, how just a humiliation!" ' (p. 208).

In the epistemological readings of the novel this moment, of course, occupies pride of place. At this point Elizabeth's education is felt to be essentially complete. But the insistent exclamation marks here (as in later passages at Pemberley) are perhaps Jane Austen's way of marking a phase of over-compensation, a certain unbalanced identification with Darcy. Elizabeth, overwhelmed for the moment by the facts Darcy has presented, capitulates entirely, and unreasonably, to his view of things, seeming even to enjoy her own humiliation.[38] It is plausible to suggest that she is reacting to him, accepting his view, dominated by his understanding, in a phase of what a psychoanalyst might call 'identificatory assimilation'. If this reading is tenable, then one is able to chart through the second half of the novel, not a uniform psychological state of receptiveness, but a succession of disparate phases of feeling, a dialectic of repair and breakdown in which Elizabeth experiences moments of chagrin, bouts of enthrallment to Darcy's views, and moments of rebellion.

A certain interpretive challenge persists through the novel's second half, which is whether Elizabeth's differing reactions are to be read as expressions of momentary feeling, or as settled developments, whether and how much they are to be regarded, in other words, with irony. For example, Jane Austen represents Elizabeth, a few days after receiving the letter, thinking of Darcy: 'His attachment excited gratitude, his general character respect; but she could not approve him; nor could she for a moment repent her refusal, or feel the slightest inclination ever to see him again' (p. 212). Is she deceiving herself, underestimating even at this point her own interest in him? What I have called an 'interpretive challenge' is, of course, in other words, the novel's fascination, and keeping the reader on tenterhooks is its design. But I do not think at this point we are meant to feel that Elizabeth is mistaken, nor do I think that Elizabeth is ever – here or earlier – unconsciously, in the normal sense of the words, 'in love with' Darcy.[39] What we can be sure of is that Elizabeth is now free from hating him, that is, freed from experiencing him as a focus of projective identifications. She can now accord him justice, but the process by which this condition of respect for him turns into love is complex. Passage after passage charts Elizabeth's oscillating responses, gratitude towards, even identification with, him balancing self-recovery and consciousnesss of independence. Darcy's complementary self-analysis, however, is largely out of the picture.

'How you must have hated me after *that* evening?' (p. 369): after the second proposal, Elizabeth is no doubt about the usual consequences of her unintentional deception. Similarly, when she tells Mrs Gardiner that Wickham has moved on to Miss King, she declares she now understands that she never was much in love with him, 'for had I really experienced that pure and elevating passion, I should at present detest his very name, and wish him all manner of evil' (p. 150). This is just what might be expected, in fact, of Darcy's response to his rejection. Earlier Elizabeth has accepted Mrs Gardiner's suggestion that she avoid becoming too involved with Wickham, and the narrator has commented that this is 'a wonderful instance of advice being given on such a point, without being resented' (p. 145). Darcy's letter is a similarly 'wonderful' instance of an assault on the ego being sustained, not resented. Not only the material information in the letter, but the moderation of its tone, and the evidence of the writer's struggle towards impartiality, contribute to its power to convince Elizabeth. His letter contains no reproaches, nor does it make any attempt at reconciliation. Most importantly, except perhaps at the opening, it does not retaliate. Darcy is himself, as he later confesses, 'tortured' by her rebuke about his manner, but it is his pride, paradoxically, that saves him from detesting her very name.

Andrew Davies, the scriptwriter of the BBC film, has remarked that 'the central motor which drives the story forward is Darcy's sexual attraction to Elizabeth'.[40] This seems true enough; but Darcy's feelings are certainly more complex after Elizabeth's repudiation. The crucial 'motor' of the second half of the novel, even more hidden than the first, is not Darcy's passion, but his struggle to overcome his pride. 'Pride' in this context is shorthand for his self-image, his previously formed conception of his own coherent identity. To recognise that the other really exists is to risk being destroyed by the other, and Darcy has to digest Elizabeth's rebukes, to allow them to alter his inner life. As we have seen, Winnicott thought the analyst's capacity to survive the patient's destructive attacks was crucially important. He or she takes the force of the patient's criticisms (which in the intimacy of analysis may well cut to the quick) and experiences them as true, but is not so overwhelmed by them that he or she succumbs to hatred of the patient. Similarly, it is Darcy's capacity to survive Elizabeth's attack – not in his abused, bruised and humiliated state to find relief in loathing – that marks the transition in the novel from one form of love relation to another. Darcy's survival of Elizabeth's destructiveness is made plain in his demeanour when they meet, and it is this in turn which enables Elizabeth herself to think of him freely. For the first time at Pemberley, she is able to imagine him, walking about the grounds, as a separately existing being.

All this has to be constructed retrospectively, and Darcy on his re-appearance at Pemberley is scarcely less enigmatic than in the first volume. The text continues its focus on Elizabeth and on the evolution of her responses to Darcy, a process that calls forth some of Austen's most adroit and tactful writing. It is sometimes quite casually said that Elizabeth 'falls in love' with Darcy.[41] But Elizabeth's emotions are presented carefully as a graduated set of adjustments, often interrupted and stimulated by outside events, which allow the reader to assume that she eventually 'loves' Darcy but which never explicitly declare this until after the second proposal, and then as reassurances, in Jane's own idiom, to her sister. Instead, Elizabeth is invested with the capacity to meditate her way through her emotions, to negotiate a series of complex psychological promptings which require simultaneously acknowledg-ment of feelings and evaluation of their character. After meeting Darcy again at Pemberley, Elizabeth cannot sleep:

She lay awake two whole hours, endeavouring to make [her feelings] out. She certainly did not hate him. No; hatred had vanished long ago, and she had almost as long been ashamed of ever feeling a dislike against him, that could be so called. The respect created by the conviction of his valuable qualities, though at first unwillingly admitted, had for some time ceased to be repugnant to her feelings; . . . Such a change in a man of so much pride, excited not only astonishment but gratitude – for to love, ardent love, it must be attributed; and as such its impression on her was of a sort to be encouraged, as by no means unpleasing, though it could not be exactly defined. She respected, she es-teemed, she was grateful to him, she felt a real interest in his welfare; and she only wanted to know how far she wished that welfare to depend upon herself, and how far it would be for the happiness of both that she should employ that power, which her fancy told her she still possessed, of bringing on the renewal of his addresses. (p. 265–66)

This is a remarkable presentation of someone 'falling in love'. In contrast to the exclamatory excitement that has marked earlier phases of Elizabeth's psychological journey, it is slow-moving, temperate, indirect. But though indirect it is not arch, and Jane Austen nowhere hints at the presence of surreptitious motives or impulses, as she was to do with such skill in the Chawton novels. Instead narrator and character seem at one in the attempt to evoke velleities and obscurities of feeling and to give as much credit as possible to the conscious and rational processes by which Elizabeth gets in touch with them and reaches her conclusions. Elizabeth does not capitulate in any sense to Darcy, though gratitude towards him is an increasingly important facet of her response. What is most notable is that having worked out what these feelings are, moved herself along a continuum towards 'love', she still leaves that feeling, or any approach to it, in suspense, and still reserves judgement as to whether it would be 'for the happiness of both' that they should marry. Moreover – one might take note of the word – the passage comes to rest on a registration of her, rather than his, 'power'. This is very far from surrender of the self, of that identificatory assimilation of the other which might have been presaged in Elizabeth's immediate reaction to Darcy's letter. The sentiment of gratitude is harvested into a more complex response.

'The object, if it is to be used, must necessarily be real in the sense of being part of shared reality, not a bundle of projections,' Winnicott comments.[42] Contemporary psychoanalysis however can offer little help with the shared vocabulary, the binding ideological system, which is crucially important in understanding what has occurred within Darcy to facilitate this change in Elizabeth. For what enables Darcy to convert his pain and anger into other emotions is in part the valency of the notion of the 'gentleman'. As Elizabeth famously declares:

You are mistaken, Mr Darcy, if you suppose that the mode of your declaration affected me in any other way, than as it spared me the concern which I might have felt in refusing you, had you behaved in a more gentleman-like manner. (p. 192)

So piercing is the criticism that it has an effect on the actual physical being of her listener. Elizabeth does 'see' Darcy start at this, but it is only later in the novel that the woundingness of her rebuke becomes apparent. 'Those were your words. You know not, you can scarcely conceive, how they have tortured me; – though it was some time, I confess, before I was reasonable enough to allow their justice' (pp. 367–68). The shock that Elizabeth's remark gives to Darcy presages his possible recuperation. It is as if this term, 'gentleman', summons up a whole intersubjective, non-personal realm to which both he and Elizabeth subscribe. When Elizabeth declares to Lady Catherine that she is a gentleman's daughter the term is being used as a designator of social status, but for both main characters the word resonates with values that are deeply held. The notion of the 'proper' is associated with a group of similar ideas which refer equally to the private self and to a person's reputation in the world, and are invested with similar mandatory force. 'You thought me then devoid of every proper feeling', Darcy continues (p. 368). 'By you, I was properly humbled', he insists. 'Indeed he has no improper pride' (p. 376) Elizabeth in turn tells her father. The concept of the 'proper', summoned up in such moments of the text, is clearly pivotal. Like 'gentleman', it signifies a field or domain in which these two figures can relate, regardless of their personal attributes. Thus the 'two person field' of intersubjectivity which in Benjamin's thought replaces psychoanalysis's original focus on the single psyche, is also too circumscribed: *Pride and Prejudice* would seem to insist that selves relate not just to other selves but within a historically situated matrix of communicative interaction that is not of their own making.

Darcy's public self is integral to himself: that is, his 'character' (his reputation in the world) is not a mask, or a role, intermittently enacted, but goes all the way down. To put this another way: the psychological relations that constitute Darcy's 'self' are with his family, understood both dynastically and privately, his servants, his tenants, and, more broadly, with the nation. That is why Mrs Reynolds's testimony at Pemberley is so important. This is the selfhood that he has articulated so clumsily and pompously at Longbourn and Netherfield. In her reproach about his lack of gentlemanliness Elizabeth makes herself the spokesperson, the embodiment of this assembly of internal presences. And – paradoxically – because Elizabeth's assault focuses on that, she throws him a lifeline.

Recognition, Benjamin stresses, is 'a dimension of psychic capability' not a normative social ideal.[43] But in effect the notion of recognition can readily be applied to the understanding of political events, as she exemplifies.[44] Recognition can clearly evidence itself in social treatment and interaction. Darcy's internal 'recognition' of Elizabeth Bennet is thus manifested in or can be read off from, the transformed manners with which he greets her and her companions at Pemberley. He acknowledges them as social equals: he seeks to include them within the house and garden, this house and garden being both literally and metaphorically expressive of his selfhood. But such recognition when played out in the social sphere does not mean the adoption of the point of view of the other, or surrender to the other's whole reasoning – that is to reinscribe domination in another form. This is not a love wrought out of mutual sympathy or affinity (as with Jane and Bingley) but a much more difficult and stronger love built out of awareness of the other's difference. An important component of this difference is public status and power.

This is where the novel's definition of love becomes further entangled with its invasive and shadowing alternative, domination, which for Benjamin, as for Hegel, is part of the human condition.[45] In his politically 'radical' reading of the novel, Edward Neill has recently argued indeed that the relation of Darcy and Elizabeth is conducted always within 'the master–slave dialectic'. 'We never leave the terms of the master–slave relationship (whichever way things happen to tilt)' he writes.[46] He understands Darcy as enjoying his power over Elizabeth, and 'succumbing to his desire to master her'.[47] Several acute contemporary feminist critics besides Neill also read the second half of the narrative as the story of Elizabeth's subjugation by or surrender to Darcy's wealth, authority and superior judgement. They see this, and the happy marriage with which the novel ends, as registering Austen's own, if temporary, capitulation to that patriarchal system which invests all males with more power than females. They see Elizabeth as dwindling into a wife.[48]

Susan Fraiman, whose chapter on the novel is called 'The Humiliation of Elizabeth Bennet', argues that the figure, introduced as reliable, is re-presented, in the context of her marriageability, as prejudiced, 'her true identity' drowned out by the social world.[49] Maaja Stewart too suggests that its action shows Elizabeth making a transition from witty woman to sentimental and vulnerable one, bashful before Darcy like a Burney heroine. 'After Elizabeth reads Darcy's letter', she writes, 'she accepts his interpretation of their shared experience. When she visits Pemberley and understands Darcy's power, she looks at his portrait and directs his gaze – which she had earlier avoided – upon herself, thus subjecting not only their shared experience but herself to his interpretation.'[50] In her view the narrative is a 'failure', because it does not 'maintain a balance between Elizabeth's energy and Darcy's power'.[51] Similarly, Neill perceives 'an inner crumpling' in Elizabeth's attitude to Darcy.[52] All three critics are hard on the character, who is presented as the very embodiment of autocracy, 'par excellence the "governor" type', enjoying his 'realm of raw power' with a faint touch of sadistic pleasure.[53] They have little but contempt for Darcy's actions in the second half of the novel, and accuse Austen of capitulation to hidebound conservative ideology as well as routine narrative contrivance in making him act so handsomely, and earning Elizabeth's hand in marriage.

These readings certainly upset the traditional critical emphasis on the novel's balance or reconciliation of discordant qualities. But they underestimate the novel's psychological and ethical insight. Back at Longbourn, Elizabeth has Darcy much in her thoughts. 'She began now to comprehend that he was exactly the man, who, in disposition and talents, would most suit her . . . by her ease and liveliness, his mind might have been softened, his manners improved, and from his judgment, information, and knowledge of the world, she must have received benefits of greater importance' (p. 312). Both Fraiman and Stewart quote this passage, assume this assessment has the text's concurrence and take 'greater importance' as paradigmatic of the gender imbalance of the novel.[54] But Austen goes on to remark that '[n]o such happy marriage could now teach the admiring multitude what connubial felicity really was' – one moment in the eventful and changing course of Elizabeth's attitudes towards Darcy in which irony, however muted, is certainly present. It is enough to suggest how little weight should be placed on Elizabeth's rhapsodising daydreaming at this moment, that her overvaluation of Darcy as against herself is a consequence of her present chagrin at apparently losing him forever.

No reading of *Pride and Prejudice* which is concerned avowedly with political and social power can afford to neglect Elizabeth's confrontation with Lady Catherine. This triumphant worsting of her enemy certainly restores Elizabeth to narrative authority. It is notable also that after she has sent Lady Catherine packing, Elizabeth Bennet is in a mood to see off Darcy too, and the balance swings the other way. If he is swayed by his aunt, she thinks, let him 'be as happy, as dignity unblemished could make him' (p. 361); *she* certainly won't be spending any time in regrets – a startling assertion so late in the romance, and an indication of how far, even at this stage, Austen is willing to go in highlighting her character's insouciance. (There is little here to suggest an ironic registering of this as a merely temporary, and self-deceiving, bout of rebellion, though Austen is certainly amused in this part of the novel by the volatility of her heroine's reactions (p. 337).) But it is a mistake to devolve or reduce all issues of relationship in the novel to matters of political power. 'Against the broad chest of Darcy's logic, Elizabeth pounds the ineffectual fists of her own', Fraiman writes with some feeling,[55] and indeed one senses something unavailing in the attempt of criticism to turn this novel into a 'failure'. By default, these critiques seem to suggest that *Pride and Prejudice* asks for a reading which understands 'power' to have different modalities. It cannot be disputed that the novel is, from one point of view, a conservative romance, but one should not confuse social 'domination' with psychological domination. The difficult, undemocratic fact is that the novel's ethical narrative is incommensurate with and may override and subsume these political readings.

Darcy's social and economic standing is a vital component of his masculine otherness. It is a premise of the novel's action that Darcy is an important figure, who occupies a sphere which is distinct from Elizabeth's as a country gentlewoman.[56] He is related to nobility, owns a large estate, with an income of ten thousand a year. Crucially, he has an intellectual and personal authority that certainly doesn't come inevitably with his property, as a comparison of other people with more money (Mr Rushworth in *Mansfield Park*, for instance) in Jane Austen's novels would suggest. It is part of her achievement in *Pride and Prejudice* to convince the reader of Darcy's 'aweful' qualities, which Bingley teases him about (p. 50), but which are manifested alongside his more pompous side, in his dexterous handling of Miss Bingley's sycophancy, in his self-restraining silences, perhaps most of all in his capacity always to transform bantering conversation into something significant – if only the reader would understand him. But Darcy is not a sensitive new-age guy. When Elizabeth thinks hard about him, as in the passage quoted above, the very deliberative nature of her thinking processes reflects her sense of Darcy as rather remote, substantive, compellingly distinct from herself.

Nor does Austen relinquish her grasp of Darcy as a formidable figure in the novel's concluding sequences. She never presents him as if he were now to be understood as wholly within the space of Elizabeth's psychology, as a lovably equal object. Whilst Elizabeth is amused, for example, at his assumptions about Bingley (and despite telling herself she mustn't yet tease him, comes very close to it) Darcy's inflexibly demanding superego (the 'I' in these sentences that instructs some other part of the self) is still being reinscribed: 'I was obliged to confess one thing, which for a time, and not unjustly, offended him. I could not allow myself to conceal that your sister had been in town three months last winter, that I had known it, and purposely kept it from him' (p. 371). The contrast between Elizabeth's impulses to playfulness and mischief and Darcy's inflexible need to act rightly and to be square with his conscience is sustained. This is not a relationship in which each mirrors the other but of distinct subjectivities whose very alterity is the ground of their rapport. This means that, since the novel's point of view continues to be mostly Elizabeth's, Darcy remains out of reach, an enigma, other, to the end. This in turn may explain why for so many readers, he remains a focus of fantasy.

The novel's play on the visual, with treating the other as an object, and as other than an object, is most brilliantly articulated in the sequence at Pemberley in which Elizabeth Bennet contemplates Darcy's portrait. I shall round up this argument by commenting on this, for it is the apotheosis of the novel's complex understanding on the nature of recognition. Partly because it has been led up to by the novel's reiterated association of visuality and knowledge, this moment, as most readers and critics feel, has a significance out of proportion to its duration. Miss Bingley's early attempts to tease Darcy about Elizabeth's low connections – 'Do let the portraits of your uncle and aunt Philips be placed in the gallery at Pemberley' (pp. 52–53) have followed from Darcy's assertion that an artist 'taking' a picture of Elizabeth would find it difficult to catch the expression of her eyes. A portrait, unlike a 'sketch', or 'picture' then has already been loaded with public, dynastic, implications. 'At last it arrested her – and she beheld a striking resemblance of Mr Darcy, with such a smile over the face, as she remembered to have sometimes seen, when he looked at her.' 'As she stood before the canvas, on which he was represented, and fixed his eyes upon herself, she thought of his regard with a deeper sentiment of gratitude than it had ever raised before; she remembered its warmth, and softened its impropriety of expression' (pp. 250–51).

The BBC film's presentation of the whole Pemberley sequence is strikingly different.[57] The viewer sees the housekeeper leading Elizabeth and the Gardiners down a long gallery, the camera looking at them first from one direction and then from the other, increasing anticipation.

Her ecstatic 'There!' on the soundtrack accompanies a shot of Elizabeth gazing upwards, and then the portrait itself. The film thus pays tribute to the significance of this moment in the novel. But because the picture is placed high on the wall, there is no possibility of Elizabeth 'fixing his eyes upon her', as in the text.[58] Nor does the portrait show Darcy smiling. Instead, its position, and the sombreness of Darcy's demeanour replicate the technique that the film has used in its previous presentations of the hero. Elizabeth's silent gaze upwards to the picture is intercut with a sequence in which Darcy is seen riding through the trees towards Pemberley, with plaintive, even tragic, woodwind themes on the soundtrack. Sitting by a pond, he takes off his jacket, unties his cravat, and plunges into the water. This shift from the public portrait – the landowner in his estates, whose eyes contemplate the viewer, not Elizabeth Bennet – to a graphic illustration of the young man seeking relief from responsibility (a modern rather than an eighteenth-century conception) effectively wrests the climactic force of the picture away from Elizabeth's and onto Darcy's psychological life, his semi-nakedness a figure for 'raw' emotions, supposedly transcending class and social boundaries. The novel's complex figuration of recognition is replaced by a call to identify with him, and at the same time his body is re-presented as an object. At this crucial moment then, the film replaces the key episode of the novel with a key of its own, a male writer's redefinition of its centre. And despite several nominally feminist appreciations, one perceives that it is Darcy's drama, not Elizabeth's, that the viewer is seduced into sharing.[59]

Elizabeth in gazing at Darcy's portrait is reminded of his smile, a smile which she had previously overlooked. The text's earlier notation of Darcy's smiling may have been picked up by the reader, or it may not. If he or she inhabits Elizabeth's psyche, perhaps it passes unnoticed; if he or she is aligned with Darcy, perhaps it sounds a warning or complicating note. But since identification is multiple, serial or alternating, both these possibilities have been kept in play. What occurs now is literally a revision, by which what was previously registered in some form is now, stimulated by the present, recovered, remembered – another version of, rather than a parallel to, Elizabeth's earlier mistaken 'remembering' of his 'boasting' of his resentments, in which she rather recalled her own reactions than his words. Now, the complexity and plasticity of memory is reaffirmed, and rather than portraying, perhaps this opens a vista into, this character's psychology. Elizabeth recovers what she had earlier not registered consciously, and the word 'regard' is allowed to hover, felicitously, between gaze and esteem, so that she can retrospectively acknowledge both his desire and his respect for her individual being.

The moment when Elizabeth contemplates the portrait then is a textual representation of the psychic capacity Jessica Benjamin names 'recognition'. It is difficult to give graphic form, to convey to the reader in writing, the real presence of the unspoken psychological transactions which crisscross the consulting room; hence 'recognition' in Benjamin's work, like 'use' in Winnicott's, remains a shade abstract, theoretic. But the portrait scene in the novel offers a kind of condensed, symbolic representation of the meaning of that insight into a rare capacity of human interaction when others are encountered as equals. It is an aesthetic rehearsal for that drama of recognition which the following chapters of the novel will play out in detail, and it is followed, in one of the novel's more daring moments, a short paragraph later, by the reappearance of Darcy himself.

Softened by her thinking about him, Elizabeth is able to 'see' what she had previously not seen, to know something, it is suggested, about Darcy that she had not previously known. In a literally magical moment, the portrait becomes animated. And why – since a Reynolds has just placed Darcy in 'an aimiable light' (p. 249) – should I not say too that this encounter with a surely very good painting is a metaphor for the power of art, a branch of which is practised by Jane Austen herself? For in the presence of art we become enchanted into the belief that the past is alive at the same moment as we are ourselves and *Pride and Prejudice* looks at us with its own eyes.[60] Elizabeth envisages Darcy as a real other being whose smile now becomes the living index of that otherness whose significance she had formerly disregarded. As Rachel Brownstein writes: 'What she loves, and sees, is what goes on between them.'[61] Submission, if it occurs, is rather a necessary tendering of self in return for the other's regard. Which of the two 'fixes' their eyes on the other? If Elizabeth allows herself to be looked at, puts herself momentarily in the position of the looked at, the object, she is simultaneously the subject of the action and the subject who is acting. It would be hard indeed to find a more compressed figuration of the interplay of alterity, submission and possession that makes up the drama of recognition. The gaze she now sees in the portrait, and the gaze she returns, is not one of domination, but of love.

CHAPTER 6

The genius and the facilitating environment

In health: the False Self is represented by the whole organisation of the polite and mannered social attitude, a 'not wearing the heart upon the sleeve,' as might be said. Much has gone to the individual's ability to forego omnipotence . . . the gain being the place in society which can never be attained or maintained by the True Self alone.

D. W. Winnicott, 'Ego Distortion in terms of True and False Self'[1]

There's a scene in *Clueless* when Cher Horowitz, nervously searching for an outfit to wear to her biggest challenge, the driving test, offhandedly asks the maid, Lucy, to have a word with the gardener for her, since she 'speaks Mexican'. Lucy indignantly replies that she's not Mexican and flounces off. When Cher tells Josh she doesn't understand why Lucy is so upset, Josh tells her Lucy is from El Salvador and rebukes her: 'You get upset if someone thinks you live below Sunset.'

For some commentators, this is one of the film's parallels or analogies with *Emma*. It mimics that important exchange in the novel when Emma, thrown off her stroke at the Box Hill picnic, lashes out – the spite not the less pointed for the politeness of the address – at the vulnerable, accommodating spinster, Miss Bates, who has just taken up Mr Weston's invitation to entertain the company, if not with wit, then with 'three things very dull indeed': 'That will just do for me, you know. I shall be sure to say three dull things as soon as ever I open my mouth, shan't I? – (looking round with the most good-humoured dependence on every body's assent) – Do not you all think I shall?':

Emma could not resist.
'Ah! ma'am, but there may be a difficulty. Pardon me – but you will be limited as to number – only three at once.' (*Emma*, p. 370)

This is a moment to make readers of the novel shiver, its sudden irruption into the supposedly convivial scene well caught in the Douglas

McGrath film of *Emma*, as the camera is allowed to dwell upon Miss Bates's face, her nervous words spelling out the full significance of the jibe, only implied in the novel.[2] Reginald Farrer described it in his 1917 appraisal of Austen's work as a violent slap in the face,[3] but for me it is more like a wound, something rather terrible that opens up suddenly in the midst of the uneasy comedy that characterises the narrative at this point. But in *Clueless*, Lucy (who has not appeared in the movie before, and never appears after) responds not with chagrin but with indignation, and though Cher has made a politically insensitive error, as Josh points out, little more comes of it. In *Emma*, the insult to Miss Bates is critical, so crucial because it suddenly opens to our unwilling and disbelieving observation a hinterland of meaning, a truth that the action of the novel has so long kept out of sight.

We know that Miss Bates is a perpetual irritant to Emma. Only the day before, at Donwell Abbey, Emma at her best, immediately responding to Jane Fairfax's appeal for help, seeing her off 'with the zeal of a friend' (p. 363), drops without a break into Emma at her worst as she addresses this 'friend' in soliloquy: 'Such a home, indeed! such an aunt! ... I do pity you. And the more sensibility you betray of their just horrors, the more I shall like you', empathy immediately curdling into resentment. We know that when Harriet has happened to mention Emma and Miss Bates in the same breath – 'But then, to be an old maid at last, like Miss Bates!' – she has launched Emma into her most formidable, and most revealing, defensive speech: 'If I thought I should ever be like Miss Bates! so silly – so satisfied – so smiling – so prosing – so undistinguishing and unfastidious – and so apt to tell every thing relative to every body about me, I would marry tomorrow' (pp. 84–5). We know that when Mrs Weston confides to Emma her suspicions that Mr Knightley might have his eye on Jane Fairfax, this too touches a raw nerve, and releases a vein of spiteful parody: 'How would he bear to have Miss Bates belonging to him? – To have her haunting the Abbey, and thanking him all day long for his great kindness in marrying Jane? – "So very kind and obliging! – But he always had been such a kind neighbour!" And then fly off, through half a sentence, to her mother's old petticoat. "Not that it was such a very old petticoat either – for still it would last a great while – and, indeed, she must thankfully say that their petticoats were all very strong"' (p. 225).

'For shame, Emma! Do not mimic her. You divert me against my conscience.' Yet Mrs Weston does laugh, however shamefacedly, and the reader with her. Even Mr Knightley knows that Miss Bates is a bore, escapes from her as fast as decently possible, and admits that she is 'absurd', though it is 'harmless absurdity'. Mr Perry too, hints that Miss Bates, 'though his very old friend' would be a most trying companion (p. 389). Highbury, it seems fair to say, finds Miss Bates tiresome; and Emma's jibe then expresses what oft was thought. The reader who has skipped or hurried over the long passages given to Miss Bates's talk, thereby imitating in their reading practice the same indifferent half attention Emma gives to the boring spinster, is implicated too: the reader who identifies with Emma, and who has enjoyed her spirit, her intelligence, her kindness, who has felt the frustration that underlies her various schemes, colludes, if only for a moment, in Emma's insult. When she says the forbidden thing – or expresses the forbidden emotion – we recognise ourselves. For a moment, the petticoat (and what is beneath the petticoat)[4] shows. Baffled by the ambivalence of Frank Churchill's signals, frustrated by the smallness and pettiness of Highbury, forced to be in the party of Mrs Elton, a woman for whom, to put it mildly, she has 'a very great dislike', caught in the cross-currents of feeling between Frank and Jane, Emma's words are not spoken by her alone, but, involuntarily, as by the group – for 'Emma could not resist': and the reader is a co-conspirator.

Perhaps the most influential piece of Austen criticism ever written is D. W. Harding's essay 'Regulated Hatred', first published in 1940.[5] References to Harding's argument, though often misunderstood, still circulate in Austen criticism, as if it represents a stimulant or irritant that has not yet been wholly assimilated. Indirectly, perhaps, he inaugurated what is in effect the mainstream of current Austen commentary. (And in this concluding chapter I seek to draw this book, largely attentive to other matters, into this stream.) The narrator's dealings with Miss Bates are an important exhibit in the case Harding makes. He quotes a passage which occurs in an early chapter of the novel where Austen is scene setting – laying the foundations of its social world. Highbury, we are told, 'was reckoned a particularly healthy spot' and the context makes it plain that this is to be taken without irony, unlike Isabella's effusions, a few chapters later, about the 'remarkably airy' situation of London's Brunswick Square (p. 103). As part of that scene setting Miss Bates is described in benevolent terms: 'She was a happy woman, and a woman whom no one named without good-will. It was her own universal good-will and contented temper which worked such wonders . . . The simplicity and cheerfulness of her nature, her contented and grateful spirit, were a recommendation to every body and a mine of felicity to herself' (p. 21). 'A mine of felicity'?: this does not sound like Jane on her toes. It is all perhaps a bit bland.

But the passage picked on by Harding comes a little earlier when Miss Bates is introduced. 'Miss Bates stood in the very worst predicament in the world for having much of the public favour; and she had no intellectual superiority to make atonement to herself, or frighten those who might hate her, into outward respect.' He writes that 'Jane Austen was herself at this time "neither handsome, young, rich, nor married", and the passage perhaps hints at the functions which her unquestioned intellectual superiority may have had for her.'[6] He suggests that this is only one of many small slips or inadvertencies in the novels which open a momentary window onto the author's unofficial and personal self, a self, he suggests, radically at odds with the polite world that surrounded her. Harding's essay in general elides distinctions between narrator and author, and tends to attribute to Jane Austen opinions and passages which a modern reader might more cautiously ascribe to the narrator. At this point, though, his move is made plausible because of the slight incompatibility or tension within what he calls this 'amiable context' of the mention of 'those who might hate her' followed by the (recuperative) assurance that Miss Bates was a woman 'whom no one named without good-will'.

In other words, Emma's attack on Miss Bates originates in, and gives fictional release to, impulses that are present in the author herself. Here Emma expresses the hatred – if that is too fierce a word, the impatience, the resentment, the contempt for mindlessness – that has been running through her head for the course of the novel. Miss Bates is undistinguishing and unfastidious: she is everything that Emma is not and Austen was not, and yet her situation is uncomfortably close to one and the other. But Miss Bates herself is not a sufficient provocation, and if Emma's insult is disturbing that is because the spinster is the target for tensions which arise from within Emma's experience of the whole social group, or perhaps even from within human society itself. As Julia Prewitt Brown writes, 'We understand it not through its overt causes – Emma's impatience and boredom, her exasperated attempt to entertain herself since no one else will entertain her – but through its covert reality: there is no reason for it: it is simply a case of unrestrained human hostility.'[7] Emma's action is both social, in the sense that it arises out of the tensions of that particular occasion, and anti-, or non-social, for these tensions cannot wholly explain or excuse it. And because the reader knows and shares that impulse, at this point Austen's work definitively transcends the comedic tradition in which her novels are conceived. At Box Hill, one might say, the novel forces the reader to contemplate the insurgency of evil (for Emma's remark will be lastingly wounding to Miss Bates) in the ethical topography of everyday life.[8]

Harding's argument has been roundly attacked, as well as often slighted, read as if he were proposing a merely satirical and misanthropic writer, 'full of hatred.'[9] Yet the stress of his argument is on Jane Austen's novels as a mode of reconciliation to the social environment, not expressions of her antagonism towards it. As he writes: 'To her the first necessity was to keep on reasonably good terms with the associates of her everyday life; she had a deep need for their affection and a genuine respect for the ordered, decent civilisation that they upheld. And yet she was sensitive to their crudenesses and complacencies and knew that her real existence depended on resisting many of the values they implied. The novels gave her a way out of this dilemma.'[10] It is this 'dilemma' that is expressed most exactly in *Emma* by explicitly making the circumscribed community – 'the Highbury world' – its subject matter, and that is resolved in the novels by irony at one level and through the agency of the romantic plot at another. Harding's argument was that 'hatred', when it is implicated in Jane Austen's writing, is always severely curtailed, hidden, detectable only in passages when it is 'regulated' by its context. As soon as Emma is made to realise what she has said, she is overcome: 'How could she have been so brutal, so cruel to Miss Bates!' Not mincing words in her self-castigation, she finds the picnic is to be 'abhorred in recollection' (p. 377). So the two sides of Austen's characteristic 'dilemma' are here brought together: on the one hand, impatience, frustration, contempt for the petty-mindedness of society, on the other a deep respect for convention, and for the reality of other people, and above all the concern for one's standards of behaviour that is pride in one's own moral life. The writer Harding found was no genteel satirist, pandering to the comfort of middle-class readers, but one whose work displays a sophisticated negotiation between solidarity with the society that nourished her (and would buy her novels!) and intense critical scrutiny.[11]

Austen's irony then, as Prewitt Brown puts it, is a 'benevolent compromise', not a mode of social detachment from others, but one of adjustment.[12] In an essay, closely aligned with Harding's, on the role of aggression in Austen's novels, Ian Watt shows how Austen's own characteristic technique is instantiated in such a figure as Elinor Dashwood.

Faced with the mercenary and self-deceiving platitudes of her half-brother, she does not argue with him: instead her 'adroitly ironic duplicity' preserves both her self-respect and amicable relations. Aggression is thus manifested and simultaneously controlled.[13] Irony, practised in all sorts of styles by all sorts of characters in Austen's novels, from Elinor to Mr Bennet to Charlotte Heywood in *Sanditon*, is perceived by the novelist as essential to the satisfactory commerce of communal life. It is 'a way of maintaining social integrity without compromising personal integrity'.[14] 'People saw the harm that excessive candor can do', as Audrey puts it in *Metropolitan*. One might add that irony is normally a means of expressing hostility without inflicting damage. But one of the most awful things about Emma's remark to Miss Bates is that it is ironic.

Harding was by profession a psychologist, and one would suppose that, working in London in the nineteen twenties and thirties, he would have come across the ideas circulating in the British Psycho-Analytic Society after the advent of Melanie Klein in 1926. His discussion of the 'Cinderella' motif in the novels, in the much less influential second half of his essay, apparently draws upon Freud's notion of the 'family romance'.[15] At the very least it is a remarkable coincidence that Harding's thinking about Austen's relation to the social group of which she formed a part, should parallel, and perhaps anticipate, the thought of members of the British psychoanalytic school, who were influenced by Klein's presentation of the infant's conflicting attitudes towards the mother, and extended this into thought about social life. Winnicott was hardly writing when Harding formulated his ideas, but his work on the 'maturational process and the facilitating environment', to use the umbrella phrase he used for a collection of his essays, overlaps with Harding's – and Austen's – presentation of these issues.[16] Winnicott's idea of 'holding', for instance, derives from the physical nursing of the mother a conception that encompasses her psychological capacity to sustain her infant's emotional life, and extends this to a conception of the psychological function of the social group.[17] His colleague, Wilfred Bion, developed a rather similar idea, that the infant's violent and destructive impulses are 'contained' by the mother who moderates and returns them, in an altered and matured form.[18] Earlier, Bion had formulated concepts about the interdependence of individuals and groups that are clearly relevant to Harding's and to Austen's work. Winnicott's attention was always on the healthy, ordinary process of maturing: Bion, on the other hand, was interested in how the genius, a figure whom he called the 'mystic', both depends upon and, if given their head, will destroy their enabling, but also stultifying, environment.[19] When Harding writes that Jane Austen 'knew that her real existence' depended upon resisting many of the values of the world about her, his formulation may be compared with Winnicott's invocation of a 'True Self', which is needed to understand the 'False Self' endlessly impinged upon, distracted by, and compliant to social reality.[20]

As is widely understood, in novels which notably abstain from other than ordinary metaphorical language, settings and places in Austen tend to take on a figural aspect. One might argue in fact that the complex processes nominated in Winnicott's and Bion's terms, 'holding' and 'containing', are already present in Austen's deployment of the spatial tropes that structure her novel. Threaded through *Emma* is a series of incidents which cannot avoid bringing to the reader's attention the facilitating and constraining features of its physical world, a material environment which is to be read simultaneously as psychological. The elaborate discussion that takes place about whether the Crown Inn will accommodate the proposed ball is an example, and when Frank Churchill taunts Mr Woodhouse about young people throwing up windows it is evident that the exchange is readable metaphorically as well as literally (pp. 251–52). Frank (frank! – Austen never misses a trick) here is both an anarchic spirit and a liberationary one: if he teases Mr Woodhouse he is both transgressing the unwritten code that holds the community together, and letting in some conceptual air. Scene after scene – the inquisition about Jane Fairfax's trips out to the post office, the depiction of the house and grounds of Donwell Abbey, the long wet July evening in which Emma paces the drawing room at Hartfield – inflect in various ways the ambivalent qualities of an environment that both (or intermittently) holds and imprisons, that both contains and stifles.[21] 'English verdure, English culture, English comfort,' thinks Emma complacently at Donwell (p. 360), only a few minutes before Jane Fairfax is to beg her for help, crying 'Oh! Miss Woodhouse, the comfort of being sometimes alone!' (p. 363).

Whilst 'happiness' tends to be the word that rings through the earlier novels, this 'comfort', with its associations of maternal sustenance, of nursing, of solace, is the notion whose promises, and traps, Austen savours and tests in the Chawton novels, and especially in *Emma*.[22] 'Oh! Miss Woodhouse, do talk to me and make me comfortable again', similarly begs Harriet, upset after her re-encounter with the

Martins (p. 179): the word here, as in many other instances of its usage in *Emma*, represents a seductive foreclosure of the psyche against disturbing perceptions of reality. 'Comfort' at one end of the spectrum is pandering to Mr Woodhouse's need for only those entertainments that never take him beyond the gate of Hartfield, or out of himself. Yet 'comfort' is a word with much deeper resonances than those which, retrospectively associating it with material provision, we tend to assume. In Johnson's *Dictionary* of 1755, the word is still defined as meaning 'consolation, support under calamity or danger'. At the other end of the spectrum, this more august, and indeed religious, sense of 'comfort'[23] names a fundamental human need, an equilibrium at once psychological and social – that equilibrium among competing urgencies which, Harding suggests, is the instigating design of Austen's art. And Austen's interest in the notion of what 'comfort' might mean also raises matters that are pertinent to the history of her critical and cultural reception.

As Brian Southam points out, many critics before Harding had noticed the acerbic, or 'cruel' streak in Austen's writing.[24] That is not the reason why his essay is important. He extends that initial recognition in two directions, inwards towards the author's psychology, and outwards towards the social and intellectual environment in which she wrote. As a psychologist, his focus is on mental and emotional health, and his fundamental argument, I think, goes towards explaining why Austen is so treasured in our culture. Harding's essay is at once a psychological appraisal of the individual author's relation to her social group (the psychology of which was his professional field), and an acute reading of an 'aspect' of her texts – a reading that he declares is 'deliberately lop-sided' so as to redress a balance that has fallen the other way.[25] It is a misreading to suggest that he considers Austen's novels merely as 'a form of personal therapy':[26] he seeks rather to explain how they arose from, but sorted out, tensions within the writer and are thus in their successful equilibrium able to bring comfort – in the older and more exalted meaning of the word – to readers who necessarily experience similar dilemmas within civil life. Another way of saying this is that they speak to and conserve the 'true self' of the reader. This book's use of psychoanalytic theory is perhaps in the tradition of his thinking, but his main influence was in a radically different direction.

The hostility that is sometimes directed towards 'Regulated Hatred' can be justified by its subsequent impact on Austen studies. The article certainly lay behind a group of aggressively argued works which emphasised the destructive, misanthropic and defensive aspects of Austen's writing, and diminished its negotiatory or reconciliatory qualities.[27] It is said to have inaugurated the 'subversive' school of Austen criticism, though the term can be misleading. More productively, Harding's writing opened the possibility of reading Austen 'politically'. His focus was on a notional object – the strains and dilemmas within the authorial psyche, understood as open to and challenged by its group environment. But his work served to turn Austen studies towards the writer's relation to her society, more broadly and historically conceived. In the decades after his essay was published, attention shifted onto the cultural circumstances in which Austen's novels were embedded. The reservations or tensions that Harding detected in Austen's attitudes to her social group were now understood in a wider context, and evidence was found in her novels for attitudes that – especially given the capacity of this term since the 1960s to include personal and sexual material – became political. Extrapolated into the field of public affairs and culture, Austen's complex and ambivalent presentations of genteel society became readable as interventions into current debates. Though she does not mention his article, Mary Poovey's *The Proper Lady and the Woman Writer* (1984) was the most cogent continuation of Harding's conception of a writer negotiating between insurgency and conformity, convincingly detailing the artistic 'strategies' that ' "resolved" – at least at the level of art' the ideological contradictions of her age.[28]

Inculcated in each reader is a spirit who harbours some of the feelings which inadvertently slip out of Emma's mouth at Box Hill. Her capacity to say what she says is an index of her distinction, her wit, almost, one might say, of her creativity – that irreducibly personal and individual spiritedness which Mrs Weston and Knightley agree on in calling her 'the picture of health'. If there is a sexual antagonism somewhere lurking here, too, that is not something in Emma we would simply wish away. So one might conceivably cheer this moment of liberation or dissent, this sudden breaking into the stiflingly petty, proper and genteel atmosphere of a middle-class picnic in *Emma* of something like honesty. It's only a step further to find Mr Knightley's almost immediately delivered rebuke a paternalistic sermon, re-enforcing all the conservative and repressive strategies this figure has articulated in the course of the novel, and that the novelist, apparently, here endorses – a male figure and a writer who together bring about 'the humiliation of Emma Woodhouse'.[29] The novel can be read as 'policing' the reader, as constructing a net around him or her, so that we are forced whilst reading to subscribe to the traditional conceptions of ethical value and social duty Mr Knightley stands for.

How can Emma's moment of unconstrained wit be both evil and creative? A reading of *Emma* demands the toleration of this paradox. But Harding's presentation of an Austen whose attitude to her social group resembles the mature individual's ability to entertain simultaneous hatred and love for the same object has tended to be recursively split. Now Austen may be presented as belonging to one of two incompatible camps – the radical or subversive, and the conservative or nostalgic. Subversive readers (whose image of the author might be represented in the biographies of John Halperin and David Nokes) discover in the novels evidence of narrative duplicities and tension, express dismay at their romantic, and conservative, resolutions, and are unwilling to believe that Austen could be other than deeply hostile to a society in which she was a dependent genius. They find evidence of 'transgressive' qualities in the novels, read them and her letters for hints of lesbian, anarchic and anti-imperialist motifs, of a 'gloriously insolent spirit' of rebellion against conformity.[30] They tend, as Janet Todd has suggested, to project contemporary anxieties and controversies onto the texts.[31] On the other hand, conservatives (who may not consciously think of Austen herself as a Tory) stress their love of her books, and tend towards a celebratory attitude towards them, and the 'world' they supposedly represent (or, in some versions, reflect). This in turn becomes for the radicals, the propagation of a sentimental, idealised Englishness, and even an instrument of colonialist educational subjugation. For each group, 'Jane Austen' becomes the repository of projections, yearnings and ambitions.

The appearance of a new generation of film versions of the novels on the scene has inflected this division in a new way, or perhaps simply deepened an already existing rift. This book has offered no systematic commentary on these representations of the novels, preferring to approach the issues they raise about reading more obliquely, but it is clear that these films are marketed to an audience for whom the appeal of 'Jane Austen' is that she represents a privileged, genteel, amusing and consoling world – in fact a form of comfort. You might show Mr Woodhouse a Jane Austen video, even if you could never get him out of the house to see the movie. Discussing the 'heritage' film, James N. Loehlin writes that Merchant Ivory offer 'popular anglophilic adaptations of anglophobic Forster novels'.[32] Something similar might apply to the Miramax treatments of Austen novels, in which any residual satire seems safely banished into the historical distance, any confrontation mitigated by exquisite acting and costly mise en scène.

The films thus offer a reincarnation of the reading of Austen that Harding found so intolerable and inaccurate. But indeed, their romantic nostalgia is hard to resist. There have been moments when I have hated even the best of these movies, hated their endemic substitution of sensuous pleasures for the intellectual dexterity and irony of the texts. I have feared their immediacy, their power to linger in the memory, their tendency to usurp mine and my students' reading of the novels. Sometimes one feels, like many academic writers, that one must rescue Jane Austen from the films, as Harding felt one had to rescue her from her admirers of the thirties. I have tried to demonstrate in the course of this book that it is possible to overcome this impulse. The films are readings, mostly made in good faith; before them, one compares and tests, and perhaps reignites, one's own inner reading of Jane Austen.

In this context, though, Patricia Rozema's *Mansfield Park* (1999) is a major challenge. Itself a 'heritage' piece, with all the accessories of the genre, beautiful cinematography, elegant costumes, sweeping panoramas, and the obligatory ball, the film seeks to modify, perhaps contest, the genre from within. Its indebtedness to Moira Ferguson, Terry Castle and other recent commentators on Jane Austen manifestly aligns it with the intellectual 'subversive' tradition, and its portrayal of a young Jane Austen accepts that tradition's view of her as a sardonic, detached observer of a selfish world.[33] In many ways the film is the apotheosis of these variously political readings of Jane Austen: it certainly represents a meeting point or site of infiltration by academic commentary into the mass media. Rozema's *Mansfield Park* itself may be seen as aimed at the nostalgic reader of the novelist, forcing the viewer to confront 'what some read Austen to avoid: politics',[34] and what, it might be reasonably argued, Austen's own novel treats circumspectly. But I rather think that what the film represents is the marketing of a new 'Jane Austen' to a post-feminist audience now receptive to its reinvention of the novel.

An informed and articulate opponent of slavery, the film's Fanny Price is made to realise her own and the family's dependence on the vicious institution that supports them and secures their material comfort. This conception involves a rewriting of the character of Sir Thomas Bertram, in the novel essentially well-meaning, if culpably obtuse at times and clumsily inadequate when dealing with the younger generation, into a Montoni-like monster of depravity. Confronted at the film's climax by the Goyaesque horrors depicted in Tom's plantation sketchbook, Fanny can do nothing but retreat in dismay from her uncle, in a slow-motion sequence, shot in darkness, which seems to register that she is both appalled and impotent. The scenes of rape and cruelty in the notebook are capped almost immediately by Fanny's horrified glimpse of Tom and Maria copulating. The linked darkness and revulsion define Mansfield as a site of masculine sexual licentiousness and exploitation. But after this climax, the film returns to a mode of stylised comedy, and the issues so dramatically raised simply vanish. One might read this as a conscious reinflection of Harding's notion of an Austen who is both deeply critical of, yet necessarily dependent upon, a social world to which she has attachments, but this seems unlikely.

The truth is, perhaps, that the film itself cannot cope with the material it feels ideologically driven to contain. An attack on colonialism, it is itself a neo-colonialist enterprise, the promotion of 'Jane Austen'.[35] And at the heart of this *Mansfield Park* is another version of the identificatory fantasy I began this book by discussing. If in the sentimental school of Austenian biography there is an inveterate tendency to blend 'Jane Austen' into her own heroines, here is a new variation on the same theme, played in a subversive key. The film's Fanny Price, with 'a tongue like a guillotine', is an incarnation of the figure sketched in David Nokes's biography, 'rebellious, satirical and wild'. Austen's youthful writing is presented in the film, just as it is in the Life, as an activity of 'impromptu rebellion', of 'defiance'.[36] 'If I am a wild beast I cannot help it', declares Fanny Price, saddling her horse in the night, and riding off into the thunderstorm. At this point the script appropriates a passage from one of Austen's letters,[37] itself wildly misread by Nokes in order to serve his scheme of exposing what he declares are the 'dark secrets' suppressed in the received view of the author and her world.[38]

Addressed to the camera, composed in her upstairs room, her writing marks this budding author as a figure isolated from a hostile environment. (In reality, as Poovey puts it, Austen's early writings were part of the fabric of her family relationships.[39]) There is something inveterately romantic about this conception of the artist's relation to society, and it feels deeply at odds with the gestating impulses of Austen's work, as Harding and many others have understood them. Perhaps one can see this most clearly in the film's treatment of imprisonment – the bondage of young women that it links (as did Mrs Elton) with the slave trade. 'I cannot get out, as the starling said': Fanny's cousin Maria is trapped within this patriarchy, but a newly imagined and more sympathetic Henry Crawford offers Fanny an escape, symbolised by the birds he contrives shall be released for her amusement in Portsmouth. When she is distressed at her uncle's treating her, too, as a vassal, this 'wild' Fanny Price rides off into the darkness. At the film's conclusion, the figure of escape is miraculously enacted: as the camera swings high over the various locations in which the characters' futures are to be led, and Fanny's voice describes them, the film identifies her genius with her romantic fulfilment, and these – gift of montage, gift of the camera – with the flight of the bird. But this is a fantasy at odds with the very premises of Austen's art. Few critics, whether conservative or more radical, would dispute what Lionel Trilling wrote in his magisterial essay on *Mansfield Park* first published in 1954: 'What we may call Jane Austen's first or basic irony is the recognition of the fact that the spirit is not free, that it is conditioned, that it is limited by circumstance.'[40]

This film, then, is a re-visioning or remaking carried out far from the spirit of homage. *Mansfield Park* presents a heroine whose outspokenness about slavery implies that the original author could not, or would not, write openly about the abuses she founded the setting and action of her novel upon: implicitly, then, it condemns the text from which it derives, just as Tom flings back at his father the word 'principles' on which the novel sets such store. But the film is arguably far less radical than the novel, if one means by 'radical' the challenging of current dispositions. As Trilling and other commentators since have pointed out, *Mansfield Park* remains disturbing because it contains a critique of modernity. Fanny is a difficult figure because her psychological struggles precede not actions, but acquiescence. Not movement, but stability, not progress but continuity, not exogamy but endogamy are what the novel honours. The energetic, whip-swinging, tearaway Fanny Price who replaces Austen's heroine, image erasing script, vitality substituting for goodness, is a figure who reflects back to contemporary audiences the traits most acceptable to and encouraged in, late capitalist society.

Praised as an instance of 'creative vandalism',[41] *Mansfield Park* is a test case for the theory of adaptation sketched in this book. This film is a clear example of Bloom's 'strong' rereading, but by the same token it demonstrates how inadequate that notion is to explain the genesis of any genuine re-creation. 'The making of *Sense and Sensibility*', declares the dustjacket of Emma Thompson's screenplay, 'has been a labour of love'.[42] Such claims, reiterated in the publicity surrounding other Austen adaptations, in themselves mean little: much 'love' of Jane

Austen is a version of what Freud called 'transference love' – an artefact of the consulting room, which needs be transcended and discarded if the patient is to learn to live. Fidelity is what the traditionalist producers of *Jane Austen in Manhattan* pretend to, and the result is a mummified production. But it probably means something when the director reveals in interviews that she was commissioned to make the film, and that on reading the novel, she could not figure out why Austen wrote such a shy, reticent central character.[43] In other words, initial love for, and understanding of, *Mansfield Park* seem, as one views the film, to be missing, another way of putting an argument I have made in Chapter 4. The film seems to embody everything a structuralist critique of a revision would recognise. But in replacing Austen's Fanny with an upbeat, proto-feminist figure, in finding in Austen's austere conservative prose a Gothic darkness – ruins, cruelty, storm, incest, secrets – the movie actively resists the novel's most disturbing aspects, unsettling, among other things, to the popular conception of a 'romantic', safely painless 'Jane Austen'. The comfort of a contemporary audience will hardly be disturbed by being shown that slavery is evil, or that a patriarch is corrupt. There *is* a heart of darkness in Austen but it lies elsewhere, often in the psychological violence of woman against woman, like Mrs Norris's persecution of Fanny, or Emma's half-inexplicable burst of spite. Rozema's film is not then 'subversive' in the sense that much Jane Austen criticism can claim to be, a perception of that subversion within Austen's texts which allows the artist to preserve her real, true self.

I began this book with Helen Fielding's commentary, in the *Diary of Bridget Jones*, on popular versions of the classics. The second volume of the Diary, *Bridget Jones: the Edge of Reason*, contains an even more cheeky reworking of Jane Austen. Appearing the same year, it offers a contrast to Patricia Rozema's treatment of *Mansfield Park* in being utterly different from, yet sympathetic to, the original. In a chapter called 'Persuasion', the role of Lady Russell is taken by Bridget's friends, Jude and Shazzer. Rather against her will they get Bridget to break off her relationship with Mark Darcy, who's been seen with another woman, Rebecca. Despite Mark's sleeping with Rebecca (Bridget has an awful moment when she finds the Newcastle United boxer shorts she bought him for Valentine's Day neatly folded on Rebecca's bedspread), he is still keen on Bridget. But every time he comes near her and tries to tell her so, another man gets in the way, particularly a colleague of his called – no surprises – Giles Benwick. Benwick is depressed by his wife's seeking a divorce, and Bridget is helping him find support and consolation in self-help books. Then the next day, sitting behind a hedge in the garden, Bridget overhears a conversation between Rebecca and Mark. 'If I decide I love someone then nothing will stand in my way', declares Rebecca. After lunch, despite Mark's protests – 'I trust my own judgement' – she jumps off a bridge. The water isn't deep enough and she twists her ankle. Bridget reaches in her bag for the mobile phone and rings for a doctor.[44]

Like the references to *Pride and Prejudice* in Nora Ephron's script for *You've Got Mail* (1998)[45] the borrowings are entertaining, unpretentious, and part of an authentic contemporary context in which lots of other amusing things occur. Such 'use' of Austen is quite different from the sentimental and conventionally symbolic status attached to the name 'Jane Austen' and can accommodate, in the case of Ephron's script, the character Joe Fox's disparagement of the figure and text he is unwittingly re-enacting. (Where have we come across this before, I wonder?) But Jane Austen, as I have emphasised, is a writer who transcends comedy and romance, who engages the reader's deepest responses to the dilemmas of civil society. Helen Fielding's books have none of the tautness of structure and not much of the underlying personal urgency of Austen's. But she is not prone to the fantasy of inhabiting Jane Austen's mind or imagination, like the writers of biographies, prequels and sequels: instead her novels engage familiarly with their originals, treating them cavalierly as only those who are secure in their relation to the mother text can. Like Austen's own handling of earlier authors, including Shakespeare, they are expressions of affectionate authorial consanguinity, having fun with, and even recreating, Jane Austen.

Notes

INTRODUCTION   'JANE AUSTEN' AND JANE AUSTEN

1 The script for *Metropolitan* is in Whit Stillman, *Barcelona & Metropolitan: Tales of Two Cities*, Boston, Mass. and London: Faber, 1994. The text on p. 177 differs slightly from the filmed version.

2 Helen Fielding, *Bridget Jones's Diary*, London: Picador, 1997; Helen Fielding, *Bridget Jones: the Edge of Reason*, London: Picador, 1999.

3 Fielding, *Diary*, p.101.

4 Harriet Hawkins, *Classics and Trash*, Hemel Hempstead: Harvester Wheatsheaf, 1990.

5 Michèle Willems uses this term to define the 'concessions' needed in translating from one system of signs (the Shakespeare play) to another (television); 'Verbal-Visual, Verbal-Pictorial or Textual-Televisual? Reflections on the BBC Shakespeare series', in Antony Davies and Stanley Wells, eds., *Shakespeare and the Moving Image*, Cambridge: Cambridge University Press, 1994, pp. 69–85, p. 72.

6 Emma Tennant, *Pemberley*, London: Hodder and Stoughton, 1993; Janet Aylmer, *Darcy's Story from Pride and Prejudice*, Bath: Copperfield Books, 1996.

7 See, for example, the series of pictures of Salisbury Cathedral in Stewart Brand, *How Buildings Learn; What Happens After They're Built*, revised paperback edn, London: Pheonix Illustrated, 1997, pp. 36–37.

8 Meagan Morris, 'Feminism, reading postmodernism', in Thomas Docherty, ed., *Postmodernism: a Reader*, Hemel Hempstead: Harvester Wheatsheaf, 1993, p. 371, originally published in *The Pirate's Fiancée*, London: Verso, 1988.

9 Linda Troost and Sayre Greenfield, eds., *Jane Austen in Hollywood*, Lexington, Ky.: University Press of Kentucky, 1998; Virginia L. Macdonald and Andrew F. Macdonald, eds., *Jane Austen on Screen*, Cambridge: Cambridge University Press, forthcoming.

10 Kristin Flieger Samuelian, '"Piracy Is Our Only Option": Postfeminist Intervention in *Sense and Sensibility*', in Troost and Greenfield, *Jane Austen in Hollywood*, pp. 148–58, p. 150.

11 Rebecca Dickson, 'Misrepresenting Jane Austen's Ladies: Revising Texts (and History) to Sell Films', in Troost and Greenfield, *Jane Austen in Hollywood*, pp. 44–57, p. 56.

12 Devoney Looser mentions that Amy Heckerling refused to alter *Clueless* for Twentieth-Century Fox. 'Paramount stepped in and the film was made with its focus intact' ('Feminist Implications of the Silver Screen Austen', Troost and Greenfield, *Jane Austen in Hollywood*, p .168).

13 'You will be glad to hear that every copy of S&S is sold & that it has brought me £140 besides the copyright, if that sh^d be of any value – I have now therefore written myself into £250 – which only makes me long for more' (Jane Austen, letter of 3 July 1813). Many similar remarks are quoted in Jan Fergus's *Jane Austen, a Literary Life*, London: Macmillan, 1991.

14 Andrew Dudley, *Concepts in Film Theory*, Oxford: Oxford University Press, 1984, Chapter 6, 'Adaptation', p. 103.

15 Walter Benjamin, 'The task of the translator', in *Illuminations*, London: Collins, 1973, p. 69.

16 Pierre Bourdieu, *Distinction*, trans. Richard Nice, Cambridge, Mass.: Harvard University Press, 1984.

17 W. J. T. Mitchell, 'The violence of public art: *Do The Right Thing*', in *Picture Theory*, Chicago, Ill.: University of Chicago Press, 1994, p. 375.

18 'The writer can only imitate a gesture that is always anterior, never original. His only power is to mix writings' (Roland Barthes, 'The Death of the Author' [1968], in Stephen Heath, ed., *Image Music Text*, London: Flamingo [1977] 1984, p. 146).

19 Fielding, *Diary*, p. 102.

20 Winnicott's phrase actually applies to 'transitional phenomena' rather than works of art. 'An essential part of my formulation of transitional phenomena is that we agree never to make the challenge to the baby: did you create this object, or did you find it conveniently lying around?' ('The Location of Cultural Experience', in *Playing and Reality* [1971], London and New York: Routledge, 1991, p. 96.).

21 See, for example, the interviews collected in Anne Clancier and Jeannine Kalmanovich, *Winnicott and Paradox, from Birth to Creation*, trans. Alan Sheridan, London: Tavistock, 1987.

22 Jacques Lacan, 'The Freudian Unconscious and Ours', in Jacques-Alain Miller, ed., *The Four Fundamental Concepts of Psychoanalysis*, Harmondsworth: Penguin Education, 1979, p. 21.

23 Mary Ann Doane, 'Sublimation and the psychoanalysis of the aesthetic', *Femmes Fatales: Feminism, Film Theory and Psychoanalysis*, New York and London: Routledge, 1991, pp. 249–67.

24 See, for example, Meredith Skura, *The Literary Uses of the Psychoanalytic Process*, New Haven, Conn.: Yale University Press, 1981, pp. 185–90.

25 Stephen Mitchell, *Hope and Dread in Psychoanalysis*, New York: Basic Books, 1993, p. 9.

26 Jan Kott, *Shakespeare, Our Contemporary*, trans. Boleslaw Taborski, preface by Peter Brook, 2nd edn., rev., London: Methuen, 1967.

27 *Mansfield Park*, Chapter 43.

28 Eve Kosofsky Sedgwick, *Tendencies*, Durham, N.C.: Duke University Press, 1993, pp. 109–29.

29 Witold Rybczynski, *Home: a Short History of an Idea*, New York: Viking Penguin, 1986, pp. 120–21.

30 Andrew Davies, *B. Monkey*, London: Minerva, 1993, p. 44.

31 I write in Australia, where such prejudices are often acute. I take these issues up briefly in the discussion of Patricia Rozema's film of *Mansfield Park* in the concluding chapter.

32 Sedgwick, *Tendencies*, p. 125

33 David Lodge, *Changing Places, a Tale of Two Campuses*, [1975] London: Penguin, 1978, p. 213.

34 Howard Mills, *Working with Shakespeare*, Hemel Hempstead: Harvester Wheatsheaf, 1993, p. 13.

35 Nigel Nicolson, *The World of Jane Austen*, London: Weidenfeld and Nicolson, 1991, p. 79.

36 Lodge, *Changing Places*, p. 250.

37 Reginald Farrer, 'Jane Austen, ob. July 18 1817', *Quarterly Review* 452 (July 1917), p. 5.

38 See for instance, G. M. Polya, *Jane Austen and the Black Hole of British History*, privately published, Melbourne, 1998. Polya coins the term 'Austenization' for the denial of historical atrocities.

39 See Stephen Greenblatt's opening to *Shakespearian Negotiations: the Circulation of Energy in Renaissance England*, Oxford: Clarendon Paperbacks, 1990, p. 1.

I   IMAGINING JANE AUSTEN'S LIFE

1 Henry James, *The Art of the Novel*, Critical Prefaces, with an Introduction by Richard P. Blackmur, New York: Scribner's, 1934, p. 164.

2 Constance Pilgrim, *Dear Jane: a Biographical Study*, Durham: Pentland Press, 1991.

3 Pilgrim, *Dear Jane*, p. 19. R. W. Chapman, 'Romance', in *Jane Austen: Facts and Problems*, Oxford: Clarendon Press, 1948, p. 68, covers this episode. See also W. Austen Leigh, R. A. Austen-Leigh and Deirdre Le Faye, *Jane Austen; a Family Record*, London: British Library, 1989, pp. 126–27.

4 Pilgrim, *Dear Jane*, p. 50.

5 Deirdre Le Faye, ed., *Jane Austen's Letters*, 3rd edn, Oxford: Oxford University Press, 1995. (Preface to the 3rd edn, p. xv.)

6 J. E. Austen-Leigh, *A Memoir of Jane Austen by her Nephew James Edward Austen-Leigh*, R. W. Chapman, ed., Introduction by Fay Weldon, London: Folio Society, 1989, p. xi.

7 Le Faye, *A Family Record*, London: The British Library, 1989.

8 Pilgrim, *Dear Jane*, p. 83.

9 W. J. Bate and Albrecht B. Strauss, eds., *The Yale Edition of the Works of Samuel Johnson*, vol. III, *The Rambler*, New Haven and London: Yale University Press, 1969, p. 11.

10 See Jennifer Scott's useful *After Jane, a Review of the Continuations and*

Completions of Jane Austen's Novels, privately printed, 1998, p. 31.

11 Le Faye, *A Family Record*, p. 181.

12 David Nokes, *Jane Austen: a Life*, London: Fourth Estate, 1997, p. 257.

13 Katherine Mansfield, *Novels and Novelists*, London: Constable, 1930, p. 304.

14 Among the more recent are: Jane Aiken Hodge, *The Double Life of Jane Austen*, London: Hodder and Stoughton, 1972; Joan Rees, *Jane Austen: Woman and Writer*, New York: St Martin's Press, 1976; David Cecil, *A Portrait of Jane Austen*, London: Constable, 1978; John Halperin, *The Life of Jane Austen*, Baltimore, Md.: Johns Hopkins University Press, 1984; Park Honan, *Jane Austen, her Life* [1987], rev. edn, 1997; Jan Fergus: *Jane Austen: a Literary Life*, London: Macmillan, 1991; Valerie Grosvenor Myers, *Obstinate Heart: Jane Austen, a Biography*, London: Michael O'Mara, 1997; Nokes, *Jane Austen, a Life*, Claire Tomalin, *Jane Austen, a Life*, London: Viking, 1997.

15 For example, Brian Wilks, *The Life and Times of Jane Austen*, London: Chancellor Press, 1984; Susan Watkins, *Jane Austen's Town and Country Style*, New York: Rizzoli, 1990; Nigel Nicolson, *The World of Jane Austen*, London: Weidenfeld and Nicolson, 1991; Mavis Batey, *Jane Austen and the English Landscape*, London: Barn Elms, 1996.

16 Terry Castle, 'Sister-Sister', *London Review of Books*, 5 August 1995, p. 3.

17 Julian Wilmot Wynne, *Jane Austen and Sigmund Freud: an interpretation*, London: Plume Publications, 1998, p. x.

18 J. E. Austen-Leigh, *Memoir of Jane Austen* by her nephew James Edward Austen-Leigh, ed. R. W Chapman, Oxford: Clarendon Press, 1926, p. 102.

19 In *A Room of One's Own* Virginia Woolf took it as emblematic of the confinement of the female writer; upon her idea Sandra M. Gilbert and Susan Gubar build their argument about Jane Austen, 'Jane Austen's Cover Story'. Austen 'hides a distinctly unladylike outlook behind the "cover" or "blotter" of parody' in the juvenilia (p. 153): in her mature novels Austen shows her heroines submitting to male authority in order to survive, but this is a 'cover' for the 'rebellious anger' detected elsewhere in the novels (p. 169). See Sandra M. Gilbert and Susan Gubar, *The Madwoman in the Attic: the Woman Writer and the Nineteenth-Century Literary Imagination*, New Haven, Conn.: Yale University Press, 1979.

20 Winnicott gives many accounts of this process, as in, for instance, 'Ego Distortion in Terms of True and False Self' [1960] in D. W. Winnicott, *The Maturational Process and the Facilitating Environment, Studies in the Theory of Emotional Development*, London: Karnac, 1990, p. 145–48.

21 Park Honan, *Authors' Lives: on Literary Biography and the Arts of Language*, New York: St Martin's Press, 1990, p. xiii.

22 Richard Holmes, *Footsteps, Adventures of a Romantic Biographer*, Harmondsworth: Penguin Books, 1986, p. 67.

23 Elizabeth Jenkins, *Jane Austen* [1938], London: Cardinal, 1973, pp. 42–43.

24 Defined in the *OED* as 'a thin soft silk used for linings'.

25 Peter Gay, ed., *The Freud Reader*, London: Vintage, 1995, p. 442.

26 F. Robert Rodman, ed., *The Spontaneous Gesture: Selected Letters of*

D. W. Winnicott, London and Cambridge, Mass.: Harvard University Press, 1987, p. 123.

27 Victor Turner, 'Liminality and Communitas', in *The Ritual Process; Structure and Anti-Structure* [1969], New York: Aldine de Gruyter, 1995, Chapter 3, pp. 94–130; F. R. Leavis, *The Living Principle*, London: Chatto and Windus, 1975, pp. 36, 62.

28 Bernard Crick, Introduction, 'Biography and Character', in *George Orwell, a Life*, London: Secker and Warburg, rev. edn, 1981, Introduction, p. xxiii.

29 *Ibid.*

30 David Ellis, *Literary Lives; Biography and the Search for Understanding*, Edinburgh: Edinburgh University Press, 2000, pp. 13, 12 and *passim*.

31 Le Faye, *A Family Record*, pp. 83–84.

32 D. W. Harding provides cogent reasons for thinking that Cassandra's memory misled her and that it was *Pride and Prejudice*, not *Sense and Sensibility*, which was elaborated from an earlier manuscript in letter form. 'Appendix A. The supposed letter form of *Sense and Sensibility*', in *Regulated Hatred and Other Essays on Jane Austen*, London: Athlone Press, 1998, pp. 211–17.

33 Jenkins, *Jane Austen*, p. 61.

34 Among many examples: 'Jane Austen clearly wrote the book [*Sense and Sensibility*] in a foul mood: the nastiness is everywhere' (Halperin, *Life of Jane Austen*, p. 85); 'That Mrs Norris is a malicious portrait of the resented aunt of the Austens is obvious' (p. 238). When Jane Austen was accused of having 'pourtrayed' an acquaintance as Mr Collins, she is said to have expressed 'a very great dread of what she called "such an invasion of the social proprieties"' (Le Faye, *A Family Record*, p. 210.)

35 Halperin, *Life of Jane Austen*, p. 110.

36 Nokes, *Jane Austen: a Life*, pp. 5–6.

37 'Realism' in this, non-doctrinal, sense is defined in one standard text, Watt's *The Rise of the Novel*, as 'the premise or primary convention, that the novel is a full and authentic report of human experience, and is therefore under an obligation to satisfy its reader with such details of the story as the individuality of the actors concerned, the particularities of the times and places of their actions, details which are presented through a more largely referential use of language than is common in other literary forms' (Ian Watt, *The Rise of the Novel: Studies in Defoe, Richardson and Fielding*, Berkeley, Calif.: University of California Press, 1964, p. 32).

38 Le Faye, *Letters*, p. 68 (Letter 29).

39 Quoted by Leela Gandhi in a review of Kathryn Hughes, *George Eliot: the Last Victorian*, in *The Australian's Review of Books*, May 1999, p. 17.

40 Henry James, 'The Art of Fiction' [1884], in Morris Shapira, ed., *Henry James: Selected Literary Criticism*, London: Heinemann, 1963, p. 51.

41 Deirdre Le Faye, *Newsletter of the Jane Austen Society*, October 1998, p. 9.

42 D. W. Winnicott, *Playing and Reality* [1971], London and New York: Routledge, 1994, p. 51.

43 Le Faye, *Letters*, pp.328–29.

44 Honan, *Authors' Lives*, pp. 6–7.
45 Honan, 'Richardson's Influence', in *Authors' Lives*, pp. 74–84, p. 78.
46 Honan, *Jane Austen: her Life*, pp. 191–96.
47 Honan, *Jane Austen: her Life*, p. 120.
48 For examples, *ibid.*, pp. 46 and 129.
49 This occurs too in an earlier biography, Hodge's *Double Life* (1972).
50 Tomalin, *Jane Austen: a Life*, p. 121.
51 See, for example, Elizabeth Waites, 'Transference Dimensions of Biography', *Psychoanalytic Review*, 82: 1, 1995, pp. 107–24.
52 James, 'The New Novel' [1914], in *Henry James, Selected Literary Criticism*, p. 317.
53 Bruce Redford, ed., *The Letters of Samuel Johnson*, The Hyde Edition, Oxford: Clarendon Press, 1992, vol. III, pp. 89–90.
54 Nadia Radovici, *A Youthful Love?: Jane Austen and Tom Lefroy*, Braunton: Merlin Books, 1995, pp. 14–15.
55 *Ibid.*, pp. 11, 14–15, 7, 29–30.
56 Le Faye, *A Family Record*, p. 85.
57 Nokes, *Jane Austen: a Life*, p. 158.
58 *Ibid.*, p. 158–59, 161.
59 Honan, *Jane Austen: her Life*, pp. 106–07.
60 Le Faye, *Letters*, p. 2.
61 Honan, *Jane Austen: her Life*, pp. 107–08.
62 See also the remarks of John Worthen on Tomalin's earlier life of Ellen Ternan, in 'The Necessary Ignorance of a Biographer', in John Batchelor, ed., *The Art of Literary Biography*, Oxford: Clarendon Press, 1995, pp. 227–44, p. 242.
63 The best of these are: Fergus, *Jane Austen: a Literary Life*; Oliver MacDonagh, *Jane Austen: Real and Imagined Worlds*, New Haven, Conn. and London: Yale University Press, 1991; and Irene Collins, *Jane Austen and the Clergy*, London: Hambledon Press, 1994.
64 Castle's original review, headed 'Sister-Sister', appeared in *The London Review of Books*, 3 August 1995, pp. 3–6.
65 Jocelyn Harris, 'Jane Austen and the Burden of the (Male) Past: The Case Re-examined', in Devoney Looser, ed., *Jane Austen and Discourses of Feminism*, New York: St Martin's Press, 1995, p. 98.
66 *London Review of Books*, 5 October 1995, p. 4.
67 Nigel Nicolson, *The World of Jane Austen*, London: Weidenfeld and Nicolson, 1991, p. 79.
68 Esther Sonnet, 'From *Emma* to *Clueless*: Taste, Pleasure and the Scene of History', in Deborah Cartmell and Imelda Whelehen, eds., *Adaptations: from Text to Screen, Screen to Text*, London and New York: Routledge, 1999, pp. 57–59, p. 59.
69 D. W. Winnicott, 'The Location of Cultural Experience', in *Playing and Reality* [1971], London: Routledge, 1991, pp. 95–103, p. 99.

2 RECREATING JANE AUSTEN: *JANE AUSTEN IN MANHATTAN, METROPOLITAN, CLUELESS*

1 Walter Benjamin, *Illuminations*, London: Collins, 1973, p. 255.

2 Adrienne Rich, 'When We Dead Awaken: Writing as Re-Vision', in *On Lies, Secrets and Silence, Selected Prose 1966–1978*, New York: Norton, 1979, p. 35.

3 See Susan Wiseman, 'The Family Tree Motel: Subliming Shakespeare in *My Own Private Idaho*', in Linda E. Boose and Richard Burt, eds., *Shakespeare, the Movie, Popularising the Plays on Film, TV and Video*, London and New York: Routledge, 1997, pp. 225–39.

4 Caroline Cakebread, 'Remembering *King Lear* in Jane Smiley's *A Thousand Acres*', in Christy Desmet and Robert Sawter, eds., *Shakespeare and Appropriation*, London and New York: Routledge, 1999.

5 I take this word from Kate Chedgzoy, *Shakespeare's Queer Children: Sexual Politics and Contemporary Culture*, Manchester and New York: Manchester University Press, 1995, who notes the 'many writers and artists from culturally oppressed or marginalised groups who have succeeded in plundering Shakespeare's texts to their own ends' (p. 21). Other books which discuss contemporary revisions of Shakespeare include Peter Erickson, *Rewriting Shakespeare, Rewriting Ourselves*, Berkeley, Calif. and London: University of California Press, 1991, and Marianne Novy, ed., *Cross-Cultural Performances: Differences in Women's Re-visions of Shakespeare*, Urbana, Ill.: University of Illinois Press, 1993. See also Antony Davies, *Filming Shakespeare's Plays*, Cambridge: Cambridge University Press, 1988.

6 Peter Erickson, 'Adrienne Rich's Revision of Shakespeare', in *Rewriting Shakespeare*, pp. 146–66.

7 Michael Dobson, *The Making of the National Poet, Shakespeare, Adaptation and Authorship, 1660–1769*, Oxford: Clarendon Press, 1992, pp. 164–81.

8 The first typology is by Geoffrey Wagner (*The Novel and the Cinema*, Rutherford, N.J.: Fairleigh Dickson University Press, 1975); the second by Dudley Andrew (*Concepts in Film Theory*, Oxford and New York: Oxford University Press, 1984). See R. Giddings, K. Selby and C. Wensley, *Screening the Novel: the Theory and Practice of Literary Dramatization*, London: Macmillan, 1990, Chapter 1, 'The Literature/Screen debate: an overview', pp. 1–27.

9 Howard Mills, *Working with Shakespeare*, Hemel Hempstead: Harvester Wheatsheaf, 1993, p. 217. See also Jean Marsden, ed., *The Appropriation of Shakespeare: Post Renaissance Reconstructions of the Works and the Myth*, Hemel Hempstead: Harvester Wheatsheaf, 1991.

10 Brian Southam, ed. and transcribed by, *Jane Austen's 'Sir Charles Grandison'*, foreword by Lord David Cecil, Oxford: Clarendon Press, 1980, p. 17.

11 *Ibid.*

12 Jocelyn Harris, 'Jane Austen and the Burden of the (Male) Past: The Case Re-examined', in Devoney Looser, ed., *Jane Austen and Discourses of Feminism*, New York: St Martin's Press, 1995, pp. 87–100, p. 92.

13 Brian McFarlane, *Novel to Film, an Introduction to the Theory of Adaptation*, Oxford: Clarendon Press, 1996, pp. 26–27.

14 Howard D. Weinbrot, *The Formal Strain: Studies in Augustan Imitation and Satire*, Chicago, Ill. and London: University of Chicago Press, 1969, p. 21.
15 *Ibid.*, p. 29.
16 Niall Rudd, ed., *Johnson's Juvenal*, Bristol: Bristol Classical Press, 1981.
17 Harold Bloom, *The Anxiety of Influence, a Theory of Poetry*, New York: Oxford University Press, 1973.
18 *Ibid.*, p. 30.
19 *Ibid.*, p. 11. Sandra M. Gilbert and Susan Gubar (*The Madwoman in the Attic: the Woman Writer and the Nineteenth-Century Literary Imagination*, New Haven, Conn.: Yale University Press, 1979) extend Bloom's Freudian paradigm to women writers, arguing that the anxiety of influence transmutes in the female writer to 'an even more primary "anxiety of authorship"'' (p. 48).
20 Harris, 'Jane Austen and the Burden of the (Male) Past', pp. 88–89.
21 Jessica Benjamin, *The Bonds of Love, Psychoanalysis, Feminism, and the Problem of Domination* [1988], London: Virago Press, 1990, p. 30.
22 'The Most of It' (1942).
23 D. W. Winnicott, 'The Use of an Object and Relating through Identifica-tions', *Playing and Reality* [1971], London and New York: Routledge, 1991, pp. 86–94.
24 Sigmund Freud, 'Observations on Transference-Love' [1915], *Standard Edi-tion of the Works of Sigmund Freud*, James Strachey *et al.*, eds., vol. xii.
25 Adam Phillips, *Winnicott*, London: Fontana Modern Masters Series, 1988, p. 131.
26 'There to receive the communication', like so many of Winnicott's phases, disarmingly throw-away, means 'able to take the other's feelings on board, to experience them, without being disturbed by them'. It resembles his colleague, W. R. Bion's notion of 'containing'. I discuss this further in Chapter 6.
27 Jessica Benjamin, *Like Subjects, Love Objects, Essays on Recognition and Sexual Difference*, New Haven, Conn. and London: Yale University Press, 1995, p. 40.
28 Bloom, *Anxiety*, p. 51. No reference is given.
29 Peter Brooks, 'Changes in the Margins', *Psychoanalysis and Storytelling*, Oxford: Blackwells, 1994, Chapter 2.
30 Southam, 'Introduction', in *Jane Austen's 'Sir Charles Grandison'*, p. 10.
31 McFarlane, *Novel to Film*, pp. 9–10; H. Elizabeth Ellington, 'A Correct Taste in Landscape', in Troost and Greenfield, *Jane Austen in Hollywood*, p. 108; Julian Wilmot Wynne, *Jane Austen and Freud: an Interpretation*, London: Plume Publications, 1999, p. 162.
32 Morris Beja, *Film and Literature*, New York: Longman 1979, quoted in McFarlane, *Novel to Film*, p. 9.
33 Esther Sonnet, 'From *Emma* to *Clueless*, Taste, Pleasure and the Scene of History', in Deborah Cartmell and Imelda Whelehen, eds., *Adaptations: from Text to Screen, Screen to Text*, London and New York: Routledge, 1999, pp. 51–62, p. 60.

34 Sue Parrill, 'Metaphors of Control: Physicality in *Emma* and *Clueless*', *Persuasions On-Line* 20: 1, p. 3.
35 James Servin, 'Totally Clueless', *Vogue Australia*, October 1995, pp. 129–30.
36 Carol M. Dole, 'Austen, Class, and the American Market', in Linda Troost and Sayre Greenfield, eds., *Jane Austen in Hollywood*, Lexington, Ky.: University Press of Kentucky, 1998, pp. 48–78, p. 74.
37 I discuss the absence of Miss Bates from *Clueless* further in Chapter 6.
38 I owe my understanding of voice-over in *Clueless* to a paper by Laura Carroll, forthcoming in *Film and Literature Quarterly*.
39 *Minor Works*, ed. R. W. Chapman, Oxford: Clarendon Press, 1954, p. 97. The references to films often resemble the wild allusions of Austen's juvenilia. 'Love and Freindship' at one moment parodies Ophelia's madness, at another Boswell's *Tour to the Hebrides*. *Clueless* at one moment accompanies a shot of a mobile phone with the apocalyptic chords of 'Thus Spake Zarathustra' used in *2001*, and Cher's climactic distress is accompanied by visual reminders of Audrey Hepburn in *Breakfast at Tiffany's*.
40 Lesley Stern, '*Emma* in Los Angeles: Remaking the Book and the City', in James Navemore, ed., *Film Adaptation*, New Brunswick, N.J.: Rutgers University Press, 2000, pp. 221–38.
41 'In Defense of Mixed Cinema', in André Bazin, *What is Cinema?*, selected and trans. Hugh Gray, Berkeley, Calif.: University of California Press, 1967, p. 67. I owe this reference to Laura Carroll.
42 Sonnet, 'From *Emma* to *Clueless*', p. 61.

3 AN ENGLISHWOMAN'S CONSTITUTION: JANE AUSTEN AND SHAKESPEARE

1 Early 1770s: quoted in Michael Dobson, *The Making of the National Poet: Shakespeare, Adaptation and Authorship 1660–1769*, Oxford: Clarendon Press, 1992, p. 173. Murphy is parodying Garrick.
2 The images were the Martin Droeshout engraving of Shakespeare first published on the title page of the first Folio (1623) and the Victorian engraving of Jane Austen from the sketch by her sister, c. 1810. S. Schoenbaum calls the Droeshout 'the most hackneyed icon in the English literary tradition', 'Artist's images of Shakespeare', in W. Habicht, D. J. Palmer and R. Pringle, eds., *Images of Shakespeare*, Delaware, Md.: University of Delaware Press, 1988, p. 30.
3 B. C. Southam, ed., *Jane Austen, the Critical Heritage, 1811–1870*, London: Routledge and Kegan Paul, 1968, pp. 97–98.
4 *Ibid.*, p. 98.
5 Thomas Babington Macaulay, 'Madame d'Arblay', in *Critical and Historical Essays* [1903], arranged by A. J. Grieve, Everyman's Library: London: Dent, 1967, pp. 563–612, p. 603; originally in the *Edinburgh Review*, 76, January 1843.
6 Southam, *Critical Heritage*, p. 125.

7 Quoted in the Introduction, Southam, *Critical Heritage*, p. 24.

8 A. C. Bradley, *A Miscellany*, London: Macmillan, 1929, p. 32. Bradley's words seem to be echoed by Virginia Woolf's description of Austen as being 'as inscrutable in her small way as Shakespeare in his vast one' (*Collected Essays*, vol. II, p. 275, quoted by Janet Todd, 'Who's Afraid of Jane Austen?', in *Gender, Art and Death*, New York: Continuum 1991, p. 162). R. Brimley Johnson, in *Jane Austen*, London: Sheed and Ward, 1927, writes that '[e]very critic must find occasion, it seems, of comparing Jane Austen with Will Shakespeare' and suggests that she displays a similar freedom in her use of sources (p. 117).

9 Southam, *Critical Heritage*, p. 260.

10 *Ibid.*, p. 256.

11 Brian Southam, ed., *Jane Austen: the Critical Heritage volume II: 1870–1940*, London: Routledge, 1987, p. 246.

12 Brian Southam, 'Janeities and Anti-Janeites', in J. David Grey, ed., *The Jane Austen Handbook*, London: Athlone Press, 1986, p. 239.

13 See also Edmund Wilson, 'A Long Talk about Jane Austen', in Ian Watt, ed., *Jane Austen: a Collection of Critical Essays*, Englewood Cliffs, N.J.: Prentice Hall, 1963, p. 35.

14 F. B. Pinion, *Jane Austen Companion*, London: Macmillan, 1973, p. 179. Pinion suggests that 'the music, the moonlight and the inner harmony' are matched in the two texts. K. C. Phillips, (*Jane Austen's English*, London: Andre Deutsch, 1970), points out that the 'Shakespearean' '*in* such a night as this' occurs in *Northanger Abbey*: 'I do not know that, in such a night as this, I could have answered for my courage' (p. 167). F. W. Bradbrook (*Jane Austen and her Predecessors*, Cambridge: Cambridge University Press, 1966, p. 107) suggests the mediating influence of Radcliffe.

15 Park Honan, *Jane Austen, her Life*, London: Weidenfield and Nicholson, 1997, p. 312.

16 W. K. Wimsatt, ed., *Dr Johnson on Shakespeare*, Harmondsworth: Penguin Shakespeare Library, 1969, p. 57, fn 36, p. 152.

17 Isobel Armstrong, *Mansfield Park*, Harmondsworth: Penguin Critical Studies, 1988, p. 98.

18 Roger Gard, *Jane Austen's Novels: the Art of Clarity*, New Haven, Conn. and London: Yale University Press, 1992, pp. 182–86. The quotation is from p.13. Claire Tomalin compares *Mansfield Park* with *The Merchant of Venice* but only to suggest how 'Shakespeare's play and Austen's novel are both so alive and flexible as works of art that they can be interpreted now one way, now another' (Claire Tomalin, *Jane Austen: a Life*, London: Viking, 1997, p. 229). 'Like *Mansfield Park*, Shakespearean drama characteristically pivots upon the performance of a play within a play', claims Nina Auerbach, who compares Fanny Price's reluctance to act with Hamlet's ('Jane Austen's Dangerous Charm', in Judy Simons, ed., *Mansfield Park and Persuasion*, London: Macmillan, 1997, p. 278).

19 Gard, *Jane Austen's Novels*, pp. 77–78. This resemblance was also pointed out by Honan, *Jane Austen, her Life*, p. 278.

20 Armstrong, *Mansfield Park*.

21 Isobel Armstrong, *Sense and Sensibility*, Harmondsworth: Penguin Critical Studies, 1994, pp. 8–9, 64.

22 Jocelyn Harris, *Jane Austen's Art of Memory*, Cambridge: Cambridge University Press, 1989; Jocelyn Harris, 'Jane Austen and the burden of the (male) past: the case reexamined', in Devoney Looser, ed., *Jane Austen and Discourses of Feminism*, New York: St Martin's Press, 1995, pp. 87–100. Harris claims that '*Emma* draws all its main elements from *Midsummer Night's Dream*' (p. 93). Clare Tomalin, on the other hand, finds that the parallels between *Mansfield Park* and *A Midsummer Night's Dream* are 'obvious' (*Jane Austen: a Life*, p. 329).

23 Among many other studies: Bradbrook, *Jane Austen and her Predecessors*; Harris, *Jane Austen's Art of Memory*; Park Honan, 'Richardson's Influence' and 'Sterne and Jane Austen's Talent', in *Authors' Lives: On Literary Biography and the Arts of Language*, New York: St Martin's Press, 1990, pp. 73–94; Isobel Grundy, 'Jane Austen and Literary Traditions' in Edward Copeland and Juliet McMaster, eds., *The Cambridge Companion to Jane Austen*, Cambridge: Cambridge University Press, 1997, pp. 189–210.

24 'She is the daughter of Dr Johnson', C. S. Lewis, 'A Note on Jane Austen', in Ian Watt, ed., *Jane Austen: a Collection of Critical Essays*, Englewood Cliffs, N.J.: Prentice Hall, 1963, p. 34; Peter L. De Rose, *Jane Austen and Samuel Johnson*, Washington, D.C.: University Press of America, 1980; Claudia L. Johnson, 'The "Twilight of Probability": Uncertainty and Hope in *Sense and Sensibility*', *Philological Quarterly* 62, 1983, pp. 171–86; Claudia L. Johnson, 'The "Operations of Time, and the Changes of the Human Mind"': Jane Austen and Dr Johnson Again', *Modern Language Quarterly* 44: 1, 1983, pp. 28–38. I discuss Austen's indebtedness to the Johnson of Boswell and Mrs Piozzi's memoirs in *Jane Austen's 'Dear Dr Johnson'*, The Eighth Fleeman Memorial Lecture, Melbourne: Johnson Society of Australia, 2001.

25 Armstrong, *Sense and Sensibility*, p. 15.

26 Sigmund Freud, *The Interpretation of Dreams* [1900], in *The Standard Edition of the Complete Psychological Works of Sigmund Freud*, trans. James Strachey, vols. IV and V, London: Hogarth Press and the Institute of Psycho-Analysis, 1953. Armstrong mentions neither Freud nor this text.

27 The number of plots being finite, and human relations being fairly constant, one might imagine similar relations between any Austen novel and any Shakespeare play. What about *Mansfield Park* and *King Lear*? After all, *Mansfield Park* contains brothers called Edmund and Tom: by a process of reversal, typical of the dream-work, Edmund the wicked brother of the play might become the benevolent figure, loyal to his father, of the novel; Edgar would then be hidden under the name of Tom, just as he is hidden under the name of Poor Tom in the play, 'such is the perverse inventiveness of the dream structure' (Armstrong, *Sense and Sensibility*, p. 16). Fanny is surely a shadowy reworking of Cordelia, the virginal right-thinking heroine who opposes the will, and braves the fury, of the patriarch, and is banished from

his domain to Portsmouth, just as Cordelia is banished to France. Maria and Julia are a transposed Goneril and Regan, who both desire Crawford, as the rapacious sisters desired Edmund. 'Never, never, never, he never will ucceed with me', Fanny cries. Can the attentive reader of Jane Austen fail to detect the text's allusion to *Lear* here?

28 Alice Chandler, ' "A Pair of Fine Eyes": Jane Austen's Treatment of Sex', in Harold Bloom, ed., *Jane Austen, Modern Critical Views*, New York: Chelsea House, 1986, pp. 27–42, p. 19.

29 For example, Darcy's comment that 'There is, I believe, in every disposition a tendency to some particular evil, a natural defect' refers, as Bradbrook points out, to Hamlet's soliloquy in Act I, scene 4 (Bradbrook, *Jane Austen and her Predecessors*, p. 72). It seems designed to suggest that bookishness of Darcy which is traceable in his reponse to Elizabeth discussed below, as well as in his remark about libraries (*Pride and Prejudice*, p. 38).

30 Harris, *Jane Austen's Art of Memory*, p. 169.

31 She is certainly (mis)quoting Shakespeare, but behind that may well be a reference to Johnson. 'Art thou so bare and full of wretchedness / And fear'st to die?' Romeo asks the Apothecary 'The world is not thy friend, nor the world's law' (*Romeo and Juliet*, v, ii, 68–69). Like Emma at this stage of her story, Romeo's speech has developed a grave and mature note. In *Rambler* 107, a correspondent, Amicus, applies his words to 'those forlorn creatures, the women of the town.' His letter is a plea for Christian charity to be extended to prostitutes, often the victims of the very men who scorn them. Jane Austen may simply be remembering Shakespeare, but the intervening application to exploited women certainly deepens the resonance of the quotation to Jane's situation. The letter in *Rambler* 107 is not in fact by Johnson, but by his old Lichfield friend Joseph Simpson.

32 Marianne Novy, *Engaging with Shakespeare: Responses of George Eliot and Other Women Novelists*, Athens, Ga. and London: University of Georgia Press, 1994, p. 23.

33 Jonathan Bate, *Shakespearean Constitutions: Politics, Theatre, Criticism 1730–1830*, Oxford: Clarendon Press, 1989.

34 I am indebted here to an unpublished paper by Marcia McClintock Folsom, 'Part of an Englishwoman's constitution.'

35 Mary Russell Mitford, *Recollections of a Literary Life: or, Books, Places, and People*, 3 vols., London: Richard Bentley, 1852, vol. II, p. 97, quoted by Valerie L. Gager, *Shakespeare and Dickens: the dynamics of influence*, Cambridge: Cambridge University Press, 1996, p. 32.

36 Margaret Anne Doody, Robert L. Mack and Peter Sabor, eds., *The Wanderer*, Oxford: World's Classics, 1991, p. 116. Sarah Harriet Burney, Burney's half-sister, similarly very often quotes Shakespeare in her letters. Lorna J. Clark, ed., *The Letters of Sarah Harriet Burney*, Athens, Ga. and London: University of Georgia Press, 1997.

37 Jonathan Bate, *The Genius of Shakespeare*, London: Picador, 1997, pp. 226–30.

38 Fanny 'was in the middle of a very fine speech of that man's' according to

Lady Bertram when they are interrupted by Crawford. She assures him 'as soon as he mentioned the name of Cardinal Wolsey, that he had got the very speech' (*Mansfield Park*, p. 304).

39 Valerie L. Gager, *Shakespeare and Dickens: the Dynamics of Influence*, Cambridge: Cambridge University Press, 1996. Marianne Novy, *Engaging with Shakespeare*, demonstrates George Eliot's lifelong preoccupation with Shakespeare. She makes the interesting point that Lewes developed the idea of a Shakespeare–Austen tradition into which he 'tried to insert' Eliot (pp. 23, 49).

40 Deirdre Le Faye, ed., *Jane Austen's Letters*, 3rd edn, Oxford: Oxford University Press, 1995, pp. 256, 257 (March 1814).

41 Gager, *Shakespeare and Dickens*, pp. 32–34. Gager's exemplary study includes a 115 page catalogue of Dickens's references to Shakespeare, pp. 251–369.

42 Phillipps, *Austen's English*, p. 200.

43 Jonathan Bate discusses the origins of the notion of influence in *Shakespeare and the English Romantic Imagination*, Oxford: Clarendon Press, 1986, pp. 22–23.

44 *Ibid.*, p. 180. Seneca writes that food 'passes into tissue and blood only when it has been changed from its original form. So it is with the food which nourishes our higher nature . . . we must digest it; otherwise it will merely enter the memory and not the reasoning power', Seneca, *Ad Lucilium Epistolae Morales*, 3 vols., London: Loeb Classical Library, Heinemann, 1920, vol. II, Letter 84, pp. 279–81.

45 Ben Jonson, *Timber, or Discoveries, being Observations on Men and Manners* [1641], London: Dent and Co., 1898, p. 119.

46 Freud, 'Negation' [1925], in *Standard Edition*, vol. XIX: 'The Ego and the Id and Other Works', p. 237.

47 More correctly, it is the fantasies accompanying feeding that are the model or blueprint for later fantasies of introjection. See R. D. Hinselwood, *A Dictionary of Kleinian Thought*, London: Free Association, 2nd edn, 1991, p. 333.

48 D. W. Winnicott, 'The Sense of Guilt' [1958], in *The Maturational Process and the Facilitating Environment, Studies in the Theory of Emotional Development* [1965], London: Karnac, 1990, p. 22.

49 D. W. Winnicott, 'The Use of an Object and Relating Through Identifications', in *Playing and Reality* [1971], London and New York: Routledge, 1991, pp. 86–94.

50 *Critical Review*, March 1813, in Southam, *Critical Heritage*, vol. I, p. 45.

51 As for example in their first exchange: 'Benedick: What, my dear Lady Disdain, are you yet living? / Beatrice: Is it possible disdain should die whilst she hath such food to feed it as Signor Benedick?' (*Much Ado About Nothing*, I, i, 112–13).

52 Novy, *Engaging with Shakespeare*, p. 26.

53 D. W. Winnicott, 'The Capacity to be Alone', in *The Maturational Process and the Facilitating Environment*, pp. 29–36.

54 Martin Price, Introduction, in M. Price, ed., *Dickens: a Collection of Critical Essays*, Engelwood Cliffs, N.J.: Prentice-Hall, 1967, p. 1.

55 Macaulay, 'Madame D'Arblay', in *Critical and Historical Essays*, pp. 605, 604.

56 'The striking and powerful contrasts in which Shakespeare abounds could not escape observation; but the use he makes of the principle of analogy to reconcile the greatest diversities of character and to maintain a continuity of feeling throughout, have not been sufficiently attended to' (William Hazlitt, *Characters of Shakespear's Plays*, in P. P. Howe, ed., *Complete Works*, 21 vols., vol. IV, p. 183, quoted by Bate, *Shakespearean Constitutions*, p. 151).

57 A. P. Rossiter, *Angel with Horns, and other Shakespearean Lectures*, ed., Graham Storey, London: Longmans, 1961, p. 52.

58 G. K. Hunter, *English Drama 1586–1642: the Age of Shakespeare*, Oxford: Clarendon Press, 1997, p. 392.

59 Graham Bradshaw, *Misrepresentations: Shakespeare and the Materialists*, Ithaca, N.Y. and London: Cornell University Press, 1993, pp. 63–80.

60 *Much Ado About Nothing*, II, i, 64–65.

61 Julia Prewitt Brown similarly comments on *Emma* as 'a system of interdependence' in which 'events and characters are likened to one another in subtle ways, like so many hues of one color'. Suggesting how 'transformation as repetition' is characteristic of the novel, she then alludes to its 'almost Shakespearean imaginative continuity'. See Julia Prewitt Brown, *Jane Austen's Novels, Social Change and Literary Form*, Cambridge, Mass.: Harvard University Press, 1979, pp. 104, 105.

62 Claudia L. Johnson notes the 'carefully elaborated cross-referencing' of the characters in *Pride and Prejudice*. 'The very method of the novel', she writes, 'obstructs the impulse to make a tidy moral' (*Jane Austen: Women Politics, and the Novel*, Chicago, Ill.: University of Chicago Press, 1988, p. 77).

4   FROM DRAMA, TO NOVEL, TO FILM: INWARDNESS IN *MANSFIELD PARK* AND *PERSUASION*

1 Grigory Kozintsev, *'King Lear', the Space of Tragedy: the Diary of a Film Director*, Mary Mackintosh, trans., London: Heinemann Educational, 1977, p. 55.

2 Frances Burney, *Camilla or A Picture of Youth* [1796], Edward A. Bloom and Lilian D. Bloom, eds., London: Oxford University Press, 1972, pp. 191–92.

3 In a note at the back of her copy in the Bodleian there are the pencilled words: 'Since this work went to the press a circumstance of some assistance to the happiness of Camilla has taken place, namely that Dr Marchmont has since died' (Margaret Anne Doody, *Frances Burney: the Life in the Works*, Cambridge: Cambridge University Press, 1988, pp. 272, 416, fn. 26). I take this to be a comment on the artificial stratagems and impediments that Burney contrives to block her heroine's progress towards happiness.

4 Marilyn Butler, *Jane Austen and the War of Ideas*, Oxford: Clarendon Press, new edn, 1987, p. 237.

5 Moreland Perkins discusses Austen's presentation of her heroines' inner

thoughts in *Reshaping the Sexes in 'Sense and Sensibility'*, Charlottesville, Va.: University Press of Virginia, 1998. He shows with great persuasiveness how intelligent Elinor Dashwood is, but his analyses of her thinking do not touch on such questions as sub-textual currents, or gaps in the sequence of ideas, which I go on to discuss in the case of Fanny Price. See especially Chapter 3, 'Elinor's Emotions', pp. 69–103.

6 Dorrit Cohn, *Transparent Minds: Narrative Modes for Presenting Consciousness in Fiction*, Princeton, N.J.: Princeton University Press, 1978. See especially Chapter 3, pp. 99–140. Cohn distinguishes three kinds of representation, 'psycho-narration', 'quoted monologue' and 'narrated monologue', all of which Jane Austen used, and all of which continually blend into each other in her writing. 'Psycho-narration summarizes diffuse feelings, needs, urges; narrated monologue shapes these inchoate reactions into virtual questions, exclamations, conjectures; quoted monologue distils moments of pointed self-address that may relate only distantly to the original emotion' (pp. 135–36). Austen tends to use different combinations of these modes according to the character: thus the presentation of Emma involves much more 'quoted monologue'; and less 'psycho-narration' than does the presentation of Fanny Price.

7 Raymond Williams offers a taxonomy in 'On Dramatic Dialogue and Monologue (particularly in Shakespeare)', *Writing in Society*, London: Verso, 1983, pp. 31–64.

8 Daniel Seltzer, 'Prince Hal and Tragic Style', *Shakespeare Survey* 30, 1977, pp. 13–27.

9 *Ibid.*, p. 19.

10 *Ibid.*, p. 18.

11 *Ibid.*, p. 21.

12 W. K. Wimsatt, ed., *Dr Johnson on Shakespeare*, Harmondsworth: Penguin Books, 1969, p. 67.

13 For the reception of *All's Well* see Joseph G. Price, *The Unfortunate Comedy: A Study of 'All's Well That Ends Well' and its Critics*, Toronto: University of Toronto Press, 1968.

14 Jonathan Bate, *The Genius of Shakespeare*, London: Picador, 1997, p. 152.

15 Describing the style of the novels of sensibility, Janet Todd remarks that it 'rather resembled the semiotic, pre-rational irruptions beloved of psychoanalytical feminists of the 1970s. It was unbalanced, hyperbolic, eccentric and fragmented, suggesting suppressed thought by extraverbal devices like the exclamation mark and dash.' She gives an example from Mary Hays's *Emma Courtney*. Todd, 'Jane Austen, Politics and Sensibility', in *Gender, Art and Death*, New York: Continuum, 1993, pp. 136–54, p. 143.

16 Emmanuel Levinas, *Of God Who Comes to Mind*, Bettina Bergo, trans., Stanford, Calif.: Stanford University Press, 1998, p. 129. I owe this reference to Paul Komesaroff.

17 Cohn, *Transparent Minds*, Chapter 1, pp. 21–47.

18 *Ibid.*, p.11.

19 As in *Hamlet*, i, i, 135: 'to his confine'.
20 Frank Kermode, *Shakespeare's Language*, London: Allen Lane, 2000, p. 10 and *passim*.
21 *Ibid.*, pp. 12, 16.
22 Norman Page, *The Language of Jane Austen*, Oxford: Basil Blackwell, 1972, p. 131.
23 Linda Bree, 'Introduction', in L. Bree, ed., Jane Austen, *Persuasion*, Peterborough, Ontario, Broadview Literary Texts, 1998, pp. 26, 27.
24 Reginald Farrer, 'Jane Austen, ob. July 18 1817', *Quarterly Review* 452, July 1917, p. 7.
25 An American silent film version of *Anna Karenina*, produced by J. Gordon Edwards was released in 1915. There was a Russian film in 1914 and a Hungarian one in 1918. The next was the Garbo film of 1935.
26 Virginia Woolf, 'The Movies and Reality', *New Republic* 47, 4 August 1926, reprinted as 'The Cinema' in *The Captain's Death Bed and Other Essays*, New York: Harcourt, Brace, 1950, pp. 180–86, pp. 182–83.
27 Judith Mayne, 'Dracula in the Twilight: Murnau's *Nosferatu* (1922)', in Eric Rentschler, ed., *German Film and Literature: Adaptation and Transformation*, New York: Methuen, 1986, p. 25.
28 *Persuasion* (BBC and WGBH): released by Sony Picture Classics, 1995.
29 Elizabeth Dalton, 'Mourning and Melancholia in *Persuasion*', *Partisan Review* 62, Winter 1995, pp. 49–59. Quotations of this article in the text are from pp. 50–51. See also Loraine Fletcher, 'Time and Mourning in *Persuasion*', *Women's Writing* 5: 1, 1998, pp. 81–90.
30 Mary Waldron, *Jane Austen and the Fiction of her Time*, Cambridge: Cambridge University Press, 1999, p. 143.
31 Jessica Benjamin, *The Bonds of Love*, London: Virago Press, 1990, p. 30.
32 Woolf, 'The Cinema', p.184–85.
33 *Mansfield Park*, written and directed by Patricia Rozema, BBC/Miramax, 1999.
34 *The Letters of Gustave Flaubert*, vol. 1, p. 230, quoted in Casey Finch and Peter Bowen, ' "The Tittle-Tattle of Highbury": Gossip and the Free Indirect Style in *Emma*', *Representations* 31, Summer 1990, pp. 1–18, p. 3.
35 Claudia L. Johnson, 'Run Mad, But Do Not Faint', review of *Mansfield Park*, *Times Literary Supplement*, 31 December 1999, pp. 15–17.
36 Jan Fergus, *Jane Austen and the Didactic Novel*, London: Macmillan, 1983, pp. 121, 127.
37 'Love and Freindship', which is the principal source of Fanny's comments, is dated 13 June 1790.
38 Susan Fraiman, *Unbecoming Women, British Women Writers and the Novel of Development*, New York: Columbia University Press, 1993, p. 68.
39 Further comments on this film will be found in Chapter 6.
40 As in Garrick's 'Ode' at the Shakespeare festival in 1769: 'Nature's glory, fancy's child; / Never, sure, did witching tongue / Warble forth such woodnotes wild!' (Alan Kendall, *David Garrick, a Biography*, London: Harrap, 1985, p. 138).

41 Morris Shapira, ed., *Henry James: Selected Literary Criticism*, London: Heinemann, 1963, p. 228 ('Gustave Flaubert', 1902); Brian Southam, ed., *Jane Austen, the Critical Heritage, vol. ii 1870–1940*, London: Routledge, 1987, p. 230 ('The Lesson of Balzac', 1905).
42 B. C. Southam, ed., *Jane Austen, The Critical Heritage, 1811–1870*, London: Routledge and Kegan Paul, 1968.
43 Thanks to Jim Aubrey for this suggestion.

5 *PRIDE AND PREJUDICE*, LOVE AND RECOGNITION

1 Edward D. McDonald, ed., *Phoenix, the Posthumous Papers of D. H. Lawrence* [1936], London, Heinemann, 1961, p. 528.
2 Lilian S. Robinson, 'Why Marry Mr Collins?', in *Sex, Class and Culture* [1978], London: Methuen, 1986, pp. 178–199, p. 179.
3 Sue Birtwistle and Susie Conkin, *The Making of 'Pride and Prejudice'*, London: Penguin Books, BBC Books, 1995, Introduction, p. v.
4 As in the added scene in which Elizabeth (not quite by accident) comes across Darcy playing billiards.
5 John Halperin, *The Life of Jane Austen*, Baltimore, Md.: Johns Hopkins, 1984, p. 69; Martha Satz, 'An Epistemological Understanding of *Pride and Prejudice*: Humility and Objectivity', in Janet Todd, ed., *Jane Austen: New Perspectives*, New York: Holmes and Meier, 1983, pp. 171–86; Marcia McClintock Folsom, ' "Taking different positions": knowing and feeling in *Pride and Prejudice*', in Marcia McClintock Folsom, ed., *Approaches to Teaching Austen's 'Pride and Prejudice'*, New York: Modern Language Association, 1993, pp. 100–14, p. 100.
6 Tony Tanner, *Jane Austen*, London: Macmillan, 1986, p. 105.
7 Marilyn Butler, *Jane Austen and the War of Ideas*, Oxford: Clarendon Press, 1975, p. 215.
8 Rachel M. Brownstein, '*Northanger Abbey, Sense and Sensibility, Pride and Prejudice*', in Edward Copeland and Juliet McMaster, eds., *The Cambridge Companion to Jane Austen*, Cambridge: Cambridge University Press, 1997, p. 50.
9 Julian Wilmot Wynne argues that Elizabeth in effect projects her emotions onto her sister Jane; *Jane Austen and Sigmund Freud; an Interpretation*, London: Plume Publications, 1998, pp. 100–1.
10 D. W. Harding, 'Character and caricature in Jane Austen', in Monica Lawlor, ed., *Regulated Hatred and Other Essays on Jane Austen*, London: Athlone Press, 1998, pp. 80–105, pp. 88–89.
11 Claudia L. Johnson, *Jane Austen: Women, Politics and the Novel*, Chicago, Ill.: University of Chicago Press, 1988, p. 85.
12 Robert M. Polhemus, 'The fortunate fall; Jane Austen's *Pride and Prejudice*', in *Erotic Faith, Being in Love from Jane Austen to D. H. Lawrence*, Chicago, Ill. and London: University of Chicago Press, 1990, pp. 28–54. This is a fine commentary on the novel.

13 D. W. Winnicott, 'The Use of an Object and Relating through Identifica-tions', in *Playing and Reality* [1971], London and New York: Routledge, 1982, pp. 86–94, p. 87.

14 *Ibid.*, p. 92.

15 Jessica Benjamin, *The Bonds of Love, Psychoanalysis, Feminism and the Problem of Domination* [1988], London: Virago, 1990; Jessica Benjamin, *Like Subjects, Love Objects, Essays on Recognition and Sexual Difference*, New Haven, Conn. and London: Yale University Press, 1995; Jessica Benjamin, *Shadow of the Other: Intersubjectivity and Gender in Psychoanalysis*, London and New York: Routledge, 1998. In this presentation I draw mostly on Chapter 3, 'The Shadow of the Other Subject: Intersubjectivity and feminist theory', in *Shadow of the Other*, pp. 79–108.

16 J. Laplanche and J.-B. Pontalis, *The Language of Psychoanalysis*, London: Karnac, 1973, p. 351.

17 Similar observations are made by Butler, *Austen and the War of Ideas*, p. 105.

18 Johnson, *Jane Austen, Women, Politics and the Novel*, p. 82.

19 Benjamin, *Like Subjects*, p. 27.

20 Rachel M. Brownstein, *Becoming a Heroine, Reading about Women in Novels* [1982], New York: Columbia University Press, 1994, p. 116.

21 Emily Brontë, *Wuthering Heights*, Chapter 9, Penguin Classics edition, p. 82.

22 Benjamin, *Like Subjects*, p. 41.

23 Tanner, *Jane Austen*, p. 105.

24 *Ibid.*, pp.105–6, suggests the novel's affinity with Locke.

25 'The other is in no way another myself, participating with me in a common existence. The relationship with the other is not an idyllic and harmonious relationship of communion or a sympathy through which we put ourselves in the other's place, we recognise the other as resembling us, but exterior to us; the relationship with the other is a relationship with a Mystery.' See *Time and the Other*, p. 75, quoted in Colin Davis, *Levinas, an Introduction*, Notre Dame, Ind.: University of Indiana Press, 1996, p. 31. 'Sympathy' refers to Husserl's concept of *einfürlung*, in which the other is known because all others reflect the self.

26 Letter of Friday 29 January 1813, Deidre Le Faye, ed., *Jane Austen's Letters*, 3rd edn, Oxford: Clarendon Press, 1995, p. 202.

27 Reuben Brower, 'Light and Bright and Sparking: Irony and Fiction in *Pride and Prejudice*', in *The Fields of Light, An Experiment in Critical Reading*, New York: Oxford University Press, 1951, pp. 164–81, p. 172.

28 Butler, *Austen and the War of Ideas,* p. 216.

29 Mary Waldron, *Jane Austen and the Fiction of her Time*, Cambridge: Cambridge University Press, 1999, p. 51.

30 An exemplary discussion of the dialogue in Chapter 10 is in Jan Fergus, *Jane Austen and the Didactic Novel*, London: Macmillan, 1983, pp. 110–15.

31 Howard Babb, 'Dialogue with Feeling, a note on *Pride and Prejudice*', in Donald J. Gray, ed., *Pride and Prejudice*, Norton Critical Edition, 1966, p. 428.

32 Gerald Edelman, *Bright Air, Brilliant Fire; on the Matter of the Mind,*

Harmondsworth: Penguin, 1994; Gerald Edelman, *The Remembered Present, A Biological theory of Consciousness*, New York: Basic Books, 1989.

33 I am indebted in this paragraph to a discussion with Justin Kelly, SJ.

34 Benjamin, *Shadow of the Other*, p. 97.

35 *Ibid.*, p. 93.

36 This feature is observed by Susan Fraiman, *Unbecoming Women: British Women Writers and the Novel of Development*, New York: Columbia University Press, 1993, p. 77.

37 *Ibid.*, p. 85.

38 Tanner, *Jane Austen*, p. 113.

39 I am grateful to Professor Elaine Bander for putting me right on this point.

40 Birtwistle and Conkin, *Making of 'Pride and Prejudice'*, p. 3.

41 Elizabeth is 'wholly complicit with patriarchal evaluations when she falls in love with Darcy', Maaja A. Stewart, *Domestic Realities and Imperial Fictions: Jane Austen's Novels in Eighteenth-Century Contexts*, Athens, Ga. and London: University of Georgia Press, 1993, p. 41.

42 Winnicott, *Playing and Reality*, p. 88.

43 Benjamin, *Like Subjects*, p. 22.

44 Benjamin, *Shadow of the Other*, pp. 94, 98–99.

45 Alexander Kojève, *Introduction to the Reading of Hegel* [1947], Ithaca, N.Y.: Cornell University Press, 1989, p. 40.

46 Edward Neill, *The Politics of Jane Austen*, London: Macmillan, 1999, p. 52. My argument is the converse of his.

47 *Ibid.*, p. 58.

48 Judith Lowder Newton, *Women, Power and Subversion, Social Strategies in British Fiction, 1778–1860*, New York: Methuen, 1985, quoted in Fraiman, *Unbecoming Women* (see note 36 above), p. 62.

49 Fraiman, *Unbecoming Women*, p. 82; see also Susan Fraiman, 'Peevish accents in the Juvenilia: A Feminist Key to *Pride and Prejudice*', in Marcia McClintock Folsom, *Approaches to Teaching Austen's Pride and Prejudice*, New York: Modern Language Association, 1993, pp. 74–80.

50 Stewart, *Domestic Realities*, p. 71.

51 *Ibid.*, p. 42.

52 Neill, *Politics of Jane Austen*, p. 52.

53 *Ibid.*, p. 62; Stewart, *Domestic Realities*, p. 56; Fraiman, *Unbecoming Women*, p. 79.

54 Fraiman, *Unbecoming Women*, p. 81.

55 *Ibid.*, pp. 78–79.

56 'Why Darcy would not have married Elizabeth Bennet' ran the headline in the *London Review of Books* on 3 September 1998. Austen, Linda Colley writes,

took it for granted that her contemporaries would appreciate (as late twentieth-century readers sometimes do not) the extent to which *Pride and Prejudice*, say, is a deliberate essay in fantasy. An Eliza Bennet, fetching daughter of a small country gentleman, niece to a Cheapside attorney, might well be invited to a one-off county ball given by a Mr Bingley with a rented house and £5,000 per annum. But a Mr

Darcy with an inherited landed estate of £10,000 per annum would have been most unlikely to seek her hand for a dance, much less for marriage. Indeed, real-life Darcys would scarcely have wasted their precious bachelor youth on rural Hertfordshire. London, with its indulgences, its political life and its marriage market offering more eligible future wives even than Miss Bingley, would have been the automatic draw.

Did Austen's contemporary readers think the book's action a fantasy? Annabella Milbanke's, the future Lady Byron, comments in a letter to her mother in 1813 are well-known: 'I have just finished a novel called Pride and Prejudice . . . I really think it is the *most probable* fiction I have ever read'. M. Elwin, *Lord Byron's Wife*, London, 1962, p. 159 (quoted O. MacDonagh, *Jane Austen: Real and Imagined Worlds*, p. 136–37); Le Faye, *A Family Record*, p. 175. But Colley's insistence points to the great gulf that does exist between the two main figures.

57 H. Elizabeth Ellington, ' "A Correct Taste in Landscape": Pemberley as Fetish and Commodity', in Linda Troost and Sayre Greenfield, eds., *Jane Austen in Hollywood*, Lexington, Ky.: University Press of Kentucky, 1998, pp. 90–110.

58 The filming of these scenes replicates the earlier BBC adaptation (1979) with script by Fay Weldon. In this version, similarly, the housekeeper gestures towards the portrait, which is positioned high on the wall, Elizabeth looks up to it, and the Darcy is unsmiling. In voice-over Elizabeth says 'Brother, landlord, master – how many people's happiness are in your hands. I am very thankful for your regard for me. How stark you look in your portrait. But I remember your warmth and would soften that look.' Clumsy as this is, it seems that here too, the emphasis is on Darcy's lonely authority, and the film implicitly subordinates Elizabeth to it at this moment.

59 Lisa Hopkins, 'Mr Darcy's Body: Privileging the Female Gaze', in Troost and Greenfield, *Jane Austen in Hollywood*, pp. 111–21; Esther Sonnet, 'From *Emma* to *Clueless*: Taste, Pleasure and the Scene of History', in Deborah Cartmell and Imelda Whelehan, eds., *Adaptations: from Text to Screen, Screen to Text*, London and New York: Routledge, 1999, p. 58. And see Helen Fielding, *Bridget Jones: the Edge of Reason*, London: Picador, 1999, p. 45.

60 Compare Berenson's remarks on 'the aesthetic moment', Bernard Berenson, *Aesthetics and History* [1948], New York: Doubleday, 1965, p. 93.

61 Brownstein, *Becoming a Heroine*, p. 130.

6   THE GENIUS AND THE FACILITATING ENVIRONMENT

1 D. W. Winnicott, 'Ego Distortion in terms of True and False Self (1960)', in *The Maturational Process and the Facilitating Environment* [1965], London: Karnac, 1990, pp. 140–52, p. 143.

2 *Emma*, written and directed by Douglas McGrath, Miramax Films, 1996.

3 'Emma's abrupt brutality to her on Box Hill comes home with the actuality of a violent sudden slap in our own face' (Brian Southam, ed., *Jane Austen: the*

Critical Heritage volume II: 1870–1940, London: Routledge 1987, p. 268).

4 Emma has earlier spoken of Jane sending her aunt the pattern of a stomacher, or knitting a pair of garters for her grandmother. Why does Emma's imagination revert to the Bates's underclothing? Compare the passage in *Pride and Prejudice* where the seduced Lydia writes to Kitty 'I wish you would tell Sally to mend a great slit in my worked muslin gown' (*Pride and Prejudice*, p. 292).

5 D. W. Harding, 'Regulated Hatred: an Aspect of the Work of Jane Austen', in Monica Lawlor, ed., *Regulated Hatred and Other Essays on Jane Austen*, London: Athlone Press, 1998, pp. 5–26. (Originally published in *Scrutiny* 7, 1940, pp. 342–62.) Claudia L. Johnson argues that Harding inaugurates 'modern Austenian criticism'. See 'Austen cults and cultures', in Edward Copeland and Juliet McMaster, eds., *The Cambridge Companion to Jane Austen*, Cambridge; Cambridge University Press, 1997, pp. 211–26, p. 213.

6 Harding, 'Regulated Hatred', p. 10.

7 Julia Prewitt Brown, *Jane Austen's Novels, Social Change and Literary Form*, Cambridge, Mass.: Harvard University Press, 1979, pp. 119–20. Prewitt Brown goes on to cite Harding but (paradoxically) with hostility.

8 I am indebted to 'The experience of evil', an unpublished paper by Paul A. Komesaroff for this phrase.

9 Park Honan, *Author's Lives: on Literary Biography and the Arts of Language*, New York: St Martin's Press, 1990, p. 13. Marilyn Butler groups Harding with Garrod and Forster as a critic who 'attacks' Jane Austen, *Jane Austen and the War of Ideas*, Oxford: Clarendon Press, new edn, 1987, p. ix. Julian Wilmot Wynne says he descends into '(baseless) psychobiography', (*Jane Austen and Sigmund Freud: an Interpretation*, London: Plume, 1999, p. 34). Mary Waldron reiterates Harding's stress that Austen was not a satirist, but claims that his essay 'hardly engages in a positive way with what the novels did achieve' (*Jane Austen and the Fiction of Her Time*, Cambridge: Cambridge University Press, 1999, p. 7).

10 Harding, 'Regulated hatred', pp. 11–12.

11 Harding's emphasis on Austen as beleaguered intellectual assumes that she shares the characteristic stance of *Scrutiny*.

12 Prewitt Brown, *Social Change and Literary Form*, p. 105.

13 Ian Watt, 'Jane Austen and the traditions of comic aggression', in Harold Bloom, ed., *Jane Austen: Modern Critical Views*, New York: Chelsea House, 1986, pp. 191–201.

14 Prewitt Brown, *Social Change and Literary Form*, p. 105.

15 Peter Gay, ed., *The Freud Reader*, London: Vintage, 1995, pp. 298–300. Harding's only reference to a 'Freudian' interpretation of Austen's novels is hostile, but it is to 'the mechanical application of Freudian ideas', not necessarily to the ideas themselves (*Regulated Hatred*, p. 131). The Cinderella theme in Austen's novels is discussed at length in Derek Brewer, *Symbolic Stories: Traditional Narratives of the Family Drama in English Literature*, London and New York: Longmans, 1988, pp. 148–67, without reference to Harding.

16 D. W. Winnicott, *The Maturational Process and the Facilitating Environment* [1965], London: Karnac, 1990. The first publications listed are from the twenties.

17 'Society holds the family', in D. W. Winnicott, selected and compiled by Claire Winnicott, Ray Shepherd and Madeleine Davis, *Home is Where We Start from, Essays by a Psychoanalyst*, New York: Norton, 1986, p. 107.

18 I should add that the notion that 'holding' and 'containing' are similar concepts would be hotly disputed in some psychoanalytic circles. To consider the relevance of Bion's thinking about groups (*Experiences in Groups*, London: Tavistock, 1961) to Austen would take another book.

19 W. R. Bion, *Attention and Interpretation, a Scientific Approach to Insight in Psychoanalysis and Groups*, London: Tavistock, 1970, pp. 72–82. See also Gerard Bleandonu, *W. R. Bion, his Life and Works, 1897–1979*, trans. Claire Pajaczkowski, London: Free Association, 1994, pp. 227–29.

20 Winnicott, 'True and False Self', p. 148.

21 Suvendrini Perera argues, for example, that '[t]he almost palpable affirmations emanating from Donwell become constraining as well as reassuring, like the multiple reiterations of "sweetness and Englishness" in the landscape' (Suvendrini Perera, *Reaches of Empire; the English Novel from Edgeworth to Dickens*, New York: Columbia University Press, 1991, p. 42).

22 Among many examples, Fanny Price's 'nest of comforts' (*Mansfield Park*, p. 152) is one of the most interesting.

23 As in the opening tenor aria of Handel's *Messiah*, 'Comfort ye, comfort ye, my people.'

24 Brian Southam, ed., 'Introduction', *Critical Heritage, 1870–1940*, p. 127–29.

25 Harding became Professor of Psychology at the University of London in 1945: his book *Social Psychology and Individual Values* was published in 1953 (London: Hutchinson). Harding says that his essay is 'not offered as a balanced appraisal of [Austen's] work' (p. 25).

26 Mary Waldron, *Jane Austen and the Fiction of her Time*, Cambridge: Cambridge University Press, 1999, p. 7.

27 Prominent among these are Marvin Mudrick, *Jane Austen: Irony as Defense and Discovery*, Berkeley, Calif.: University of California Press, 1952, and Sandra Gilbert and Susan Gubar, *The Madwoman in the Attic: the Woman Writer and the Nineteenth-Century Literary Imagination*, New Haven, Conn.: Yale University Press, 1979.

28 Mary Poovey, *The Proper Lady and the Woman Writer*, Chicago, Ill.: University of Chicago Press, 1984, p. xvii.

29 Mark Shorer, 'The Humiliation of Emma Woodhouse', in Ian Watt, ed., *Jane Austen, a Collection of Critical Essays*, Englewood Cliffs, N.J.: Prentice Hall, 1963.

30 David Nokes, *Jane Austen, a Life*, London: Fourth Estate, 1997, p. 402.

31 Janet Todd, 'Jane Austen, Politics and Sensibility', in *Gender, Art and Death*, New York: Continuum, 1993, pp. 136–54.

32 James N. Loehlin, ' "Top of the World, Ma", *Richard III* and cinematic

convention', in Linda E. Boose and Richard Burt, eds., *Shakespeare, the Movie: Popularising the Plays on Film, Television and Video*, London and New York: Routledge, 1997.

33 Miramax/BBC Films 1999. The influence of Edward Said's reading of *Mansfield Park* is clear ('Jane Austen and Empire', in *Culture and Imperialism*, London: Vintage, 1994, pp. 95–116): less so perhaps is the association of lesbian feeling in scenes of attention to dress that picks up the similar suggestion in Terry Castle's review and subsequent letter (*London Review of Books*, 24 August 1995, p. 4). See also Frank Gibbon, 'The Antiguan Connection: Some New Light on *Mansfield Park*', *The Cambridge Quarterly* 11, 1982, pp. 298–305; Moira Ferguson, '*Mansfield Park*, Slavery, Colonialism, and Gender', *The Oxford Literary Review* 13, 1991, pp. 118–39.

34 Claudia L. Johnson, 'Run Mad But Do Not Faint', review of *Mansfield Park*, *Times Literary Supplement*, 31 December 1999, p. 15.

35 A BBC/Miramax film, it was partly funded by the British Arts Council.

36 Nokes, *Jane Austen*, pp. 7, 403.

37 Deirdre Le Faye, ed., *Jane Austen's Letters*, 3rd edn, Oxford: Oxford University Press, 1995, p. 212. 'I should like to meet Miss Burdett, but am rather frightened by hearing that she wishes to meet *me*. If I *am* a wild Beast, I cannot help it.' Chapman's note is 'the secret of authorship was leaking out': the reference has nothing to do with Austen's temperament or personality.

38 Nokes, *Jane Austen*, Chapter 11, 'Wild beast', pp. 397–431, p. 1.

39 Poovey, *Proper Lady*, p. 203.

40 Lionel Trilling, '*Mansfield Park*', in *The Opposing Self*, London: Secker and Warburg, 1955, pp. 206–30, p. 207.

41 Antony Lane, 'All Over the Map', *The New Yorker*, 29 November 1999, p. 140.

42 Emma Thompson, *Jane Austen's 'Sense and Sensibility': the Screenplay and Diaries*, London: Bloomsbury, 1995. The producer Lindsay Doran underlines this in her Introduction to the volume (p. 11). This film, neglected in this book, is a considerable achievement.

43 Patty-Lynne Herlevi, *Mansfield Park – a Conversation with Patricia Rozema*, http//movie-reviews, colossus.net/comment/111599.htm. Accessed 14/07/00.

44 Helen Fielding, *Bridget Jones: the Edge of Reason*, London: Picador, 1999, Chapter 9, 'Social hell', pp. 235–60.

45 Warner Brothers, 1998.

A note on films cited

In this book I have used the catch-all term 'film' to cover both products made for television and those made for cinema release. It can be argued that the 1995 *Persuasion*, originally shown on television, and only later released for the cinema, benefits from being made for a medium which fosters a more intimate focus. Its camera-work and mise en scène seem influenced by Terence Davies's *Distant Voices, Still Lives* (1988) – also originally made for television.

Films discussed (however briefly) in this book are:

Clueless (Paramount 1995) written and directed by Amy Heckerling.

Emma (Miramax 1996) written and directed by Douglas McGrath.

Jane Austen in Manhattan (Contemporary Films/Merchant Ivory Productions 1980) written by Ruth Prawer Jhabvala, directed by James Ivory.

Mansfield Park (Miramax/BBC 1999) written and directed by Patricia Rozema.

The Last Days of Disco (Castle Rock/Westerly 1998) written and directed by Whit Stillman.

Metropolitan (Westerly 1990) written and directed by Whit Stillman.

Northanger Abbey (BBC and A&E 1987) written by Maggie Wadley and directed by Giles Foster.

Persuasion (Granada 1971) written by Julian Mitchell and directed by Howard Baker.

Persuasion (BBC and WGBH 1995) written by Nick Dear and directed by Roger Michell.

Pride and Prejudice (MGM 1940) written by Aldous Huxley and Jane Murfin and directed by Robert Z. Leonard.

Pride and Prejudice (BBC and A&E 1979) written by Fay Weldon and directed by Cyril Coke.

Pride and Prejudice (BBC and A&E 1995) written by Andrew Davies and directed by Simon Langton.

Sense and Sensibility (Columbia) written by Emma Thompson and directed by Ang Lee.

Vanya on 42nd Street (Channel 4 Films/Mayfair, 1994) adapted from Chekhov by Andre Gregory and directed by Louis Malle.

You've Got Mail (Warner Bros 1999) written and directed by Nora Ephron.

It might be added that *Pride and Prejudice* is one of the classics saved from the flames in Truffaut's *Fahrenheit 451* (1966). In Ray Bradbury's novel, from which the script derives, the Great Books preserved through their devoted readers' memorising are exclusively by male writers: in many other respects Truffaut's film is an interesting example of the act of recreation discussed in this book.

Bibliography

Andrew, Dudley, *Concepts in Film Theory*, Oxford and New York: Oxford
  University Press, 1984.
Armstrong, Isobel, *Mansfield Park*, Harmondsworth: Penguin Critical Studies,
  1988.
  Sense and Sensibility, Harmondsworth: Penguin Critical Studies, 1994.
Auerbach, Nina, 'Jane Austen's Dangerous Charm', in Judy Simons, ed.,
  Mansfield Park and Persuasion, London: Macmillan, 1997.
Austen-Leigh, J. E., *A Memoir of Jane Austen by her Nephew*, Introduction by Fay
  Weldon, London: Folio Society, 1989.
Austen Leigh, W., Austen-Leigh, R. A. and Le Faye, Deirdre, *Jane Austen: A
  Family Record*, London: The British Library, 1989.
Aylmer, Janet, *Darcy's Story from Pride and Prejudice*, Bath: Copperfield Books,
  1996.
Babb, Howard, 'Dialogue with Feeling, a note on *Pride and Prejudice*', in Donald
  J. Gray, ed., *Pride and Prejudice*, Norton Critical Edition, 1966.
Barthes, Roland, 'The Death of the Author' [1968], in Stephen Heath, ed.,
  Image Music Text, London: Flamingo, 1984.
Bate, Jonathan, *Shakespeare and the English Romantic Imagination*, Oxford: Claren-
  don Press, 1986.
  Shakespearean Constitutions: Politics, Theatre, Criticism 1730–1830, Oxford: Claren-
  don Press, 1989.
  The Genius of Shakespeare, London: Picador, 1997.
Bate, W. J. and Albrecht B. Strauss, eds., *The Yale Edition of the Works of Samuel
  Johnson*, vol. III, *The Rambler*, New Haven and London: Yale University
  Press, 1969.
Batey, Mavis, *Jane Austen and the English Landscape*, London: Barn Elms, 1996.
Bazin, André, *What is Cinema?*, selected and trans. Hugh Gray, Berkeley, Calif.:
  University of California Press, 1967.
Benjamin, Jessica, *The Bonds of Love, Psychoanalysis, Feminism, and the Problem of
  Domination* [1988], London: Virago Press, 1990.
  Like Subjects, Love Objects, Essays on Recognition and Sexual Difference, New Haven,
  Conn. and London: Yale University Press, 1995.
  Shadow of the Other: Intersubjectivity and Gender in Psychoanalysis, London and New
  York: Routledge, 1998.

Benjamin, Walter, *Illuminations*, London: Collins, 1973.

Berenson, Bernard, *Aesthetics and History* [1948], New York: Doubleday, 1965.

Bion, W. R., *Attention and Interpretation a Scientific Approach to Insight in Psychoanalysis and Groups*, London: Tavistock, 1970.

Birtwistle, Sue, and Conkin, Susie, *The Making of 'Pride and Prejudice'*, London: Penguin Books, BBC Books, 1995.

Bleandonu, Gerard, *W. R. Bion, his Life and Works, 1897–1979*, trans. Claire Pajaczkowski, London: Free Association, 1994.

Bloom, Harold, *The Anxiety of Influence, a Theory of Poetry*, New York: Oxford University Press, 1973.

Bourdieu, Pierre, *Distinction*, trans. Richard Nice, Cambridge, Mass.: Harvard University Press, 1984.

Bradbrook, F. W., *Jane Austen and her Predecessors*, Cambridge: Cambridge University Press, 1966.

Bradbury, Ray, *Fahrenheit 451*, New York: Simon and Schuster, 1967.

Bradley, A. C., *A Miscellany*, London: Macmillan, 1929.

Bradshaw, Graham, *Misrepresentations: Shakespeare and the Materialists*, Ithaca, N.Y. and London: Cornell University Press, 1993.

Brand, Stewart, *How Buildings Learn; What Happens After They're Built*, revised paperback edn, London: Pheonix Illustrated, 1997.

Bree, Linda, 'Introduction', in L. Bree, ed., Jane Austen, *Persuasion*, Peterborough, Ontario, Broadview Literary Texts, 1998.

Brewer, Derek, *Symbolic Stories: Traditional Narratives of the Family Drama in English Literature*, London and New York: Longmans, 1988.

Brooks, Peter, *Psychoanalysis and Storytelling*, Oxford: Blackwells, 1994.

Brower, Reuben, 'Light and bright and sparking: irony and fiction in *Pride and Prejudice*', in *The Fields of Light, an Experiment in Critical Reading*, New York: Oxford University Press, 1951.

Brownstein, Rachel M., *Becoming a Heroine, Reading about Women in Novels* [1982], New York: Columbia University Press, 1994.

'*Northanger Abbey, Sense and Sensibility, Pride and Prejudice*', in Edward Copeland and Juliet McMaster, eds., *The Cambridge Companion to Jane Austen*, Cambridge: Cambridge University Press, 1997.

Burney, Frances, *Camilla, or A Picture of Youth* [1796], Edward A. Bloom and Lilian D. Bloom, eds., London: Oxford University Press, 1972.

The Wanderer, [1814] Margaret Anne Doody, Robert L. Mack and Peter Sabor eds., Oxford: World's Classics, 1991.

Butler, Marilyn, *Jane Austen and the War of Ideas*, Oxford: Clarendon Press, 1975. (See also new edn. 1987.)

Cakebread, Caroline , 'Remembering *King Lear* in Jane Smiley's *A Thousand Acres*', in Christy Desmet and Robert Sawter, eds., *Shakespeare and Appropriation*, London and New York: Routledge, 1999.

Castle, Terry, 'Sister-Sister', *London Review of Books*, 3 August 1995.

Cecil, David, *A Portrait of Jane Austen*, London: Constable, 1978.

Chandler, Alice, ' "A Pair of Fine Eyes": Jane Austen's Treatment of Sex', in

Harold Bloom, ed., *Jane Austen, Modern Critical Views*, New York: Chelsea House, 1986.

Chapman, R. W., *Jane Austen: Facts and Problems*, Oxford: Clarendon Press, 1948.

Chapman, R. W., ed., *Memoir of Jane Austen* by her nephew James Edward Austen-Leigh, Oxford: Clarendon Press, 1926.

Minor Works, Oxford: Clarendon Press, 1954.

Chedgzoy, Kate, *Shakespeare's Queer Children: Sexual Politics and Contemporary Culture*, Manchester and New York: Manchester University Press, 1995.

Clancier, Anne, and Kalmanovich, Jeannine, *Winnicott and Paradox, from Birth to Creation*, trans. Alan Sheridan, London: Tavistock, 1987.

Clark, Lorna J., ed., *The Letters of Sarah Harriet Burney*, Athens, Ga. and London: University of Georgia Press, 1997.

Cohn, Dorrit, *Transparent Minds: Narrative Modes for Presenting Consciousness in Fiction*, N.J.: Princeton University Press, 1978.

Colley, Linda, 'Why Darcy would not have married Elizabeth Bennet', *London Review of Books*, 3 September 1998.

Collins, Irene, *Jane Austen and the Clergy*, London: Hambledon Press, 1994.

Crick, Bernard, *George Orwell, a Life*, London: Secker and Warburg, rev. edn, 1981.

Dalton, Elizabeth, 'Mourning and Melancholia in *Persuasion*', *Partisan Review* 62, Winter 1995.

Davies, Andrew, *B. Monkey*, London: Minerva, 1993, p. 44.

Davies, Antony, *Filming Shakespeare's Plays*, Cambridge: Cambridge University Press, 1988.

Davis, Colin, *Levinas, an Introduction*, Notre Dame, Ind.: University of Indiana Press, 1996.

De Rose, Peter L., *Jane Austen and Samuel Johnson*, Washington, D.C.: University Press of America, 1980.

Dickson, Rebecca, 'Misrepresenting Jane Austen's Ladies: Revising Texts (and History) to Sell Films', in Troost and Greenfield, *Jane Austen in Hollywood*.

Doane, Mary Ann, 'Sublimation and the Psychoanalysis of the Aesthetic', *Femmes Fatales: Feminism, Film Theory and Psychoanalysis*, New York and London: Routledge, 1991.

Dobson, Michael, *The Making of the National Poet: Shakespeare, Adaptation and Authorship, 1660–1769*, Oxford: Clarendon Press, 1992.

Dole, Carol M., 'Austen, Class, and the American Market', in Troost and Greenfield, *Jane Austen in Hollywood*.

Doody, Margaret Anne, 'Jane Austen's Reading', in J. E. Grey, ed., *The Jane Austen Handbook*, London: Athlone Press, 1986.

Frances Burney: the Life in the Works, Cambridge: Cambridge University Press, 1988.

Dudley, Andrew, *Concepts in Film Theory*, Oxford: Oxford University Press, 1984.

Edelman, Gerald M., *The Remembered Present, a Biological Theory of Consciousness*, New York: Basic Books, 1989.

Bright Air, Brilliant Fire; on the Matter of the Mind, Harmondsworth: Penguin, 1994.

Ellington, H. Elizabeth, ' "A Correct Taste in Landscape": Pemberley as Fetish and Commodity', Linda Troost and Sayre Greenfield, eds., *Jane Austen in Hollywood*, Lexington, Ky.: University Press of Kentucky, 1998.

Ellis, David, *Literary Lives; Biography and the Search for Understanding*, Edinburgh: Edinburgh University Press, 2000.

Erickson, Peter, *Rewriting Shakespeare, Rewriting Ourselves*, Berkeley, Calif. and London: University of California Press, 1991.

Farrer, Reginald, 'Jane Austen, ob. July 18 1817', *Quarterly Review* 452, July 1917.

Fergus, Jan, *Jane Austen and the Didactic Novel*, London: Macmillan, 1983.

Jane Austen, a Literary Life, London: Macmillan 1991.

Ferguson, Moira, '*Mansfield Park*, Slavery, Colonialism, and Gender', *The Oxford Literary Review* 13, 1991.

Fielding, Helen, *Bridget Jones's Diary* [1996], London: Picador, 1997.

Bridget Jones: the Edge of Reason, London: Picador, 1999.

Finch, Casey, and Bowen, Peter, ' "The Tittle-Tattle of Highbury": Gossip and the Free Indirect Style in *Emma*', *Representations* 31, Summer 1990.

Fletcher, Loraine, 'Time and Mourning in *Persuasion*', *Women's Writing* 5: 1, 1998.

Folsom, Marcia McClintock, ' "Taking Different Positions": Knowing and Feeling in *Pride and Prejudice*', in Marcia McClintock Folsom, ed., *Approaches to Teaching Austen's 'Pride and Prejudice'*, New York: Modern Language Association, 1993.

Fraiman, Susan, 'Peevish Accents in the Juvenilia: a Feminist Key to *Pride and Prejudice*' in Marcia McClintock Folsom, ed., *Approaches to Teaching Austen's 'Pride and Prejudice'*, New York: Modern Language Association, 1993, pp. 74–80.

Unbecoming Women: British Women Writers and the Novel of Development, New York: Columbia University Press, 1993.

Freud, Sigmund, *The Interpretation of Dreams* [1900], trans. James Strachey, in James Strachey *et al.*, eds., *The Standard Edition of the Complete Psychological Works of Sigmund Freud*, vols. IV and V, London: Hogarth Press and the Institute of Psycho-Analysis, 1953.

'Observations on Transference-Love' in [1915], in James Strachey *et al.*, eds., *The Standard Edition of the Complete Psychological Works of Sigmund Freud*, vol. XII, London: Hogarth Press and the Institute of Psycho-Analysis.

'Negation' [1925], in James Strachey *et al.*, eds., *The Standard Edition of the Complete Psychological Works of Sigmund Freud*, vol. XIX, 'The Ego and the Id and other works'.

Gager, Valerie L., *Shakespeare and Dickens: the Dynamics of Influence*, Cambridge: Cambridge University Press, 1996.

Gard, Roger, *Jane Austen's Novels: the Art of Clarity*, New Haven, Conn. and London: Yale University Press, 1992.

Gay, Peter, ed., *The Freud Reader*, London: Vintage, 1995.

Gandhi, Leela, review of Kathryn Hughes, *George Eliot: the Last Victorian*, in *The Australian's Review of Books*, May 1999, p. 17.

Gibbon, Frank, 'The Antiguan Connection: Some New Light on *Mansfield Park*', *The Cambridge Quarterly* 11, 1982.

Giddings, R., Selby, K., and Wensley, C., *Screening the Novel: the Theory and Practice of Literary Dramatization*, London: Macmillan, 1990.

Gilbert, Sandra M. and Gubar, Susan, *The Madwoman in the Attic: the Woman Writer and the Nineteenth-Century Literary Imagination*, New Haven, Conn.: Yale University Press, 1979.

Greenblatt, Stephen, *Shakespearian Negotiations: the Circulation of Energy in Renaissance England*, Oxford: Clarendon Paperbacks, 1990.

Grundy, Isobel, 'Jane Austen and Literary Traditions', in Edward Copeland and Juliet McMaster, eds., *The Cambridge Companion to Jane Austen*, Cambridge: Cambridge University Press, 1997.

Halperin, John, *The Life of Jane Austen*, Baltimore, Md.: Johns Hopkins University Press, 1984.

Harding, D. W., *Social Psychology and Individual Values*, London: Hutchinson, 1953.

'Character and caricature in Jane Austen' in Monica Lawlor, ed., *Regulated Hatred and Other Essays on Jane Austen*, London: Athlone Press, 1998.

'Regulated Hatred: an Aspect of the Work of Jane Austen', in *Regulated Hatred and Other Essays on Jane Austen*, pp. 5–26. (Originally published in *Scrutiny* 8, 1940).

Regulated Hatred and Other Essays on Jane Austen, Monica Lawlor, ed., London: Athlone Press, 1998.

Harris, Jocelyn, *Jane Austen's Art of Memory*, Cambridge: University Press, 1989.

'Jane Austen and the Burden of the (Male) Past: the Case Re-examined', in Devoney Looser, ed., *Jane Austen and Discourses of Feminism*, New York: St Martin's Press, 1995, pp. 87–100.

Hawkins, Harriet, *Classics and Trash*, Hemel Hempstead: Harvester Wheatsheaf, 1990.

Hazlitt, William, *Characters of Shakespear's Plays*, in P. P. Howe, ed., *Complete Works*, 21 vols., New York: AMS Press, 1967, vol. IV.

Herlevi, Patty-Lynne, *Mansfield Park – a Conversation with Patricia Rozema*, http// movie-reviews, colossus.net/comment/111599.htm.

Hinselwood, R. D., *A Dictionary of Kleinian Thought*, London: Free Association, 2nd edn., 1991.

Hodge, Jane Aiken, *The Double Life of Jane Austen*, London: Hodder and Stoughton, 1972.

Holmes, Richard, *Footsteps, Adventures of a Romantic Biographer*, Harmondsworth: Penguin Books, 1986.

Honan, Park, *Authors' Lives: on Literary Biography and the Arts of Language*, New York: St Martin's Press, 1990.

Jane Austen, her Life, [1987] rev. edn., 1997.

Hopkins, Lisa, 'Mr Darcy's Body: Privileging the Female Gaze', in Troost and Greenfield, *Jane Austen in Hollywood*, 1998.

Hunter, G. K., *English Drama 1586–1642: The Age of Shakespeare*, Oxford: Clarendon Press, 1997.

James, Henry, *The Art of the Novel*, Critical Prefaces, with an Introduction by
Richard P. Blackmur, New York: Scribner's, 1934.

Jenkins, Elizabeth, *Jane Austen* [1938], London: Cardinal, 1973.

Johnson, Claudia L., 'The "Operations of Time, and the Changes of the
Human Mind": Jane Austen and Dr Johnson Again', *Modern Language
Quarterly* 44: 1, 1983, pp. 28–38.

'The "Twilight of Probability": Uncertainty and Hope in *Sense and Sensibility*',
Philological Quarterly 62, 1983, pp. 171–86.

Jane Austen: Women, Politics and the Novel, Chicago, Ill.: University of Chicago
Press, 1988.

'Austen Cults and Cultures', in E. Copeland and J. McMaster, eds., *The
Cambridge Companion to Jane Austen*, Cambridge: Cambridge University
Press, 1997, pp. 211–26.

'Run Mad, But Do Not Faint', review of *Mansfield Park*, *Times Literary
Supplement*, 31 December 1999, 15–17.

Johnson, R. Brimley, *Jane Austen*, London: Sheed and Ward, 1927.

Jonson, Ben, *Timber, or Discoveries, being Observations on Men and Manners* [1641],
London: Dent and Co., 1898.

Kendall, Alan, *David Garrick, a Biography*, London: Harrap, 1985.

Kermode, Frank, *Shakespeare's Language*, London: Allen Lane, 2000.

Kojève, Alexander, *Introduction to the Reading of Hegel* [1947], Ithaca, N.Y.: Cornell
University Press, 1989.

Kott, Jan, *Shakespeare, Our Contemporary*, trans. Boleslaw Taborski, preface by
Peter Brook, 2nd edn., rev., London: Methuen, 1967.

Kozintsev, Grigory, *'King Lear', the Space of Tragedy: the Diary of a Film Director*,
trans. Mary Mackintosh, London: Heinmann Educational, 1977.

Lacan, Jacques, 'The Freudian unconscious and ours', in Jacques-Alain Miller,
ed., *The Four Fundamental Concepts of Psychoanalysis*, Harmondsworth: Penguin Education, 1979.

Lane, Antony, 'All Over the Map', *The New Yorker*, 29 November 1999,
p. 140.

Laplanche, J. and Pontalis, J.-B., *The Language of Psychoanalysis*, London: Karnac,
1973.

Lascelles, Mary, *Jane Austen and her Art*, [1939] Oxford: Clarendon Press, 1965.

Lawrence, D. H., 'Morality and the Novel', in Edward D. McDonald, ed.,
Phoenix, the Posthumous Papers of D. H. Lawrence [1936], London: Heinemann,
1961.

Le Faye, Deirdre, *Newsletter of the Jane Austen Society*, October 1998.

Le Faye, Deirdre, ed., *Jane Austen's Letters*, 3rd edn., Oxford: Oxford University
Press, 1995.

Leavis, F. R., *The Living Principle*, London: Chatto and Windus, 1975.

Levinas, Emmanuel, *Of God Who Comes to Mind*, Bettina Bergo, trans., Stanford,
Calif.: Stanford University Press, 1998.

Lodge, David, *Changing Places, a Tale of Two Campuses*, [1975] London: Penguin, 1978.

Loehlin, James N, 'Top of the World, Ma', *Richard III* and Cinematic Convention', in Linda E. Boose and Richard Burt, eds., *Shakespeare, the Movie: Popularising the Plays on Film, Television and Video*, London and New York, Routledge, 1997.

Looser, Devoney, 'Feminist implications of the silver screen Austen', in Troost and Greenfield, *Jane Austen in Hollywood*, 1998.

Macaulay, Thomas Babington, *Critical and Historical Essays* [1903], arranged by A. J. Grieve, London: Everyman's Library, Dent, 1967, 'Madame d'Arblay', pp. 563–612; originally in the *Edinburgh Review* 76, January 1843.

MacDonagh, Oliver, *Jane Austen: Real and Imagined Worlds*, New Haven, Conn.: Yale University Press, 1991.

Macdonald, Virginia and Andrew F. Macdonald, eds., *Jane Austen on Screen*, Cambridge: Cambridge University Press, forthcoming.

Mansfield, Katherine, *Novels and Novelists*, London: Constable, 1930.

Marsden, Jean, ed., *The Appropriation of Shakespeare: Post Renaissance Reconstructions of the Works and the Myth*, Hemel Hempstead: Harvester Wheatsheaf, 1991.

Mayne, Judith, 'Dracula in the Twilight: Murnau's *Nosferatu* (1922)', in Eric Rentschler, ed., *German Film and Literature: Adaptation and Transformation*, New York: Methuen, 1986.

McFarlane, Brian, *Novel to Film, an Introduction to the Theory of Adaptation*, Oxford: Clarendon Press, 1996.

Mills, Howard, *Working with Shakespeare*, Hemel Hempstead: Harvester Wheatsheaf, 1993.

Mitchell, Stephen, *Hope and Dread in Psychoanalysis*, New York: Basic Books, 1993.

Mitford, Mary Russell, *Recollections of a Literary Life: or, Books, Places, and People*, 3 vols., London: Richard Bentley, 1852.

Modleski, Tanya, *Loving With a Vengeance*, London: Methuen, 1984.

Morris, Meagan, 'Feminism, reading postmodernism', in Thomas Docherty, ed., *Postmodernism: a Reader*, Hemel Hempstead: Harvester Wheatsheaf, 1993.

Mudrick, Marvin, *Jane Austen: Irony as Defense and Discovery*, Berkeley, Calif.: University of California Press, 1952.

Mulvey, Laura, *Visual and Other Pleasures*, London: Macmillan, 1989.

Myers, Valerie Grosvenor, *Obstinate Heart: Jane Austen, a Biography*, London: Michael O'Mara, 1997.

Neill, Edward, *The Politics of Jane Austen*, London: Macmillan, 1999.

Nicolson, Nigel, *The World of Jane Austen*, London: Weidenfeld and Nicolson, 1991.

Nokes, David, *Jane Austen: a Life*, London: Fourth Estate, 1997.

Novy, Marianne, *Engaging with Shakespeare: Responses of George Eliot and Other Women Novelists*, Athens, Ga. and London: University of Georgia Press, 1994.

Novy, Marianne, ed., *Cross-Cultural Performances: Differences in Women's Re-visions of Shakespeare*, Urbana, Ill.: University of Illinois Press, 1993.

Page, Norman *The Language of Jane Austen*, Oxford: Basil Blackwell, 1972.

Parrill, Sue, 'Metaphors of Control: Physicality in *Emma* and *Clueless*', *Persuasions On-Line* 20: 1.

Perera, Suvendrini, *Reaches of Empire; the English Novel from Edgeworth to Dickens*, New York: Columbia University Press, 1991.

Perkins, Moreland, *Reshaping the Sexes in 'Sense and Sensibility'*, Charlottesville, Va.: University Press of Virginia, 1998.

Phillipps, K. C., *Jane Austen's English*, London: Andre Deutsch, 1970.

Phillips, Adam, *Winnicott*, London: Fontana Modern Masters Series, 1988.

Pilgrim, Constance, *Dear Jane: a Biographical Study*, Durham, s.c.: Pentland Press, 1991.

Pinion, F. B., *Jane Austen Companion*, London: Macmillan, 1973.

Polhemus, Robert M., 'The Fortunate Fall; Jane Austen's *Pride and Prejudice*', in *Erotic Faith, Being in Love from Jane Austen to D. H. Lawrence*, Chicago, Ill. and London: University of Chicago Press, 1990.

Polya, G. M., *Jane Austen and the Black Hole of British History*, privately published, Melbourne, 1998.

Poovey, Mary, *The Proper Lady and the Woman Writer*, Chicago, Ill. and London: University of Chicago Press, 1984.

Prewitt Brown, Julia, *Jane Austen's Novels, Social Change and Literary Form*, Cambridge, Mass.: Harvard University Press, 1979.
  'The social history of *Pride and Prejudice*', in Marcia Folsom, ed., *Approaches to Teaching 'Pride and Prejudice'*, New York: Modern Language Association, 1993, pp. 57–66.

Price, Joseph G., *The Unfortunate Comedy: a Study of 'All's Well that Ends Well' and its Critics*, Toronto: University of Toronto Press, 1968.

Price, Martin, 'Introduction', in M. Price, ed., *Dickens: a Collection of Critical Essays*, Englewood Cliffs, N.J.: Prentice Hall, 1967.

Radovici, Nadia, *A Youthful Love?: Jane Austen and Tom Lefroy*, Braunton: Merlin Books, 1995.

Redford, Bruce, ed., *The Letters of Samuel Johnson*, The Hyde Edition, 3 vols., Oxford: Clarendon Press, 1992.

Rees, Joan, *Jane Austen: Woman and Writer*, New York: St Martin's Press, 1976.

Rich, Adrienne, 'When We Dead Awaken: Writing As Re-Vision', in *On Lies, Secrets and Silence, Selected Prose 1966–1978*, New York: Norton, 1979.

Robinson, Lilian S., 'Why Marry Mr Collins?', in *Sex, Class and Culture* [1978], London: Methuen 1986.

Rodman, F. Robert, ed., *The Spontaneous Gesture: Selected Letters of D. W. Winnicott*, London and Cambridge, Mass.: Harvard University Press, 1987.

Rossiter, A. P., *Angel with Horns, and other Shakespearean Lectures*, Graham Storey, ed., London: Longmans, 1961.

Rudd, Naill, ed., *Johnson's Juvenal*, Bristol: Bristol Classical Press, 1981.

Rybczynski, Witold, *Home: a Short History of an Idea*, New York: Viking Penguin, 1986.

Said, Edward, 'Jane Austen and Empire', in *Culture and Imperialism*, London: Vintage, 1994, pp. 95–116.

Samuelian, Kristin Flieger, ' "Piracy Is Our Only Option": Postfeminist Intervention in *Sense and Sensibility*', in Troost and Greenfield, eds., *Jane Austen in Hollywood*.

Satz, Martha, 'An epistemological understanding of *Pride and Prejudice*: humility and objectivity', in Janet Todd, ed., *Jane Austen: New Perspectives*, New York: Holmes and Meier, 1983, pp. 171–86.

Schoenbaum, S., 'Artist's images of Shakespeare', in *Images of Shakespeare*, eds. W. Habicht, D. J. Palmer and R. Pringle, Delaware, Md.: University of Delaware Press, 1988.

Scott, Jennifer, *After Jane, a Review of the Continuations and Completions of Jane Austen's Novels*, privately printed, 1998.

Sedgwick, Eve Kosofsky, *Tendencies*, Durham, N.C.: Duke University Press, 1993.

Seltzer, Daniel, 'Prince Hal and Tragic Style', *Shakespeare Survey* 30, 1977, pp. 13–27.

Seneca, *Ad Lucilium Epistolae Morales*, 3 vols., London: Loeb Classical Library, Heinemann, 1920.

Servin, James, 'Totally Clueless', *Vogue Australia*, October 1995.

Shapira, Morris, ed., *Henry James: Selected Literary Criticism*, London: Heinemann, 1963.

Shorer, Mark, 'The humiliation of Emma Woodhouse', in Ian Watt, ed., *Jane Austen, a Collection of Critical Essays*, Englewood Cliffs, N.J.: Prentice Hall, 1963.

Skura, Meredith, *The Literary Uses of the Psychoanalytic Process*, New Haven, Conn.: Yale University Press, 1981.

Sonnet, Esther, 'From *Emma* to *Clueless*: taste, pleasure and the scene of history', in Deborah Cartmell and Imelda Whelehan, eds., *Adaptations: from Text to Screen, Screen to Text*, London and New York: Routledge, 1999.

Southam, B. C., ed., *Jane Austen, the Critical Heritage, 1811–1870*, London: Routledge and Kegan Paul, 1968.

    ed. and transcribed by, *Jane Austen's 'Sir Charles Grandison'*, foreword by Lord David Cecil, Oxford: Clarendon Press, 1980.

    'Janeities and Anti-Janeites', in J. David Grey, ed., *The Jane Austen Handbook*, London: Athlone Press, 1986.

    ed., *Jane Austen: the Critical Heritage, volume II: 1870–1940*, London: Routledge, 1987.

Stern, Lesley, '*Emma* in Los Angeles: remaking the book and the city', in James Navemore, ed., *Film Adaptation*, New Brunswick, N.J.: Rutgers University Press, 2000.

Stewart, Maaja A., *Domestic Realities and Imperial Fictions: Jane Austen's Novels in Eighteenth-Century Contexts*, Athens, Ga. and London: University of Georgia Press, 1993.

Stillman, Whit, *Barcelona & Metropolitan: Tales of Two Cities*, Boston, Mass. and London: Faber, 1994.

Tanner, Tony, *Jane Austen*, London: Macmillan, 1986.

Tennant, Emma, *Pemberley*, London: Hodder and Stoughton, 1993.

Thompson, Emma, *Jane Austen's 'Sense and Sensibility': the Screenplay and Diaries*, London: Bloomsbury, 1995.

Todd, Janet, 'Jane Austen, politics and sensibility' and 'Who's Afraid of Jane Austen?', in *Gender, Art and Death*, New York: Continuum, 1993.

Tomalin, Claire, *Jane Austen, a Life*, London: Viking, 1997.

Trilling, Lionel, 'Mansfield Park', in *The Opposing Self*, London: Secker and Warburg, 1955.

Troost, Linda and Greenfield, Sayre eds., *Jane Austen in Hollywood*, Lexington, Ky.: University Press of Kentucky, 1998.

Turner, Victor, *The Ritual Process; Structure and Anti-Structure*, [1969], New York: Aldine de Gruyter, 1995.

Wagner, Geoffrey, *The Novel and the Cinema*, Rutherford, N.J.: Fairleigh Dickinson University Press, 1975.

Waites, Elizabeth, 'Transference Dimensions of Biography', *Psychoanalytic Review* 82: 1, 1995.

Waldron, Mary, *Jane Austen and the Fiction of her Time*, Cambridge: Cambridge University Press, 1999.

Watkins, Susan, *Jane Austen's Town and Country Style*, New York: Rizzoli, 1990.

Watt, Ian, *The Rise of the Novel: Studies in Defoe, Richardson and Fielding*, Berkeley, Calif.: University of California Press, 1964.

'Jane Austen and the Traditions of Comic Aggression' [1981], in Harold Bloom, ed., *Jane Austen: Modern Critical Views*, New York: Chelsea House, 1986.

Watt, Ian, ed., *Jane Austen: a Collection of Critical Essays*, Engelwood Cliffs, N.J.: Prentice-Hall, 1967.

Weinbrot, Howard D., *The Formal Strain: Studies in Augustan Imitation and Satire*, Chicago, ill. and London: University of Chicago Press, 1969.

Wilks, Brian, *The Life and Times of Jane Austen*, London: Chancellor Press, 1984.

Willems, Michèle, 'Verbal-visual, verbal-pictorial or textual-televisual? Reflections on the BBC Shakespeare series', in Antony Davies and Stanley Wells, eds., *Shakespeare and the Moving Image*, Cambridge: Cambridge University Press, 1994.

Williams, Raymond, 'On dramatic dialogue and monologue, (particularly in Shakespeare)', *Writing in Society*, London: Verso, 1983.

Wilson, Edmund, 'A long talk about Jane Austen', in I. Watt, ed., *Jane Austen: a Collection of Critical Essays*, Englewood Cliffs, N.J.: Prentice Hall, 1963.

Wiltshire, John, *Jane Austen's 'Dear Dr Johnson'*, The Eighth Fleeman Memorial Lecture, Melbourne: Johnson Society of Australia, 2001.

Wimsatt W. K., ed., *Dr Johnson on Shakespeare*, Harmondsworth: Penguin, 1969.

Winnicott, D. W., *Home is Where We Start From*, eds. Claire Winnicott, Ray Shepherd and Madeleine Davis, New York: Norton, 1986.

The Maturational Process and the Facilitating Environment, Studies in the Theory of Emotional Development, [1965], London: Karnac, 1990.

Playing and Reality [1971] London and New York: Routledge, 1991.

Wiseman, Susan, 'The Family Tree Motel: Subliming Shakespeare in *My Own Private Idaho*', in Linda E. Boose and Richard Burt, eds., *Shakespeare, the Movie, Popularising the Plays on Film, TV and Video*, London and New York: Routledge, 1997.

Woolf, Virginia, 'The Movies and Reality', *New Republic* 47, 4 August 1926; reprinted as 'The Cinema', in *The Captain's Death Bed and Other Essays*, New York: Harcourt, Brace, 1950.

Worthen, John, 'The Necessary Ignorance of a Biographer', in John Batchelor, ed., *The Art of Literary Biography*, Oxford: Clarendon Press, 1995.

Wynne, Julian Wilmot, *Jane Austen and Sigmund Freud: an Interpretation*, London: Plume Publications, 1999.

Index

Entries in bold indicate main discussions

176